TCHAIKOVSKY
HIS LIFE AND WORKS

Frontispiece.

PETER ILICH TCHAIKOVSKY.

TCHAIKOVSKY

HIS LIFE AND WORKS, WITH EXTRACTS FROM HIS WRITINGS, AND THE DIARY OF HIS TOUR ABROAD IN 1888

BY

ROSA NEWMARCH

EDITED

*WITH A COMPLETE CLASSIFIC ACCOUNT OF WORKS, COPIOUS
ANALYSES OF IMPORTANT WORKS, ANALYTICAL AND
OTHER INDICES; ALSO, SUPPLEMENT DEALING WITH
"THE RELATION OF TCHAIKOVSKY TO ART-
QUESTIONS OF THE DAY.'*

BY

EDWIN EVANS, Senr., *F.R.C.O.*

HASKELL HOUSE PUBLISHERS Ltd.

Publishers of Scarce Scholarly Books

NEW YORK. N. Y. 10012

1969

First Published 1900

HASKELL HOUSE PUBLISHERS Ltd.
Publishers of Scarce Scholarly Books
280 LAFAYETTE STREET
NEW YORK. N. Y. 10012

Library of Congress Catalog Card Number: 68-25298

Standard Book Number 8383-0310-2

Printed in the United States of America

Editor's Note

ENTRUSTED with the care of this greatly enlarged edition of the present work, my attention was first directed to the provision of chapter-headings to be focussed to a " Table of Contents "; and next to that of an " Analytical Index " as a means of bringing the varied and interesting detail with which the book abounds within immediate reach; whilst the anecdotal mention of each particular production appeared to me of such special interest that I was tempted to add a " Classific Account " of the composer's entire works, in such form as to enable the reader to couple the survey of them with a reference to cursory items of information.

In course of this it became manifest that the usefulness of the present contribution to Tchaikovsky literature would be much increased by a detailed exposition of some of the more abstruse subjects to which the opinions relate. I therefore ventured upon the dissertation, entitled, " The Relation of Tchaikovsky to Art-questions of the Day ";

but this, in its turn, revealed a further necessity. In treating "Individuality," for example, I perceived that nothing less than an exhaustive analysis could successfully lay bare to the student some of the points which came under review; and a series of essays on important works became the result.

The additions are therefore much more extensive than was at first contemplated; but, in order that they should nevertheless assume an auxiliary character, they preserve an intimate relation with the original book. In this way two objects are served; for, firstly, the two portions of the Collection are rendered mutually helpful; and, secondly, an importance is retained for the original; as the nucleus of the whole scheme.

The aspirations which have guided me are therefore, commendable enough; but whether their working-out deserves a like approval I must leave the reader to decide.

EDWIN EVANS, Senr.

London,
Jan., 1908.

Preface to the Original Edition

SIX years have now elapsed since Tchaikovsky's death, and as yet no really adequate biography has appeared, either in Russia or abroad.* The authorised *Life and Letters* has long been expected in vain. Probably the difficulty of selecting from such a vast mass of correspondence—Tchaikovsky's letters are said to be numbered by thousands—is the chief reason for the delay in publication. Meanwhile the public interest, especially in England, is steadily increasing, and almost every scrap of information concerning the composer of "The Pathetic" Symphony is eagerly sought after. In the absence of anything more complete and authoritative I venture

* It is necessary to mention that Tchaikovsky's death occurred in Nov., 1893. At the present time (1908) therefore fifteen years have elapsed; and, in the interim, we have had the "Life and Letters" written by his brother Modeste, which now constitutes the standard biography of the composer.—[ED.]

to offer this volume to the admirers of Tchaikovsky's works.

In 1897 I published in *The Musician* a series of papers upon Tchaikovsky based upon a little volume of personal reminiscences by M. N. Kashkin,* one of the Professors of the Moscow Conservatoire, and a friend and colleague of the composer. These papers, which I have been repeatedly asked to reprint, form the first part of the present volume. They have been almost entirely rewritten, and supplemented by a considerable amount of new information derived from other and more recent sources.

In 1898 appeared *The Collected Writings of Tchaikovsky*, edited, with a preface, by the well-known Russian critic G. Laroche. From this book I made a collection of extracts showing the composer's musical tastes and sympathies, and these papers appeared in the *Musical Standard* under the title, "Tchaikovsky as a Musical Critic." The fact that they were very well noticed in several Russian papers, notably the *Moscow Viedomosti*, induced me to reprint them here, with two additional chapters dealing with Tchaikovsky's attitude towards Russian music. Later on, at the suggestion of Mr. C. A. Barry, I

---

* *Reminiscences of Peter Ilich Tchaikovsky*, by N. Kashkin, Moscow, 1897. (P. Jurgenson).

undertook to translate the diary of Tchaikovsky's tour abroad in 1888, now published for the first time in English. And so the book grew to its present size.

My thanks are due to the editors of *The Musician* and the *Musical Standard* for their courteous permission to reprint such matter as has already appeared in those papers. I must also express my gratitude to M. Kashkin and M. Laroche, from whose works I have quoted freely; and particularly to M. Berezovsky, whose excellent article on Tchaikovsky contains invaluable information. To the composer's brother, M. Modeste Tchaikovsky, I am indebted for permission to republish the Diary of 1888; while M. P. Jurgenson has kindly supplied me with the facsimile from the score of the *Overture 1812*. Last, but not least, I have to thank M. Vladimir Stassov, whose ready help and sympathy first enabled me to undertake the study of Russian art.

ROSA NEWMARCH.

OPENING BARS FROM THE OVERTURE "1812."

From the MS. in the possession of P. Turgenson, Moscow.

CONTENTS

TCHAIKOVSKY—HIS LIFE AND WORKS

TCHAIKOVSKY AS A MUSICAL CRITIC

"DIARY OF MY TOUR IN 1888"
(Translated from the Russian)

Contents

SUPPLEMENT. (A)

THE RELATION OF TCHAIKOVSKY TO ART-QUESTIONS OF THE DAY

SUPPLEMENT. (B)

ANALYSES OF SELECTED WORKS

SUPPLEMENT. (C)

INDICES FOR STUDENT USE

TCHAIKOVSKY

AMONG the leaders of the New School of music in Russia Tchaikovsky occupies an exceptional place, as one who, while strongly attracted by the forward movements of his time, was restrained by his special training from acknowledging complete allegiance to the nationalist party. His character was essentially Russian, and his tendencies the liberating tendencies of the generation to which he belonged; but his musical education was cosmopolitan, and the teachers whom he most reverenced leaned towards tradition and authority. He was not, like Glinka, or, in a less degree, like Rimsky-Korsakov, consecrated to the service of nationality. In his heart a follower of Liszt, in his intellectual conscience an adherent of Classicism, Tchaikovsky composed under the sway of two conflicting influences, neither of which was strong enough to efface for long his own intense personality. Thus throughout his work we find a lack of unity which baffles dogmatic criticism, and compels us to seek in the character of the man, rather than in his

B

theories, the interpretation of all he has expressed in music. This susceptibility to the antagonistic currents of thought and feeling which surrounded him is not altogether a fault in Tchaikovsky. On the contrary, it has lent to his music qualities of pliancy, variety, and eclecticism which have proved sources of charm and attraction. It distinguishes him from most of his contemporaries, and places him in the sharpest contrast alike to Wagner, whose militant energies forced a new channel of their own, and to Brahms, whose work was mainly accomplished under the influence of a single dominant idea

> that Freedom slowly broadens down
> From precedent to precedent.

Even if we admit that this division of thought and emotion is a source of weakness in Tchaikovsky, we must also acknowledge that it has its element of popularity. At a time when the entire world of art is divided upon questions of law and liberty, this subjective confession of unsettled faith and dual allegiance puts him in closer touch with his own generation, though it may weaken his hold upon succeeding ones.

Another source alike of weakness and popularity in Tchaikovsky's music is his sympathy with the *maladie du siècle;* his command of every note in the gamut of melancholy. "A poet of one mood in all his lays," his monotony of pessimism, though it must at times weary the sane-minded individual, seems to engage the public and draw them to him most persistently in his moods of blackest despair. In this respect, foreigners consider his music typically Russian; a view not entirely just to Russian art as a whole, which is far too vigorous and healthy a growth to remain continuously under the sway of one emotional influence. Nor is Tchaikovsky's melancholy of that particular type which we associate with the Russian character: that sober, grey-tinted, resigned pessimism which is a part of the Russian nature rather than a mood, and is best exemplified in the poems of Nekrasov. Tchaikovsky's emotional and romantic despair seems to belong to other times and other lands. It echoes Chateaubriand and Byron, not Gogol and Tourgeniev.

To say that Tchaikovsky is the most accessible and the best known among Russian composers is by no means to say that he is the greatest. Unlike the majority of the school to which he—in part—belongs, he did not in his lifetime disdain popularity, and has reaped his reward in a wider fame and a stronger sway over the public taste. Setting aside his natural dislike of public appearances, he was the first of the Russians to travel in his own goods, if I may use so commercial a simile. Partly for this reason, and partly because his music possesses in the highest degree those qualities of highly-wrought emotion and brilliant workmanship which are always the first to awaken a sympathetic echo, he has made a greater impression than any of his compatriots. It is the fashion to praise Tchaikovsky for having cast aside so much of his national peculiarities as impeded his progress towards the goal of fame. This action was not so much a matter of conviction as of temperament and the circumstances of his education. It was easier for him to drop the Slav than for many of his fellow-workers. Fortunately, too, he could not altogether get rid of that imperishable fibre of race to which he owes so much that is interesting and original. There are few compensations for the sale of our birthright. Nationality in art may have its narrowing results, but the lasting influences in music, as in literature, have never been effected by the *dépaysés*.

I do not deny that Tchaikovsky possesses many of the virtues of a master artist, but we shall miss much if we let our appreciation of Russian music stop short at his works alone. In each member of the group which he partially represents, there is some individual charm or gift, some concentration of artistic purpose to a definite aim, in the highest degree interesting to the student. The wisest will let Tchaikovsky's achievement—with which we are beginning to be familiar—serve as an elucidation of the great national movement which lay behind it, and as an introduction to the music—less stirring perhaps, but not less worthy—of his immediate predecessors.

I

Peter Ilich Tchaikovsky was born 7th May 1840, at Votinsk, in the government of Viatka. His father was employed there as a mining engineer, but later on he moved to St. Petersburg, where he was appointed Director of the Technological Institute. The boy was educated at the School of Jurisprudence, and afterwards obtained a post in the Ministry of Justice.

Like most of the Russian composers, Tchaikovsky began his musical career as an amateur. Launched upon the society of the capital as an average youth of fashion, his musical gifts won him considerable popularity. At evening parties he shone in such pieces as Döhler's *Nocturne in D flat* and Weber's *Invitation à la Valse;* but he had higher ideals than these. The atmosphere of the School of Jurisprudence was decidedly musical, thanks to the influence of its patron Prince Oldenburgsky. Tchaikovsky's most intimate school friend was the future author Apukhtin, a young man of cultivated and artistic tastes, who was passionately fond of Italian music. The two friends spent their free evenings at the opera, and most of their leisure moments in discussing their favourite art. Apukhtin refers to this in one of his poems, dedicated to Tchaikovsky : —

> Do you remember how you used to drown
> Your soul in art, forget this world of men ?
> And how we dreamt of some ideal renown,
> For Music was our worshipped idol then,
> And Life a fleeting dream to us . . .

But in spite of this enthusiasm for music, it is doubtful if Tchaikovsky had any serious thoughts of it as a profession when first he took up his duties in the

Ministry of Justice. It would certainly have been considered *infra dig.* in the official circles in which he moved, besides which, it was imperative that he should begin to earn a livelihood as soon as possible. A trifling circumstance first started him upon the path that was destined eventually to become a triumphal way. Tchaikovsky had a cousin in the Mounted Grenadiers, who was also an amateur performer and a friendly rival at social evenings. One day, having met at the house of a mutual friend, they began to discuss musical questions. "Among other things," to relate the story in Tchaikovsky's own words, "my cousin said it was possible to modulate from one key to another without using more than three chords. This excited my curiosity, and to my astonishment I found that he improvised whatever modulations I suggested, even from quite extraneous keys." Tchaikovsky was piqued by this show of superior knowledge. "I asked him where he picked this up, and discovered that there were classes in connection with the Musical Society where one might learn all this wisdom."

Tchaikovsky lost no time in joining these classes, which were held at the Michailovsky Palace; but, says Kashkin, he showed so little inclination for serious work that he was at first regarded as an incorrigible dilettante. Nevertheless, about this time he began to feel a strong impulse towards music as a vocation. But besides the question of means, he was lacking in self-confidence. In December 1861, he wrote to his sister: "I told you I was studying the theory of music with considerable success. It is generally agreed that with my uncommon talents (I hope you will not take this for mere boasting) it would be a pity not to try my luck in this career. I am only afraid of a want of purpose; perhaps idleness may take possession of me and I may not persevere. You know I have power and capacity, but I am ailing with your malady, which is called 'fragmentariness,' and if I do not become enthusiastic over a thing I am easily done for."

For some months Tchaikovsky remained in this vacillating frame of mind. Without actually throwing over his official duties he entered the Conservatoire, and was placed under Zaremba in the class for counterpoint.

Anton Rubinstein often attended the harmony classes at the Conservatoire to examine the work of the students. Struck by the ability, and also by the carelessness, of Tchaikovsky's exercises, he called him aside after class, and spoke to him with such combined charm and severity that the Laodicean mood vanished for ever. Rubinstein's appeal irrevocably decided Tchaikovsky's destiny, and henceforward he cherished an adoration for the man who had pointed out his true vocation. He now resigned his official appointment, withdrew from fashionable society, and devoted himself entirely to the study of music. It is recorded of Ilia Muromets—that popular hero of Russian folklore—that he sat out the first thirty years of his life in complete inactivity. Once roused from his lethargy, however, his strength was as the strength of ten, and his deeds of prowess unparalleled. Tchaikovsky might have taken this old hero for his model, he now proved himself so full of unsuspected energy and ambition.

"Tchaikovsky worked in an astonishing way," said Rubinstein, speaking of his pupil to Kashkin in later years. "Once, at the composition class, I set him to write out contrapuntal variations on a given theme, and I mentioned that in this class of work not only quality but *quantity* was of importance. I thought perhaps he would write about a dozen variations. But not at all. At the next class I received over two hundred. To examine all these," Rubinstein concluded, with a bland smile, "would have taken me more time than it took him to write them." Tchaikovsky, on leaving the Conservatoire some three years later, received a silver medal for his diploma work—a cantata for solo, chorus, and orchestra, the text from Schiller's *Ode to Joy*. With regard to this work, it is interesting to know that the composer himself did not look upon it by any means as a weak or immature effort, and would gladly have seen it published, or at least re-performed.

In 1863 Tchaikovsky began to study orchestra- . tion in Rubinstein's class. Rubinstein, as a com- poser, wrote only for the modern orchestra, while retaining at the same time the greatest reverence for the works of the old classical writers. He impressed these views upon his pupil, and made him adopt the habit of thinking and writing in the language of the modern orchestra from the beginning of his career.

Besides the piano, Tchaikovsky studied the flute and the organ. Rubinstein helped him to earn a living by recommending him as a teacher and accompanist. In the latter capacity he frequently attended the musical evenings of the Grand Duchess Helena Paulovna. At the Conservatoire he became intimate with his fellow-student Laroche, who exercised an important influence upon his future life.

Tchaikovsky now came to be regarded, both by masters and students, as a young man of very great promise. In 1864-65, Laroche—who afterwards became one of the foremost musical critics in Russia —wrote to Kashkin in Moscow of Tchaikovsky's excellent qualities, and pointed him out as "the future star of Russian music." Since 1863 harmony classes had been held in Moscow in connection with a branch of the Russian Musical Society, under the management of Nicholas Rubinstein. Rubinstein had neither time nor inclination to devote himself to the teaching of theory, and in view of the opening of the Moscow Conservatoire, in 1866, it was thought necessary to engage a special teacher of these subjects. The choice of a good man was limited in those days, and Nicholas Rubinstein offered the post to Serov. Serov accepted, but immediately afterwards the success of his opera *Rogneda*, in St. Petersburg, made him unwilling to leave the modern capital for the less stirring atmosphere of Moscow. Rubinstein then resolved to engage the services of one of the first students who should qualify satisfactorily at the December examinations of the St. Petersburg

Conservatoire. Kashkin, on hearing of this, showed Laroche's letter to Nicholas Rubinstein, and thus Tchaikovsky was marked out as a suitable applicant. Rubinstein, having subsequently interviewed the young composer in St. Petersburg, was so favourably impressed that he determined to appoint him to the post, disregarding even the advice of Zaremba, who recommended a more mature candidate.

Tchaikovsky entered upon his duties in Moscow early in January 1866. The funds of the Musical Society were not then in a flourishing condition, and the expenses of the classes were kept as low as possible. Tchaikovsky, as teacher of harmony, was to receive fifty roubles—about £6 : 5s.—per month until the opening of the Conservatoire. He would have found some difficulty in living upon this extremely modest salary if Nicholas Rubinstein had not suggested to him to take up his quarters in his own flat, where he had already one inmate in the person of the violinist Shradik. "In external appearance," says Kashkin, "Tchaikovsky produced a very favourable appearance, but the same cannot be said as to his dress. He wore a very old fur pelisse which had been lent him by a friend, and the rest of his costume harmonised with this ancient *shuba*." Nicholas Rubinstein, who thought the young professor would be none the worse for a new frock-coat, was on the point of offering him credit at his own tailor's, when he remembered that Wieniawsky—who always stayed with him on his visits to Moscow— had, on the last occasion, left behind him a nearly new frock-coat. It was fully a year since the virtuoso had departed, and, according to Russian custom, the coat belonged to the master of the house, who presented it, therefore, to Tchaikovsky. It was a very bad fit, but Tchaikovsky did not trouble about that, and wore it, "with as much proud dignity as though it had been bought at the best tailor's in the town."

Kashkin was soon on terms of intimate friendship with his young colleague. Tchaikovsky might easily have become as great a social favourite in Moscow as he had been in St. Petersburg, but he did not care much for society, and preferred to spend his evenings quietly with Kashkin, or his friend Jurgenson, the publisher. He also frequented the Little Theatre, where the plays of Ostrovsky were the great attraction of the day. An interesting feature of Moscow life at that time was the Artists' Club, founded by Nicholas Rubinstein, Ostrovsky, and Count Odoievsky. Here the members often met to listen to the reading of some new literary work. Musical evenings were constantly organised, and every renowned virtuoso who passed through Moscow was certain to be heard at the Artists' Club. Ladies were admitted, and dances held, at which the dance-music was provided by such artists as Nicholas Rubinstein and Wieniawsky. At this club Tchaikovsky met Ostrovsky, one of the most celebrated writers of his day, who treated him with the greatest kindness, and afterwards generously provided him with the libretto of his first opera, *The Voievoda*. The earliest idols of Tchaikovsky's musical cult were

Glinka and Mozart, and he had a great veneration for the works of Beethoven. Schumann's fiery impulse and dreamy sentimentalism had a great attraction for him, and he inclined more to his music than to that of Chopin, in whom he found a note of invalidishness and a superfluity of subjective sentiment that somewhat repelled him. He greatly modified this opinion, however, after he had heard the works of Chopin interpreted by Nicholas Rubinstein. Tchaikovsky was well read in the literature of his own country, and his favourite authors were Ostrovsky and Tolstoi. He spoke French fluently, but of the German language and literature he knew very little in his younger days. Like most Russians, he was acquainted with Dickens and Thackeray through the medium of translations, but it was not until the last years of his life that he knew any English. Kashkin says that Tchaikovsky valued the morning hours for writing, and only under great pressure of work employed his evenings in composition. He would spend many hours reading music for four hands. His favourite relaxation was the game of *Yeralash* (a Russian form of whist). He was too absent-minded to become a good player, but bore the rebukes of irritable partners with the patient good-humour that seems always to have been his characteristic. "Tchaikovsky never defended himself when attacked, or began a quarrel," says Kashkin.

Tchaikovsky started his harmony class upon the system of his master Zaremba. Afterwards he became more independent in his methods, and laid great stress on the value of thorough-bass; half his harmony course consisted of exercises in this subject. He never considered himself a good teacher, and took up the work more from necessity than inclination. But his scrupulous accuracy, business-like habits, and wonderful memory for musical examples, made him a more valuable teacher than he himself believed. Shortly after his arrival in Moscow, Nicholas Rubinstein suggested to him to write something for performance at one of the concerts of the Musical Society. Rubinstein—who during two-thirds of the year taught for nearly nine hours a day —was very rarely at home, and saw next to nothing of the two young men who shared his rooms. They were not, however, very quiet quarters, for a series of pianoforte classes was held there, and this music, mingled with the strains of Shradik's fiddle, were very distracting to the young composer. He was driven to take refuge in a neighbouring inn which, though it was a favourite haunt of the University students, was generally deserted in the morning hours. In the comparatively peaceful atmosphere of "The Great Britain" Tchaikovsky worked out most of his earlier compositions. The new work —a *Concert Overture in C minor*—was duly finished and submitted to Rubinstein for approval.

The composer, however, was destined to meet with the first of a series of bitter disappointments. Nicholas Rubinstein was not favourably impressed by the work, and all idea of its performance came to an end. Tchaikovsky was hurt by what seemed to him the captious quality of Rubinstein's criticisms, but he showed no resentment. The time was too short to allow of his preparing another work, and the *Concert Overture in F major*, for small orchestra, written in St. Petersburg, took the place of the rejected composition. Here again Rubinstein demurred, and insisted upon the overture being re-scored for full orchestra, a proceeding which, according to Laroche, quite spoilt its unity of character. It was heard on 4th March 1866, at Rubinstein's benefit concert, and though it did not have an extraordinary success, it attracted the attention of musicians to its composer. "He was thirsting for support and encouragement," writes Kashkin, "but at that time he hardly found one or the other." For the rest of the winter Tchaikovsky composed very little, but he planned the sketch of his first symphonic poem, *Winter Day Dreams (Zimnia Grozi)*.

The next event of importance in his life was the opening of the Moscow Conservatoire in the autumn of 1866. After an imposing ceremony, a banquet was given, at which the directors of the institution and the members of the teaching staff were present. Tchaikovsky, in spite of constitutional shyness, was a good speaker, and in an effective speech he proposed the prosperity of the sister Conservatoire of St. Petersburg. The banquet was followed by music, and Tchaikovsky, who was resolved that the first music heard in the hall of the Conservatoire should be Glinka's, opened the impromptu concert by playing the Overture to *Russlan and Ludmilla* from memory. He would have been well received, if only from patriotic sentiments, but his technique and artistic feeling were of a quality to command attention in themselves. Nicholas Rubinstein now moved into rooms adjoining the Conservatoire, and Tchaikovsky went with him. A few months later they were joined by Laroche, who had been appointed to the Conservatoire. The presence of Laroche did much towards reconciling Tchaikovsky to life in Moscow; for though, eventually, he grew very fond of the ancient town atmosphere, during the first years of his existence there he was always regretting St. Petersburg, with its modern and more progressive musical life.

During the autumn of 1866 he was chiefly occupied upon his symphonic poem, *Winter Day Dreams*. With regard to his method of work I will quote the words of his friend Kashkin :— "Tchaikovsky has not infrequently been accused of excessive haste and negligence in his work. On what ground such an accusation is founded I do not know; for, from the beginning to the end of his career, he finished his compositions with great care, and absolutely without haste. If his works were written in an unbroken series, this can be explained simply by his industry. Every day he spent some hours in composing, and the disinclination for work was unknown to him, at least in the morning. Unknown to him, too, was the usual Russian 'some day or other' which has stolen time from so many of us:

Tchaikovsky had the immense advantage of superior discipline in his work. Perhaps he owed this to his first governess, a French lady, whose name I forget. She lived until recently in some little town in the south of France, and cherished the memory of her pupil. If I am not mistaken, he visited her a year, or less, before his death. When he told me of this visit he was evidently much touched. With all the vehemence and impressibility of his nature, Tchaikovsky was the personification of order and accuracy, especially in his work; and he always appreciated the value of time. When first he came to live in Moscow, although he was then six-and-twenty, he was still inexperienced and young in many things, especially in the material questions of life; but in all that concerned his work he was already mature, with a particularly elaborate method of work, in which all was foreseen with admirable judgment, and manipulated with the exactitude of the surgeon in operating. This knowledge saved him much time, and permitted him to work with what seemed to others an inconceivable rapidity."

As soon as the symphonic poem, *Winter Day Dreams*, was finished, Tchaikovsky started for St. Petersburg, to show the new work to his old masters, Zaremba and Anton Rubinstein. He still valued the musical appreciation of St. Petersburg far above that of Moscow, and it was his ambition to have the symphony produced at a concert of the Musical Society in that city. He was full of hope, and confident of approbation; but again disappointment awaited him. Rubinstein and Zaremba criticised the work with unsparing severity, and decided that it could not pass into the programme of the Musical Society. Zaremba objected chiefly to the second theme of the first movement, and although this was very satisfactory to the composer himself, he changed it, and made many other alterations in deference to the wish of his masters. Even then the work did not come up to their standard of excellence. Finally, by way of consolation, they agreed to give the two middle movements, but they met with no success. The symphony now exists in its original form, except for the unfortunate second theme, of which the composer could never again recall his first idea. This disappointment had the effect of detaching Tchaikovsky's sympathies from St. Petersburg. Henceforward he grew more and more reconciled to life in Moscow, and valued the appreciation he was beginning to meet with there.

C

II

IN the winter of 1866-67 Tchaikovsky was engaged upon his first opera, *The Voievoda*. During a summer holiday to Hapsaal, on the coast of the Baltic, he wrote the pianoforte pieces *Souvenir de Hapsaal* (op. 2), of which No. 3, *Chant sans paroles*, has become such a favourite. By the autumn of 1867 a considerable portion of *The Voievoda* was written, including the orchestral number, "Dances of the Serving Maids," which soon became very popular in Moscow. During that season Nicholas Rubinstein organised a concert in the Grand Theatre on behalf of the sufferers from the famine in Finland, and suggested that Tchaikovsky should conduct his own dances. This was his *début* as a conductor, and Kashkin describes the anxiety he felt on his friend's behalf. Just before the ordeal Kashkin went behind the scenes of the theatre to see how Tchaikovsky was feeling. He said that, to his great surprise, he did not feel in the least nervous, and Kashkin returned to his seat. But when the new conductor actually found himself face to face with the vast audience, all his courage ebbed away. He completely lost his head, and practically forgot to conduct at all. Fortunately the band were well acquainted with the " Dances," and thus a fiasco was averted. For twenty years after this experience Tchaikovsky never took up the baton again. But then, circumstances having obliged him to conduct a few performances of his opera *Cherevichek*, he conquered his nervousness to a great extent, and became very fond of conducting his own works. In the early spring of 1868 the symphony, *Winter Day Dreams*—rejected in St. Petersburg—met with so warm a reception in Moscow that the composer must have been partially consoled for its first failure.

Tchaikovsky, who was on good terms with the heads of the theatrical administration in Moscow, had not much difficulty in getting *The Voievoda* accepted for performance at the Grand Theatre. In this matter he also had the assistance of Nicholas Rubinstein, by far the most influential person in the musical world of Moscow. But the troubles of the unfortunate composer only began with the acceptance of his work. At that time Italian opera reigned triumphant in Russia, while Russian opera played the part of Cinderella to her more splendid sister. Old scenery, cast-off dresses, second-rate artists, were considered good enough for National Opera. Russian composers were not even permitted the advantage of the full orchestra, which was reserved exclusively for Italian nights; they had to put up with the small and inferior "ballet orchestra."

Merelli, the manager of the Italian company, rented the Grand Theatre about five nights a week, and was practically the master of the situation. At the rehearsals Tchaikovsky suffered a great deal. He was inexperienced, and does not seem to have distributed his parts judiciously, though the material at his command was, at the best, very unpromising.

Finocchi, who sang the part of the Voievoda, was a second-rate Italian singer, who had, moreover, the greatest difficulty in singing his part in the Russian language. Madame Menshikov, the soprano, who appeared as Maria Vasilievna, had a fine voice, but no discipline. The singers were not unwilling, but their capabilities, as musicians, were of a very poor order. For example, the whole of the final quartet of one act had to be cut out, because one voice part contained triplets as against two equal notes in another, and this proved an insuperable difficulty to the performers.

Tchaikovsky's shy and sensitive disposition made it extremely painful to him to criticise or find fault with the singers. At the rehearsals, too, he began to discover, too late for alteration, many of his own mistakes of inexperience. He was in despair, says Kashkin, and only longed for the ordeal to be over. Nicholas Rubinstein twice attended the rehearsals, and went away angry with the composer's apparently supine amiability, which was really only the expression of a fatalistic resignation. The first performance of

The Voievoda took place on 30th January 1869. It was given in all about ten times—not such a bad record for a national opera in those days. Kashkin, who has forgotten many of the details of the performance, thinks that the music, though not strong, was rather popular, and that the libretto, which was a kind of Italian opera travesty of Ostrovsky's fine work, was the poorest part of the work. Afterwards Tchaikovsky burnt the score, partly perhaps from a feeling of disappointment, though no doubt the fact of his having incorporated some of the music into a new opera, *The Oprichnik*, would account for this destruction of *The Voievoda*. Twenty years later Arensky wrote an opera, *A Dream on the Volga*, upon the same subject. This work Tchaikovsky admired very much, and valued more highly than his own immature effort.

The Voievoda was followed by a fantasia for orchestra, entitled *Destiny* (*Fatum*). Although the composer never revealed the fact, Kashkin thinks that some autobiographical interest attaches to this work. The following quotation from the poet Batioushkov served as a motto to "Destiny" : —

> Thou knowest what the white-haired Melchisedek
> Said when he left this life : Man is born a slave ;
> A slave he dies. Will even Death reveal to him
> Why thus he laboured in this vale of tears,
> Why thus he suffered, wept, endured—then vanished ?

These words were suggested to Tchaikovsky as an appropriate epigraph *after* the completion of the work, but the public took them as a sort of programme, and sought in the music for some definite connection with the words. The fantasia was performed on 15th March 1869, with some success. Tchaikovsky afterwards destroyed the score of *Destiny*, but as he was fully aware of the existence of all the orchestral parts, it may be presumed that a restoration of this work would not be altogether disrespectful to the wishes of the composer.

About this time he first made the acquaintance of Balakirev, the talented leader of the nationalist school. In 1867 Balakirev had succeeded Anton Rubinstein as conductor of the St. Petersburg Musical Society, and head of the Conservatoire. He took advantage of this position to forward the interests of the rising school of Russian composers, and among these he included Tchaikovsky. But these nationalist tendencies did not find favour with the committee of management, and he was compelled to resign both positions after a brief tenure of office. Tchaikovsky wrote a letter to the *Sovrimenie Lietopis*, protesting with great indignation against the injustice done to Balakirev, and this led to a friendship between the two musicians. In the spring of 1869 Balakirev moved from St. Petersburg to Moscow, and the relations grew still more intimate. To Balakirev's suggestion Tchaikovsky owed the plan of his *Romeo and Juliet* overture. "This is always associated in my mind," writes M. Kashkin, "with the memory of a lovely day in May, with verdant forests and tall fir trees, among which we three were taking a walk. Balakirev understood, to a great extent, the nature of Tchaikovsky's genius, and knew that it was adequate to the subject he suggested. Evidently he himself was taken with the subject, for he explained all the details as vividly as though the work had been already written. The plan, adapted to sonata form, was as follows: First, an introduction of a religious character, representative of Friar Lawrence, followed by an *Allegro in B minor* (Balakirev suggested most of the tonalities), which was to depict the enmity between the Montagues and Capulets, the street brawl, etc. Then was to follow the love of Romeo and Juliet (second subject in D flat major), succeeded by the elaboration of both subjects. The so-called 'development'—that is to say, the putting together of the various themes in various forms—passes over to what is called, in technical language, the 'recapitulation'—in which the first theme, *Allegro*, appears in its original form, and the love-theme (D flat major) now appears in D major, the whole ending with the death of the lovers. Balakirev spoke with such conviction that he at once kindled the ardour of the young composer, to whom such a theme was extremely well suited." Tchaikovsky returned from his holiday in September with the overture practically finished. He had put his heart into the work, which seems to throb with youthful passion and tenderness. His friends were enthusiastic over its beauties, and prophesied a great success. But an adverse fate seemed always to await the first performances of Tchaikovsky's works.

Romeo and Juliet was given at one of the concerts of the Musical Society on 4th March 1870. It chanced that just at that time a student of the Conservatoire, resenting a reprimand which had been administered by the director, Nicholas Rubinstein, brought an action against him, and, owing to the absence of any legal code applying to the institution, won a technical victory. Public opinion was all in favour of Rubinstein, and when, on the evening of 4th March, he appeared upon the platform to conduct the new overture, he was received with the most frantic demonstration, while Tchaikovsky's music was completely forgotten in the excitement. The *Romeo and Juliet* overture was afterwards published by Bote and Bock, of Berlin, in 1871, and underwent many changes before it attained its present curtailed form, as seen in a second edition of the same published in 1881. Somewhere about this time, Tchaikovsky received the plot of a fantastic opera, entitled *Mandragora*. The composer seems to have been much attracted to the subject, and only relinquished it with great regret when M. Kashkin had convinced him of its being quite unsuited for operatic treatment. Only one number of *Mandragora* was ever heard in public, the "Chorus of Insects," which was very popular, both in Moscow and St. Petersburg. It is highly melodious, and recalls in character Mendelssohn's music to *A Midsummer Night's Dream*.

Now that the announcement of some of Tchaikovsky's works is sufficient to draw a crowded and enthusiastic audience, it is pathetic to look back upon the constant series of disappointments which awaited him in his early days. Few composers have been more unlucky with their first works than this gentle and sensitive artist, possessed with an almost feminine craving for approval and encouragement. A certain hyper-sensitiveness to the criticism of his artistic schemes led to a characteristic reticence on the part of Tchaikovsky. Consequently few people ever heard of the creation and untimely end of his opera *Undine*. The idea was probably suggested by the ready-made libretto which Count Sollogoub had written for A. Th. Lvov as early as 1848, and which was republished in Smirdin's edition of this author's works. The opera was finished early in 1870, and sent to St. Petersburg for the approval of the Theatrical Direction. Once he had completed and posted the score, and thus practically burnt his boats, Tchaikovsky spoke of the opera to a few intimate friends and played them some numbers from the work. *Undine* was rejected unconditionally, and the score, mislaid by the carelessness of some official, whom Tchaikovsky was too good-natured to expose, was not returned to him until some years later, when he destroyed it. One air, "Undine's Song," afterwards appeared as Lel's air in his music to Ostrovsky's "Snow Maiden." He took the rejection of his opera more philosophically than might be expected; but his mind was already occupied with a new scheme—the opera which afterwards appeared as *The Oprichnik*.

"Tchaikovsky," says Kashkin, "did not devote himself to the serious study of music until comparatively late; consequently he had not those definite and settled views upon music which seem a part of those who have grown up from childhood in a musical environment and have imbibed certain ideas and sympathies with life itself. He was obliged to acquire all this by means of hard work and the study of musical literature. As far as I can remember at that period (1870), he did not read orchestral scores with great ease, and preferred to make acquaintance with symphonic literature by the help of pianoforte arrangements for four hands, when I was often his partner at the piano. Of chamber music—especially string quartets—he knew very little at that time, and even the very character of this kind of music he appreciated with difficulty. The mere quality and *timbre* of the string quartet provoked in him nothing but weariness in those days, and he could hardly endure Beethoven's later quartets. He confessed to me once that he could scarcely keep awake in his seat through Beethoven's great A minor quartet. As to the combination of piano and stringed instruments, he admired many works of this class, especially those of Beethoven; but said he could not imagine himself writing for such a combination of instruments." Before long, however, he greatly modified his opinion, and even set to work upon this particular form of composition. Tchaikovsky was very anxious to spend the summer of 1871 abroad, but had no funds at his disposal. At the suggestion of Nicholas Rubinstein, he resolved to give a concert for his own benefit and produce some new work. As everything had to be organised on a modest and economical scale, there was no possibility of engaging an orchestra, and Tchaikovsky was driven to write his first string quartet in D. The *Andante* of this work has an interesting history, showing how Tchaikovsky valued national airs, and the cleverness with which he made use of them on occasion.

For several mornings the composer was awakened by the singing of a plasterer working upon the house just below his window. The workman's song haunted Tchaikovsky, who wrote down the air, and afterwards, at dinner-time, he sought out the singer and asked him to sing the words. They proved uninteresting, indeed almost devoid of meaning, as is so often the case with the townsfolk's version of the peasant's songs. The melody in its original form appears as No. 14 in Rimsky-Korsakov's collection of " A Hundred National Russian Songs."

Tchaikovsky's first concert, though not a colossal success, realised a sufficient sum to allow of his carrying out his trip abroad. Among the audience was the great novelist Turgeniev, who seems to have been impressed by Tchaikovsky's genius.

In 1870, Tchaikovsky's circumstances having considerably improved, he moved—greatly to the regret of Nicholas Rubinstein—into lodgings of his own. His way of life. even then, was by no means luxurious. He kept but one servant, a young country fellow, whose culinary skill never advanced beyond an unvarying daily dish of cabbage-soup and groats. But the composer was not fastidious, and in his new home he found the absolute quiet so indispensable for his creative work.

"About this time," writes M. Kashkin, "Tchaikovsky greatly admired a lady who sang in the Italian Opera Company. He was attracted by her talent as a singer, her ready wit, and brilliant conversational powers. His friends believed that he had fallen in love with this fascinating artist, and rumour had already decided their future, when the opera company left Moscow for Warsaw. During their visit to the Polish capital a telegram arrived, announcing the unexpected news of her marriage to another member of the company. Tchaikovsky seemed more astonished than hurt; but when, during the following season, the lady reappeared in Moscow, he was moved—even to tears—at the first sight of her upon the stage. Seven or eight years later I was present at an unexpected meeting between Tchaikovsky and this singer. He had gone to call upon Nicholas Rubinstein at the Conservatoire, but, on being told that he was engaged with a lady in his private room, we sat down in the ante-room to wait until the visitor should take her departure. Presently the door opened and the lady appeared. Tchaikovsky recognised her at a glance and sprang from his seat, turning very pale. The lady gave a little cry of alarm, and in her confusion began to fumble for the door of the half-lighted ante-room.

Having found it, she fled without a word. Nicholas Rubinstein, who had followed her out, stood a silent and astonished spectator of this little scene." A year or two later Tchaikovsky met the lady once more, while travelling abroad, and resumed his friendly relations with her. He still admired her gifted and charming disposition, but his passion—if it ever existed, save in his own imagination—had quite worn itself out. At any rate, he assured M. Kashkin, his feelings at that time were purely platonic.

About the same time that he was engaged upon the opera *Undine*, Tchaikovsky wrote his first songs: Six Songs (op. 6). These songs, though by no means the best that Tchaikovsky has written, are sufficiently characteristic to foreshadow most of his virtues and defects as a song-writer. There is no denying the extraordinary charm, the penetrating sweetness and melancholy, the vocal excellence of many of Tchaikovsky's songs. At the same time, if we compare him in this respect with Schubert and Schumann, with Brahms and Franz, or with his fellow-countrymen Dargomijsky and Balakirev, it is impossible to regard him as one of the greatest among song-writers. Nearly all his songs would be condemned if tried by the standard of formal perfection. His greatest weakness as a song-writer lies in the fact that he never realised the principle that, in the ideal song, music and poetry must meet upon an equal footing. "The union of the two arts," says Cui, "appeared to Tchaikovsky in the light of a *més-*

alliance for the one which he represented." Starting
with this idea, that music is the only element of real
importance in song, Tchaikovsky does not hesitate
to mutilate the text of the greatest poets, to inter-
polate such exclamations as "good heavens," "alas,"
"woe is me," and occasionally by a stroke of his
arbitrary pen to turn fine verse into indifferent prose.
Perhaps it was on account of his contempt for poetry
as the "worser half" of music that he has set comparatively few words by the great Russian poets,
and prefers the effusions of such poetasters as
Grekov and Sourikov. A fault which is common
in Tchaikovsky's orchestral music is also noticeable
in his songs. Not always very fastidious in his
choice of musical ideas, he seems to find a difficulty
in quitting them. He will develop, vary and repeat
an idea with a kind of mechanical skilfulness which
becomes wearisome. He had not the qualities of
terseness and concentration which go to the making
of a perfect song. Another fault—though many
may consider it an added fascination—in Tchaikovsky's songs is the monotonous vein of sentimental
melancholy. The great preponderance of the "tear-
ful minor" in his songs suggests an unhealthy
condition of mind. And I would point out this
difference between Tchaikovsky's melancholy and
that of his fellow-countrymen, of whom we may take
Moussorgsky as a characteristic type : that in the
first instance it is subjective, and sometimes artificial ;
while in the second it is objective and called into
being by the sufferings of others. It is just the

difference between "la belle mélancholie," so assiduously cultivated by Lamartine and his contemporaries, and "la tristesse de la vérité," which shows
so grimly in modern realism. But although these
depreciative remarks apply to a large proportion
of Tchaikovsky's songs, especially his early ones,
there are a few which show the master-hand, many
potentially fine songs in spite of their want of form,
and many, again, which we would not have otherwise
than they are—songs we cannot criticise when
we hear them, because they take our feelings by
storm.

In 1871 the Society of the Friends of National
Science celebrated the bicentenary of the birth of
Peter the Great by what was called the Polytechnic
Exhibition. For the opening ceremony Tchaikovsky
was commissioned to write a cantata to an appropriate
libretto by the poet Polonsky. The work was heard
once, and then—with the exception of some material
introduced later on into the *Third Symphony*—all
trace of it wholly disappeared. Tchaikovsky during
the next year or two was so deeply engaged upon his
new works, especially *The Oprichnik*, that he completely forgot this composition and took no steps to
save it from oblivion. During the following year
(1872) Tchaikovsky published his *Harmony Primer*,
which has been adopted as one of the text-books at
the Moscow Conservatoire.

During the rebuilding of the Little Theatre in
1873, all the companies—dramatic, operatic, and
ballet—were obliged to take refuge on the boards

of the Great Theatre. Under these conditions it occurred to M. Begichev, the inspector of the theatrical repertory, to utilise the services of the entire force in a kind of fairy play. Ostrovsky undertook the libretto, and chose for his subject the legend of the "Snow Queen"—*Snegourotchka;* while the music was entrusted to Tchaikovsky. Both the author and the musician took immense pleasure in their task. The sudden waking of the Russian spring never failed to stir Tchaikovsky, and this season always found him in his most exalted poetical mood. The composition of the music to this legend of springtide coincided with the coming of spring itself. In little more than three weeks the score was completed, in spite of the fact that Tchaikovsky was working twenty-seven hours a week at the Conservatoire. The first performance of *The Snow Queen* took place on 11th May 1873, but although its interpretation was undertaken by the best artists, and no expense spared in the mounting of the piece, it was not a success. The lack of dramatic interest outweighed the charm of the music. Shortly after the production of *The Snow Queen*, Tchaikovsky, with M. Kashkin, Nicholas Rubinstein, and one or two of the leading artists taking part in the piece, made an excursion to Vorobiev's Hill, a favourite resort in the neighbourhood of Moscow. "It was a lovely spring day," writes the author of the *Reminiscences*, "and the gardens of the village of Vorobiev were white with a sheet of blossom. Under the influence of spring and *The Snow Queen*, we were all in a very happy mood. The peasants soon gathered round to watch 'the quality' take their meal *al fresco* on the grass, and Nicholas Rubinstein arranged a real rustic feast, having bought for the peasants such sweets and wine as he could find in the village shops. Nicholas Rubinstein was very fond of genuine folk-music, and invited the peasants to sing. They needed no pressing, and soon started their choral dances. This scene must have always remained in Tchaikovsky's mind, and it was resuscitated years later, when he wrote the variations in the Pianoforte Trio, dedicated to the memory of 'a great artist'—Nicholas Rubinstein."

The Snow Queen consists of an Introduction to the play, of several entr'actes and dances, and includes a few choruses and solo numbers. The music is fresh and melodious, though not always of a high quality. The Introduction and the second entr'acte are the most successful parts of the work. Berezovsky considers that in some parts *The Snow Queen* shows that Tchaikovsky was very much influenced by Schumann at the time. Rimsky-Korsakov has also written a fairy opera to Ostrovsky's text, which, as regards imaginative treatment and national colouring, is superior to Tchaikovsky's work.

Some time during the early spring of 1874, Tchaikovsky finished his *Second Quartet in F major,* and it was privately performed at Nicholas Rubinstein's rooms in the presence of his more illustrious brother Anton. This occasion may serve as an

D

example of the inexplicable attitude of Anton Rubinstein towards the compositions of his former pupil. "I know," writes M. Kashkin, "that Rubinstein was very fond of Tchaikovsky as a man, and valued his talent very highly, but at the same time he took an almost hostile view of the majority of his compositions, especially the great ones. As a pianist he almost ignored Tchaikovsky's works. . . . The *Quartet in F major* was played before a very small audience; besides the players Laut, Grijimal, Fitzenhagen, and Herber—who, I believe, played second violin—there were present only Albrecht, Hubert, Anton Rubinstein, and myself. All the time the music went on, Rubinstein listened with a lowering, discontented expression, and at the end, with his usual brutal frankness, he said that it was not in the least in the style of chamber music; that he himself could not understand the composition, etc. The audience as well as the players went into ecstasies; but the one listener whose appreciation meant most to the composer obstinately stuck to his own opinion. One word from him would have been more valued than all other praise or success, but Tchaikovsky was not destined to hear that word, and he was evidently deeply hurt by Rubinstein's cutting remarks. It did not, however, shake his devotion to his former master. When, about a year later, he dedicated one of his piano pieces to Tchaikovsky, the latter was delighted, and replied by dedicating to Anton Rubinstein his *Six Pieces on one Theme* (op. 21); but he received no acknowledgment, and the great virtuoso never played one of these pieces in public."

From 1872 to 1876 Tchaikovsky acted as musical critic to the *Sovremennaya Lietopis* and the *Russky Vestnik*.

III

In 1872 the Conservatoires of Moscow and St. Petersburg had the misfortune to lose their most influential patroness, the Grand Duchess Helena Paulovna. Shortly before her death she had requested her favourite composer, Serov, to write an opera upon the subject of Gogol's "Christmas Eve Revels," for which Polonsky prepared the libretto. But Serov, who was just then engaged upon his opera *The Power of Evil*, had only time to complete one number of the new work when death put an end to his labours, and he breathed his last only an hour later than his patroness the Grand Duchess. Out of respect to the memory of this remarkable woman, the directors of the Imperial Musical Society resolved to carry out her wishes respecting this opera, and a competition was organised for the best setting of *Vakoula the Smith* (*Kouznetz Vakoula*), as Polonsky's libretto was entitled.

Tchaikovsky had not hitherto been very successful in his operatic works, and he hesitated for some time to take part in this competition. Consequently,

when at last he decided to do so, he was obliged to
work very rapidly in order to finish the opera by
August 1874. Seven works were sent in for
approval, and both the first and second prizes were
awarded to Tchaikovsky's composition. All his
friends were interested in the new work, and, encouraged by his success, Tchaikovsky, contrary to
custom, volunteered to play through the whole score
to a select audience of intimate friends. He was too
nervous, however, to do justice to the work. "The
performer killed the composer," and the opera,
rendered in a pointless and spiritless fashion, produced an unfavourable impression which the audience
could scarcely disguise. Afterwards, when the
printed score appeared, his friends recognised with
astonishment that *Kouznetz Vakoula* was one of Tchaikovsky's strongest dramatic efforts. The work was first
performed at the Marinsky Theatre, St. Petersburg,
in November 1876. It was sumptuously mounted,
and the parts entrusted to picked artists. Even the
small rôle of the *Golova* (headman of the village) was
taken by Petrov, the renowned *doyen* of the Russian
stage. *Kouznetz Vakoula* was received with enthusiasm, but its success was ephemeral. The public had
expected a light comic opera in the French style,
and did not appreciate the national element in
Tchaikovsky's music. It was given about seventeen
times, and then disappeared from the repertory. The
composer himself considered this opera one of his best
works. Later on he remodelled it under the title
of *Cherevichek* ("The little Shoes").

The year 1873 saw the production of two important orchestral compositions: the *Second Symphony in C minor*, and the orchestral fantasia on the subject of Shakespeare's *Tempest*. Tchaikovsky's *Second Symphony*, which was written a year or two before the opera *Vakoula the Smith*, is one of the most interesting examples of purely Russian symphonic music, and has been aptly called the Little-Russian Symphony, because its first and last movements are based on Malo-Russian melodies. It may here be noted that the difference between the folk-music of the Great Russians and the Malo-Russians is as great as the difference in character between the two races; consequently this symphony has a peculiar character of its own to which it owes its title, and not—as one critic has sapiently observed—to the fact that it is based on *small* Russian themes. The *Second Symphony* is perhaps the most distinctively national of all Tchaikovsky's works. The first *Allegro* is preceded by an Introduction founded on a beautiful melody of an elegiac character which runs straight into the *Allegro*. The first subject of this movement is a variant of the well-known air, "Down by Mother Volga." This is one of the songs associated with the Cossack robber Stenka Razin, whose "rebellious head"—as the ballad has it—was cut off in the Red Square, at Moscow, in 1671, and it is a great favourite among Russian students. The second movement, *Andantino marciale*, has one very interesting subject which the composer borrowed from the march in *Undine*, the unpublished opera of which he had destroyed the score. The *Finale*, which is generally considered the best movement of the symphony, has two remarkable themes treated in variation form. The first of these is taken from the Little-Russian song called "The Crane"; the second —a beautiful melody—is original. The symphony is full of vitality, movement, and racy humour, and, according to Berezovsky, it shows in sentiment and workmanship a strong reflection of Glinka's influence. It was first performed in Moscow at a concert of the Russian Musical Society in 1873, and was received with great applause, but Tchaikovsky, who was easily discouraged when his own work was in question, was persuaded by some hypercritical friends to make great changes in the symphony before it was published. "I always preferred the original form," says Kashkin, "and fortunately it might be restored, at least for purposes of comparison, for the orchestral parts used at the first performance are still preserved in the library of the Moscow Conservatoire."

A work of a totally different character was the symphonic fantasia *The Tempest*, composed during a month's holiday at a country house in the government of Tambov. It was written to a programme suggested by M. Vladimir Stassov, who has so often inspired the composers for the New Russian school with subjects for musical illustration. M. Stassov in one of his letters has given me the following account of its origin : —

"In 1872 I was very intimate with Tchaikovsky, and in constant correspondence with him. As he had observed with pleasure the various subjects for overtures, operas, and symphonies which I had recently suggested to some of my friends among the Russian composers, he asked me to find him a suitable subject for an overture. At first I refused, saying that for each individual composer one must only choose a theme completely in keeping with his nature and temperament, and that I did not feel that I knew his tastes and disposition well enough to undertake the task. However, he would not accept my refusal, and wrote me several letters, pressing me to yield, and saying that *no one was more capable than myself of finding a subject which would fascinate him.* I then gave in, and having tried him with several subjects—beginning with Scott's " Kenilworth," which did not please him much—I finally proposed Shakespeare's *Tempest*, a subject I had been mad about ever since my young days. Tchaikovsky was delighted, and wrote me back a warm reply, saying nothing could have suited him better, that he was full of enthusiasm, and could think of nothing else. He accepted my programme in all its details, without the least change, and the work, he said, must and should be dedicated to no one but myself. Shortly afterwards all this was faithfully carried out."

Stassov's programme stands as follows : " The sea. Ariel, spirit of the air, raises a tempest in obedience to the will of the enchanter Prospero. Wreck of the vessel conveying Ferdinand. The enchanted island. The first shy awakening of love between Miranda and Ferdinand. Ariel. Caliban. The enamoured pair give themselves up to the magic of love. Prospero divests himself of his powers of enchantment and quits the island. The sea." The subjects are fresh and poetical. The picture of the sea, both in storm and in undulating calm, is highly effective; especially the chords for trombones in the lower register, which give a wonderful sense of strength and repose. The Ariel theme is very sprightly, and treated with appropriate lightness and grace. It is followed by a bold, rough figure, given out by celli and basses, which effectively symbolises the uncouth Caliban. Prospero's *Leitmotif*, which has almost a religious character, seems the least appropriate of all these characteristic themes. The most noticeable fault of the fantasia is one common to most of Tchaikovsky's works, namely the irritating repetition of certain phrases which finally wearies the nerves of the hearer and ends in a temporary suspension of interest. *The Tempest* was performed at the Paris Exhibition in 1873, and was enthusiastically received.

To this period belongs the *Pianoforte Concerto in B flat minor* (op. 25). M. Kashkin gives an interesting account of the birth of this work. He writes: —

" Tchaikovsky, who had long had it in his mind to compose a pianoforte concerto for Nicholas Rubinstein, set about this work in the winter of 1874. The task proved a difficult one, because the invention of passages for the piano combined with orchestra did not come easily to him; but he did not shrink from difficulties, and in February 1875 the composition was quite ready. Tchaikovsky took the finished score to Nicholas Rubinstein, and on the title-page was inscribed the dedication to him. Tchaikovsky himself was very well satisfied with his composition, upon which he had worked hard and with zeal. The composer looked forward to the fullest approval, more especially as his friend and adviser always evinced the warmest interest in his compositions and his talent generally. This time it turned out very differently. Nicholas Rubinstein, it appeared, was disagreeably surprised that Tchaikovsky —not being a pianist—had not asked his advice about the piano part, and therefore he showed prejudice and hostility as regards this work. At the trial of the concerto N. A. Hubert and myself were the only auditors. Nicholas Rubinstein, who read admirably at sight, started the concerto, and began finding fault with everything, but especially with the piano technique. He played even with a certain intentional clumsiness, finding it all unsuitably written, too difficult, and finally declaring it altogether unplayable from this point of view, and in need of great altera- tion. N. A. Hubert did not pronounce a definite judg- ment, but seemed to agree with Rubinstein; while Tchaikovsky was burning with anger against them both. Generally speaking, he had so great a respect for Nicholas Rubinstein as a pianist and musician that no doubt he would have agreed with him as to all the alterations if his criticisms had been made in a more conciliatory spirit; but so harsh a judgment merely irritated him, and he resolved to publish the

concerto without altering a single note; only the
original dedication was struck out and replaced by
one to Hans von Bülow, whose acquaintance
Tchaikovsky had made during the previous year.
Von Bülow was delighted with the concerto, as
I saw from a letter of his to Tchaikovsky, which
was shown to me; and as he was just starting on a
long concert tour in America, he included in his
programme the work which had been dedicated to
him. Thus it happened that Tchaikovsky's *B flat
minor Concerto* was heard for the first time in
Boston, U.S.A. Bülow sent Tchaikovsky a telegram
announcing the brilliant success of his work. Of
course this news gratified the composer; but just
then he happened to be very short of money, and it
was not without some compunction that he spent it
all in answering the message. In Moscow the concerto was played for the first time by S. J. Taneiev,
with great success; and afterwards Nicholas Rubinstein
actually learnt it, and his playing of it was such as
one could hardly hear from any other artist. He
had a particular success with it at the Russian concerts
at the Paris Exhibition of 1878." Speaking of this
work, Mr. C. A. Barry says: "That N. Rubinstein
was not altogether over-severe in his strictures of
Tchaikovsky's piano technique, appears from the
fact that at a subsequent date Tchaikovsky thoroughly
overhauled his work, and issued a new and revised
edition of it in 1889, when it was found that
the pianoforte part had, to a great extent, been
rewritten."

IV

TCHAIKOVSKY worked with untiring perseverance, but the occupation of teaching grew more distasteful to him year by year. He dreamt of an ideal life in some quiet country place where he could give himself up entirely to composition. But he believed such an ideal existence to be, if not quite unattainable, at least very remote. The manner in which his dream was ultimately fulfilled reads like a fairy tale. In 1878 a lady, who preferred to keep her identity concealed, and who was not personally known to the composer, made it possible by her generous initiative for him to give up his classes at the Conservatoire and devote all his time to the creation of new works. Already in 1874 his improved means had permitted him to move from the small rooms in the Gudrinsky Place into a cosy flat, where he remained until his marriage in 1877.

In 1874 Tchaikovsky completed a new opera, *The Oprichnik*, in which he incorporated a good deal of musical material from *The Voievoda* and his

symphonic poem *Destiny*. *The Oprichnik* is sometimes translated by the somewhat misleading title of
"The Lifeguardsman." The Oprichniks were a
band of dissolute young noblemen, the chosen body-
guard of Ivan the Terrible, who swore by fearful and
unnatural oaths to carry out every command of the
despot they served. Sometimes they masqueraded in
the dress of monks, but they were in reality robbers
and murderers, hated and feared by the people whom
they oppressed. Andrew Morozov, the descendant
of a noble but impoverished house, and the only son
of the widowed Lady Morozova, is in love with the
beautiful Natalia, daughter of Prince Jemchoujny.
His poverty disqualifies him as a suitor. While
desperately in need of money, Andrew falls in with
Basmanov, a young Oprichnik, who persuades him to
join the community, telling him that an Oprichnik
can always fill his own pockets. Andrew consents, and
takes the customary oath of celibacy. Afterwards
circumstances cause him to break his vow and marry
Natalia against her father's wish. Prince Viazminsky,
the leader of the Oprichniks, cherishes an old grudge
against the family of Morozov, and works for Andrew's
downfall. On his wedding-day he breaks in upon
the feast with a message from the Tsar. Ivan the
Terrible has heard of the bride's beauty, and desires
her attendance at the royal apartments. Andrew,
with gloomy forebodings in his heart, prepares to
escort his bride, when Viazminsky, with a meaning
smile, explains that the invitation is for the bride
alone. Andrew refuses to let his wife go into the

tyrant's presence unprotected. Viazminsky proclaims him a rebel and a traitor to his vows. Natalia is carried away by force, and the Oprichniks lead Andrew into the market-place to suffer the death-penalty at their hands. Meanwhile Lady Morozova, who had cast off her son when he became an Oprichnik, has softened towards him, and comes to see him on his wedding-day. She enters the deserted hall where Viazminsky, alone, is gloating over the success of his intrigue. She inquires unsuspectingly for Andrew, and he leads her to the window. Horror-stricken, she witnesses the execution of her own son by his brother Oprichniks, and falls dead at the feet of her implacable enemy.

Tchaikovsky himself is answerable for the plot of the opera, and it would be difficult to find anything more tragic, even in the gloomy and blood-stained pages of mediæval Russian history; but it certainly offers great scope for dramatic development.

The opera opens with an overture in which all the leading motives and chief situations in the opera are more or less anticipated. The curtain rises upon the garden of Prince Jemchoujny's house, where he is discovered in earnest conversation with Mitkov, his daughter's accepted suitor. After they have left the stage, Natalia enters with her old nurse and a company of young girls, and there follows a charming chorus on a well-known Russian folk-song. Then the girls beg Natalia for a song, and she complies with a pretty, plaintive melody, very vocal, but without any marked originality. Next the Oprichniks come upon the scene, and their characteristic motive is heard in the orchestra. Basmanov meets Andrew Morozov, learns the secret of his depression, and offers to lend him some money, advising him at the same time to cast in his lot with theirs. The air "Come live among us," in which Basmanov seeks to entice the young man by promising him a life of adventure and full pockets in the future, seems quite inappropriate, being an elegant *cantilena* in the minor. After the solo, the orchestra has some bars illustrating the wild life of the Oprichniks. Andrew and Basmanov leave the garden together, and Natalia reappears, and, after a short recitative, sings a pretty air, "Ah, Furious Wind," quite Italian in character. The act ends with a second chorus of maidens, which makes an abrupt transition from the Italian to the national style.

The first scene of the second act takes place in the house of the Morozovs. The orchestra reflects the anxious forebodings with which Lady Morozova awaits her son's return. Then in an admirably characteristic recitative, which seems at once to distinguish her as the type of a high-minded religious woman, she expresses her faith in God and her resignation in all her misfortunes. Andrew now returns, and brings her the money Basmanov has given him. Lady Morozova refuses to touch what she knows to be the fruits of robbery and murder, and, in a long and touching scene, implores her son not to associate himself with the hated Oprichniks. Andrew, who is devoted to his mother, promises to obey her wishes. His solo in this act, "The White Snow," is one of the most successful, and at the same time national, numbers in the whole work.

The second scene takes us into the king's palace. It opens with a chorus (*à capella*) of the Oprichniks, who, attired as monks, are seen issuing from the royal oratory. At a sacrilegious word from their leader they throw aside their monastic garb and reveal their rich robes beneath. Basmanov introduces Andrew to the community, and he takes their vow. The first sacrifice demanded of him is the complete renunciation of his mother and Natalia. The music which depicts Andrew's inward struggle before he consents to give up all for the sake of retrieving his fortunes is often full of poignant dramatic feeling. The effect is enhanced by the gloomy chorus of the Oprichniks, which forms as it were the musical basis of the whole scene. Only, here again, Andrew's solo, with its occasional reminiscences of Rossini, seems out of keeping with the rest of the music.

The third act shows a square in Moscow. The townspeople are assembled, and in the opening chorus they bewail "that the times are evil." Then with an expression of almost fatalistic resignation and submissive piety, which is realistically characteristic of the Russian poor, they turn their lament into a touching and beautiful prayer: *Andante religioso*, "Thou, God, succour us." This scene is remarkably impressive. Lady Morozova now appears. She has suffered one more misfortune in the desertion of her son. She sings a pathetic recitative, "Now am I lonely." The children in the square catch sight of

Lady Morozova, and hail her with insulting epithets
—"Mother of an Oprichnik," etc. But the older
people are sorry for her afflictions, which are even
greater than their own. She is about to enter the
church, when Natalia hastens in. She has fled from
her father and her middle-aged lover, and implores
Lady Morozova to succour her. Her father now
arrives, and orders his rebellious daughter to return
home. Natalia's reply is given in an aria, "As
before God, O father." Prince Jemchoujny will
not relent, and orders his servants to carry off
Natalia by force. His proceedings are interrupted
by the arrival of the Oprichniks, awakening terror
and hatred among the people. Andrew sees his
mother and rushes to embrace her, while the sinister
theme of the Oprichniks is heard reminding him of his
vows. Lady Morozova turns from her son, disowns
him, and solemnly curses him as an Oprichnik. The
end of this scene is full of incident, and the music
rises to a high level of dramatic interest.

The last act takes place in the king's palace.
Andrew, unable to abandon Natalia to her fate, has
determined to marry her in spite of his vows. The
curtain draws up upon the wedding-feast, and some
of the Oprichniks who are present sing a chorus in
praise of the bride. The chorus is based upon a
folk-song, and, though musically interesting, suffers
from over-repetition. It is succeeded by national
dances, for which also folk-songs are employed.
The duet between Andrew and Natalia, "Ah, let the
feast be ended soon," has two subjects, one of which

E

Tchaikovsky transferred from his unpublished symphonic poem *Destiny*. I have already described the tragic ending of the opera. The curtain falls to a chorus of the Oprichniks, heard off the stage as they return from the execution of Andrew: "Hail, hail! Like the glorious sun at midday art thou, our father and our Tsar."

The Oprichnik, though by no means a faultless work, was a great advance on Tchaikovsky's earlier operas, *Undine* and *The Voievoda*. The chief shortcomings are a want of unity in the style of the music; a lack of decision in the portrayal of many of the characters—Lady Morozova is quite the most convincing and real of all the *dramatis personæ;* an occasional want of connection between the music and the words, and perhaps, we must add, the unrelieved gloom of the libretto. In spite of all this the opera holds our attention. The music is always fluent, often very impressive, and, as might be expected from Tchaikovsky, it contains many beautiful melodies. It is not surprising, therefore, that *The Oprichnik* holds its own on the Russian stage. Its immediate success was sufficient to encourage Tchaikovsky to new efforts in the sphere of dramatic music.

In 1875 he wrote a work in the same tonality as his pianoforte concerto—the *Sérénade Mélancholique,* for violin and orchestra. It is based on two very interesting subjects : one of a melancholy nature, the other exceedingly passionate.

V

To the same year belongs his *Third Symphony in D* (op. 29), a work altogether different in style to his two earlier ones, and totally western in character. It has some emotional and intellectual affinity with the Schumann symphonies, but displays such brilliancy of orchestration as the German master never attained to. This symphony—which is exceedingly popular in Russia and abroad—has, in some mysterious way, acquired the title of "The Polish." The label is as misleading as unauthorised labels generally are. Certainly the symphony ends with an Allegro—*tempo di Polacca*, a very alien and artificial form of that genuine national dance, the polonaise; but since the second movement is *alla tedesca*, would it not be just as reasonable—and from internal evidence far more appropriate—to christen the symphony "The German"? If there is not enough that is genuinely Polish in the musical material of the work to warrant the choice of this title, the idea that Tchaikovsky here poured out his sympathy for "Poland mourning

in her oppression and rejoicing in her regeneration"
is still more untenable. When we remember that
Tchaikovsky was exceedingly Russian in his sympathies, and that as the writer of *1812*, the *Marche
Slave*, and the *Triumphal Overture on the Danish
Hymn*, he may be regarded as the official composer
of Russia, it seems quite incredible. One would as
soon expect to find Mr. Rudyard Kipling writing an
ode in praise of the Little Englanders, or Mr. Kensit
a complimentary sonnet to the Pope. Berezovsky
gives the following brief account of this symphony:
"It consists of the customary four movements. The
first opens with a magnificent funeral march, which
leads to an allegro of a festal character, broadly
planned. The second begins with a graceful valse
alla tedesca, which afterwards gives place to an
Andante elegiaco. This *andante*, for its depth of
thought, its sincere and vital emotional qualities,
is the best movement of the whole symphony, and
one of the finest of musical conceptions. Here
Tchaikovsky's genius is displayed in all its force, in
all its varied character, and in the setting of his inimitable technique. In comparison with the *Andante*,
the third movement of the symphony—a *Scherzo*—
loses a great deal. Here expression predominates
over the contents, and leaves the impression of beautiful but uninspired music. The *Finale* is better than
the *Scherzo;* it is written throughout in the major,
and the symphony ends as it were in dazzling sun-
shine. Performed in Paris in 1876, and in New
York in 1879, this work had great success, and

attracted the attention of Europe and America to its composer."

The year 1875 also saw the publication of four sets of songs, op. 16, 25, 27, and 28. The first set, op. 16, contains two of Tchaikovsky's best: the graceful "Slumber Song," and "A Modern Greek Song," founded on a *Dies Irae* of the Middle Ages, and treated with consummate skill. In op. 25 are "Reconciliation" and "Mignon's Song." Op. 27 contains, among others, two songs in mazurka form to words by Miczkievich, which are not very well known in England. Op. 28 is a very remarkable collection, containing "The Coral Necklace," one of his most dramatic songs; "Wherefore"; the charming and characteristic "He loves me well"; and "The Dread Moment," an expression of wild, despairing passion.

In March 1875 Tchaikovsky's nerves broke down, and the doctors ordered him abroad, forbidding him to touch the piano or a sheet of music-paper. He followed these orders more strictly in the letter than in the spirit. Perhaps it would have been impossible to check entirely the creative activity of his mind; in any case, he returned with a new composition complete in his brain, though not a note had been committed to paper. The violinist Laub died in the spring of 1875, and Tchaikovsky, who had the warmest admiration for his talent, honoured his memory by the *E flat Quartet*. The date upon the MS. of this quartet (in the possession of P. Jurgenson) is February 1876, but M. Kashkin seems to have no doubt as to its having been composed a year earlier. At this time the editor of the *Nouvelist*—a St. Petersburg magazine—commissioned Tchaikovsky to write twelve short pieces, to appear monthly, under the general title of *The Seasons*. An amusing anecdote is told in connection with these pieces. Tchaikovsky, who was afraid of forgetting this little commission, told his servant—who was devoted to him—to remind him when the date came round for sending off a piece. The man never forgot, and every month he used to say to his master, "Peter Ilich, this is your day for sending to Petersburg." Tchaikovsky would go to his desk, dash off the composition, and dispatch it by the next post.

Opera was the species of composition that offered the greatest attraction to Tchaikovsky, and after that some orchestral work on a large scale, though now and then he would publish a series of songs, or "romances," as the Russians call them. Like most of his fellow-countrymen, he was, at that period of his life, a devotee of the ballet, and had long cherished the idea of producing something of this kind. The opportunity came at last when Begichev, stage-manager of the Grand Theatre at Moscow, proposed to Tchaikovsky to write a ballet. The latter agreed, but stipulated for a fantastic subject from the Age of Chivalry, and Begichev himself sketched out the plot for *The Swan Lake*, for which Tchaikovsky consented to supply the music for 800 roubles—about £100. His ideal ballet in those days was

Giselle, the joint production of Théophile Gautier and Adolphe Adam. The ballet was begun and finished in the summer of 1876, and the pianoforte score was arranged by M. Kashkin. At the request of the ballet-master, a national dance—quite out of keeping with the rest—was added to the work. The success of *The Swan Lake*, if not brilliant, was fairly lasting. It continued to be given until the scenery and dresses became shabby, when the authorities did not take any steps to restore the *mise en scène*. The music, too, underwent a great many changes, being gradually replaced by airs from other ballets until only about a third of the original was left. Recently *The Swan Lake* has been very successfully revived in St. Petersburg.

Two pieces of a more or less occasional character were produced in the course of 1876. The *Triumphal Overture on the Danish National Hymn*, was written for the visit of the Princess Dagmar to Moscow, and is on the whole superior to the general run of such works. A more interesting and inspired creation is the *Marche Slave*. The war between Turkey and Servia, in 1876, was the occasion of a great display of Slavonic enthusiasm. Nicholas Rubinstein organised a concert for the benefit of the wounded, for which Tchaikovsky, who was in full sympathy with the feelings of the hour, composed a march, first known as the "Russo-Servian," but afterwards as the "Slavonic March." It had a great success, being a stirring presentment of the emotions which just then were dominant in Russia, and in some measure it was prophetic of the triumph of the Slavonic cause.

Another great work belonging to this period is the third orchestral fantasia *Francesca di Rimini*, which was originally conceived as an opera. The libretto was brought to Tchaikovsky by the author, K. I. Zvantsev, and the composer, who was well satisfied with it, was about to begin the work, when the librettist attempted to impose some impossible conditions. Zvantsev was an almost fanatical Wagnerite, and insisted that his book should be treated according to Wagnerian principles; but the Russian composer refused to relinquish his complete liberty of action, and the opera was consequently abandoned. His imagination, however, had been fired by the subject, and he could not refrain from using up his ideas in some different form. Tchaikovsky informed M. Kashkin that Doré's drawings for Dante's "Divine Comedy" had had a considerable influence upon his picture of "Hell's Whirlwind." If so, the painter's conception gained immensely in impressiveness and dignity by its reincarnation in the musician's mind. Tchaikovsky's realism is of a far more poetic quality than Doré's, and singularly free, in this instance, from mere sensationalism. Tchaikovsky prefaces his score with the following passages from Dante's "Inferno," Canto V. (Cary's translation) : —

"Dante, coming into the second circle of Hell, witnesses the punishment of carnal sinners, who are tossed about ceaselessly in the dark air by the most furious winds. Amongst these, he

meets with Francesca of Rimini, who relates her
story : —

> . . . No greater grief than to remember days
> Of joy, when misery is at hand. That kens
> Thy learn'd instructor. Yet so eagerly
> If thou art bent to know the primal root,
> From whence our love gat being, I will do
> As one who weeps and tells his tale. One day,
> For our delight we read of Lancelot,
> How him love thrall'd. Alone we were, and no
> Suspicion near us. Oft-times by that reading
> Our eyes were drawn together, and the hue
> Fled from our alter'd cheek. But at one point
> Alone we fell. When of that smile we read,
> The wished-for smile so rapturously kissed
> By one so deep in love, then he, who ne'er
> From me shall separate, at once my lips
> All trembling kiss'd. The book and writer both
> Were love's purveyors. In its leaves that day
> We read no more. Thus while one spirit spake,
> The other wailed so sorely, that heart-struck
> I, through compassion fainting, seem'd not far
> From death, and like a corse fell to the ground.

The two first movements of the fantasia—
Andante lugubre and *Piu mosso*—are clearly intended
to illustrate the prose passages from the Argument.
To the *Allegro vivo* which succeeds it is difficult to
assign a definite connection with the text; but with
the clarinet cadenza at the close of this movement,
and the lovely melody which follows it—a melody
so entirely characteristic of Tchaikovsky's genius—
we seem to hear the spirit-voice of Francesca herself,
from which all the horrors of Hell have not taken the
sweetness of human love and poignant memory.

Immediately after the completion of *Francesca di Rimini*, he made a rough sketch of his *Fourth Symphony in F minor*. But already a new conception possessed him, which for the time being drove all others from his mind—this was the idea of *Eugene Oniegin*.

VI

IN May 1877, during the examinations at the Conservatoire, Tchaikovsky first confided to M. Kashkin his intention of writing an opera on the subject of Poushkin's celebrated "novel in verse," *Eugene Oniegin*. For the germ of this idea he was indebted to the celebrated Russian singer, Elizabeth Andrecona Lovrovsky. For several evenings in succession M. Kashkin and Tchaikovsky sat up half the night, in a private room of Taistov's Restaurant, trying to sketch out a feasible plot that should not depart too much from Poushkin's poem. The task proved almost beyond their powers, and finally Tchaikovsky declared that though he despaired of adapting *Eugene Oniegin* for operatic purposes, he still felt impelled to write something on the subject, in order to use up the many ideas which had taken root in his mind. Feeling that his work might not be suitable for a big stage, he persuaded Nicholas Rubinstein to let it be performed by the pupils of the Conservatoire, and, happy in this assurance, he threw himself heart and soul into the new project, after securing the services of Shilovsky as collaborator in the libretto.

Probably no one was more astonished than Tchaikovsky himself when he found that this work, from which he expected very little beyond personal satisfaction and a pretty operatic performance for the Conservatoire students, was destined to prove not only his most successful work, but—if we except Glinka's *Life for the Tsar*—the most popular opera in all Russia. The secret of this success lies partly in the subject itself, which is known to every reading man and woman in the land; partly in the very melodious and accessible character of the music; and partly, again, in the fact that in *Eugene Oniegin* Tchaikovsky had hit upon a subject which, though it did not call forth the very greatest that was in him, was, on the whole, pre-eminently suited to his genius, and especially to his melancholy lyricism. But though the opera is by far the most successful of Tchaikovsky's works, and in respect of popularity would soon become a rival to "The Pathetic" Symphony and *Casse-Noisette Suite*, it is by no means his best. There are really great moments in *The Oprichnik;* in *Eugene Oniegin* there are moments of extraordinary weakness and banality. But the former will interest the educated minority in spite of its faults; while the latter will take "the great public" by storm, and be loved for these very weaknesses themselves. There is a great affinity—in certain moods— between the genius of Poushkin and that of Tchaikovsky. Both had at times the gift of wearing their hearts on their sleeves in a very graceful, and not too unmanly, fashion. It is the gift of all others that has most attraction for the great public, who resent nothing so much as the failure to read the man in his work. The sentimentality, the false pathos, the Byronic cynicism of *Eugene Oniegin*, would have been far less attractive but for the thinly-veiled auto-biographic interest of the story. As it is, probably every Russian youth has fancied himself an Oniegin or a Lensky; every Russian girl has played at being Tatiana. And Tchaikovsky has attuned himself without difficulty to the subjective and sentimental mood of the poet, which was so often his own most characteristic temper of mind—though not his highest. The result in both cases is a work of almost unparalleled popularity.

The characters in the story offer several strongly-marked contrasts, of which Tchaikovsky has not availed himself in his musical presentment of them. The sisters, Tatiana and Olga, are two very different types of Russian girlhood. Tatiana is dreamy, sentimental, naïve, without coquetry; capable of folly for love's sake, but incapable of dishonour. Olga— as she appears in the book of the opera—is full of animal spirits, practical, and a reckless flirt. The girls belong to any period. The young men, on the contrary, seem essentially "dated." Lensky, the sensitive, morbid, passionate youth, fresh from a German university, belongs to the Byronic period. So, too, does Oniegin, the cold-blooded, cultured, world-weary young rake, who works such havoc in the quiet home of the Lerins.

The opera opens with an Introduction founded on the dreamy, graceful subject which is Tatiana's *Leitmotif*. Later on we hear the subject of the duet between Tatiana and Oniegin, and then the music reverts to the first theme. "Thus," says Berezovsky, "the essence of the drama is revealed to us: a love episode in the life of a woman who remains essentially unchanged by the experience."

The opening scene shows the garden of the Lerins' country-house. Madame Lerin, seated under the trees, is busy preserving her fruit; her daughters, Olga and Tatiana, are seen at the open window of the drawing-room. Their duet, "Hearest thou the Nightingale?" is extremely pretty, in a delicate, sentimental style that seems to carry us back to the days of "sensibility" and clear muslin frocks. After the duet comes a quartet, in which Madame Lerin and the old nurse Philipievna take part. Then the peasantry arrive on the scene, and there follows a chorus of harvesters, based on a very original theme, which is quite national in character. At Madame Lerin's invitation they start a choral dance. Meanwhile the sisters come into the garden. Tatiana advances dreamily, book in hand. Olga rallies her sister on her romantic proclivities and sings her first solo, "I have no mind for languor or for sadness," the music of which is in complete contradiction to the words. Their neighbour Lensky, who is in love with Olga, now comes in, and begs permission to introduce his friend Eugene Oniegin. The young men wear high riding-boots and long black cloaks of Byronic fashion. When the young people are left alone, Oniegin entertains Tatiana in a somewhat colourless recitative. After these two have wandered into the garden, Lensky remains with Olga and sings his impassioned love-song, "I love you, Olga." Throughout the entire opera Lensky's music has the most vitality, and is best suited to the character it portrays. Presently the old nurse is sent to announce that tea is served. Her eyes, quickened by love, mark a subtle change in Tatiana. She guesses that her darling has already lost her heart to "the young stranger." As the curtain falls the orchestra, in a few expressive bars, suggest the emotions newly awakened in Tatiana's heart.

In the second scene of the first act, we see Tatiana's room by moonlight. The nurse comes to remind her that it is bed-time. Then there follows a long, confidential recitative between them, while the orchestra carries on a soft accompaniment based upon Tatiana's *Leitmotif*. This scene, so exquisite in every detail—and recalling a similar scene in Shakespeare's *Romeo and Juliet*—is deservedly the most popular number in the whole opera. Tatiana's part is a musical *chef-d'œuvre*, and the nurse's tale, told to an air in the style of a Russian folk-song, is excellent. When the nurse has departed, Tatiana falls into a reverie, from which she rouses to sing her beautiful little song, "Nay, though I be undone," in which she tells her love of Oniegin. But how

will he guess her secret, unless she reveals it herself?
Then she resolves to write a love-letter to him.
Meanwhile the orchestra delicately indicates all the
emotions through which Tatiana is passing. Her
modesty, her maidenly misgivings, her despair, her
ecstasy, and the final triumph of passionate first-love.
When the nurse returns, the letter is finished, and
Tatiana begs her to convey it to Oniegin. She
hesitates, but cannot refuse anything to this child of
her heart. As she reluctantly departs on her errand,
Tatiana, seated at her writing-table, sinks once more
into her dreamy mood, and the curtain falls to her
characteristic motive.

The third scene takes us back to the garden of
the Lerins' house, and opens with a chorus, based on
a folk-song, sung by the peasant girls, who have been
gathering berries. As Tatiana enters, the orchestra
depicts her ill-concealed agitation. She has not seen
the young stranger since she sent her love-letter, and
by morning light her conduct seems unmaidenly.
Presently Oniegin enters. He cannot appreciate the
directness and sweetness of Tatiana's nature. To
his jaded mind this simple country-girl is insipid;
for he is of the type who finds the savour of love
"not in the woman but the chace." He thanks her
coldly for her letter, but assures her that he is not
a marrying man; and after offering her brotherly
affection, gives her some half-cynical advice as to
the need of more maidenly reserve in future. Finally
he leaves her crushed with shame and the pain of a
first disappointment.

The fourth scene opens upon a brilliantly-lighted room in the Lerins' house. The guests are dressed in the quaint costumes and uniforms of the twenties. The ball is in honour of Tatiana's birthday. An old-fashioned slow valse is heard in the orchestra. Oniegin, whom Lensky has dragged to the ball against his will, stands apart from the guests in a mood of cynical boredom. He resolves to console himself by flirting with Olga, and carries her off to dance, leaving Lensky—who is now her accepted lover—fuming with jealousy and injured vanity. Oniegin's music in this scene is probably meant to illustrate his condition of mind, but it leaves an impression of weakness, as well as of coldness, which does not accord with his character. The complimentary couplets to Tatiana, sung to an old-fashioned French air by a typical Frenchman, Triquet, make a pleasant break in the continuous valse-rhythm which accompanies the first part of this scene. After Triquet's solo, the valse gives place to a mazurka, and Olga is again seen dancing and flirting with Oniegin. Lensky loses his self-control, and unwisely demands an explanation. Oniegin is coldly insolent, and Olga rebellious. Lensky first insults his friend, and then forces a challenge upon him. Oniegin now feels some qualms of conscience, but it is too late to retreat or apologise. He consents to go out with Lensky, and the party breaks up in consternation.

The fifth scene represents a winter landscape at dawn. The short orchestral prelude is founded on Lensky's *Leitmotif*, one of the most interesting

F

subjects in the opera. While Lensky is awaiting Oniegin's arrival he sings his aria, "My days of youth, where have they fled?" which is one of the best and most characteristic of Tchaikovsky's inspirations. After the sincere pathos of Lensky's air, the conventional duel scene which follows seems rather poor and stagey.

Some years are supposed to elapse between the fifth and sixth scenes. The curtain rises upon a reception-room in a luxurious house in St. Petersburg. The guests are seen moving to and fro to the music of a brilliant polonaise. Apart from the rest, Oniegin stands in a gloomy reflection. In a long and not very interesting recitative he tells of his remorse for Lensky's death, his wanderings in search of peace, and of his jaded spirit, which can find no satisfaction in love or folly. Meanwhile the ball goes on, and the guests are all awaiting the arrival of the acknowledged belle of society, the Princess Gremin. She proves to be Tatiana, grown into a gracious and stately woman of the world. Her husband, Prince Gremin, is a dignified nobleman, high in the diplomatic world, middle-aged, but handsome, and devoted to his beautiful young wife. Oniegin is astonished to recognise in this dazzling woman the girl whose love he had rejected. His chilly egoism is thawed, and he falls passionately in love.

The last scene takes place in the boudoir of Princess Gremin. She is reading a letter from Oniegin. Tatiana has been quietly happy with her elderly prince, but the sight of her first love has awakened her stronger emotions. His letter throws her into a state of agitation, and before she can recover her self-control, Oniegin bursts in upon her with a passionate declaration of love. In a long duet, in which emotion is kept at extreme tension, Oniegin implores her to have pity and to fly with him, while she struggles between honour and reawakened love. Finally, with a supreme effort she breaks away from him at the very moment when she has just confessed her true feeling. When the curtain falls, Oniegin, baffled and despairing, is left alone on the stage.

It would be easy to find fault with the opera of *Eugene Oniegin*, to point to the lack of musical development in the various characters, or to condemn the poverty of the libretto—which, except for a few of Poushkin's original verses—is very poor stuff indeed. But when all is said and done, we are obliged to agree with Berezovsky, that this opera "is like a woman with many faults of heart and character, but whom we love for her beauty in spite of them all."

VII

WE have now reached the supreme crisis in the life of Tchaikovsky. At the time of the examinations in May 1877, M. Kashkin thinks the composer was already engaged to be married, although he kept this a secret from all his friends. Afterwards the staff of the Conservatoire dispersed for the summer vacation, and on M. Kashkin's return to Moscow in August, he was considerably surprised at meeting the newly-married couple at a party given in their honour by the Jurgensons. This was the sole occasion upon which M. Kashkin ever saw them together. Tchaikovsky attended to his work at the Conservatoire with his usual regularity, but all his friends observed a change in him. He was reserved and absent-minded, and seemed anxious to avoid all intimate conversation. One day he came to the Conservatoire looking strangely agitated. He said that he had been summoned to St. Petersburg by Napravnik, and took a hasty leave of his colleagues. A few days afterwards the news of his serious illness reached Moscow.

At first the accounts were alarming, but they grew more reassuring after a time. Naturally his sudden departure gave cause for much gossip. Then, as time went on, Tchaikovsky's hasty marriage and its tragic consequences came to be looked upon as an amusing comedy by outsiders. Even his most intimate friends had very little clue to the mysterious catastrophe which seemed to have broken up his life. M. Kashkin, who knew his tender-heartedness and the almost feminine sensibility of his nature, was filled with the gravest apprehensions, which, as it afterwards proved, were not without some foundation. Tchaikovsky afterwards confessed that though he shrank from an act that would have brought public disgrace upon his relatives, he had tried in many ways to shake off the life which was at that time a burden to him, and had gone so far as to stand up to his chest in the river in the first sharp frost of a September night, in the hopes of literally catching his death of cold, and getting rid of his troubles without scandal. Evidently for a short time he was overwrought to the verge of insanity, and owed, perhaps, life and reason to the devoted care of his brother, who took him abroad as soon as his physical condition permitted him to travel. A very peaceful existence in the town of Clarens, on Lake Geneva, did much to restore his health, but his spirit was too bruised to recover quickly. After a short time he wrote to his friends in Moscow that he intended to return to his duties after a long rest, but neither M. Kashkin nor N. Rubinstein thought this at all probable. Some extracts from his letters written at this time will best show his condition of mind during these months of adversity. To Albrecht he writes: "I shall remain abroad the rest of this year (1877), and return about the first of September next year. It is only in absence that one learns to know all the strength of one's affection for one's friends. Now I am living amid the wonderful scenery of Switzerland, and in a week I shall leave here for the still more wonderful beauty of Italy, but my heart belongs undividedly to my dear native land. . . . I am greatly troubled to think that I have put the Conservatoire to inconvenience by my absence . . . but better to be absent for a year than to disappear for ever. Had I stayed a day longer in Moscow, I must have lost my reason and drowned myself in the waves of that stinking—but beloved—Moskva river." To M. Kashkin he writes a little later as follows: "I love Moscow as being the dwelling-place of friends for whom now—in this time of separation— I realise the full strength of my attachment. Physically I am not amiss. Like the old woman in Goburnov's tale, I am sound in one spot while I ache in another. On the whole I am robust; but as regards my soul, there is a wound there that will never heal. I think I am *homme fini*. Of course I shall return to the Conservatoire on 1st September 1878. As usual I shall take my harmony classes, and shall feel some pleasure in the proximity of my friends; but what has been can never be again. Something is broken in me; my wings are cut and I shall never fly very high again. Now I am working hard at *Eugene Oniegin* and my symphony, but I work at the instrumentation of them as though they were written by some one else. . . . It would be too long to tell you all that has happened to me since we parted. My best time was in Clarens, where my brother and I lived very peacefully in absolute solitude amid majestic surroundings. Our going to Italy was pure folly. Her riches, her dazzling luxury, only made me irritable and worried me. I had no heart left to appreciate her great monuments, which left me cold and indifferent."

The stillness of Venice he found comparatively soothing. In Vienna he came once more in contact with his own art, and a little of the old spirit and interest returned to him. In Wagner's *Walkyrie* he took no pleasure; and speaking of some new work by Brahms, he says that the enthusiasm it aroused among the German critics was incomprehensible to him.

From abroad he sent the first act of *Eugene Oniegin*, and all his friends met to hear it at Rubinstein's rooms. Taneiev played it through on the piano. "The impression was wonderful," says M. Kashkin; "it fairly took our breath away." Even the critical Nicholas Rubinstein had nothing but praise for the new work. Each time it was played, new beauties revealed themselves, and the wonderful duet between Tatiana and her old nurse made a most favourable impression. Best of all, M. Kashkin felt that it augured happily for his friend's future. This was not the music of an "*homme fini.*" By degrees the whole opera arrived, and then some uneasiness was felt as to whether the students of the Conservatoire could possibly create such parts as Tatiana Lerin, Eugene Oniegin, and Vladimir Lensky; but Tchaikovsky was contented to entrust his work to the students under such leaders as N. Rubinstein and Samarin, rather than let it take the chance of being spoilt by the *routinier* dulness of some theatrical conductor. *Eugene Oniegin* was finished by February 1878, too late for performance during that season, so the composer had to wait, though somewhat impatiently, until the following winter.

In the spring of 1878 it was necessary to appoint some one to take charge of the department of Russian Music at the Paris Exhibition. Both Davidov and N. Rubinstein agreed that Tchaikovsky would be a suitable representative. Tchaikovsky accepted the post, but when he discovered the duties it entailed he hastily resigned it. He had very little capacity for organising, and at that time was absolutely without experience as a conductor, so that his action was undoubtedly a wise one. But Rubinstein, who was a born fighter, and could not understand Tchaikovsky's depression of spirits, nor his shrinking from publicity, was offended at his withdrawal. He believed that he had hit upon a successful plan for curing what he chose to regard as a morbid feeling in Tchaikovsky, and, in a moment of irritation, he reproached him rather severely for his "idleness" and unwillingness to undertake a useful office. This caused a passing coldness between the friends, which was happily soon forgotten. Nicholas Rubinstein ended by going to Paris himself, and he was careful that Tchaikovsky's works should take a prominent place in the programmes of the Russian concerts.

While working at *Eugene Oniegin*, Tchaikovsky had also been engaged upon his *Fourth Symphony*, of which he thought very highly, speaking of it as his best production. Both compositions were sent to Nicholas Rubinstein for performance in Moscow. Rubinstein was usually very successful in his interpretation of Tchaikovsky's music, but, either because his attention was too exclusively taken up with *Eugene Oniegin*, or because this symphony did not appeal to him so strongly as the others, the performance at the Musical Society was slack and colourless. For some years the work was totally neglected, until its revival by Safonov, whose interpretation of it was far better than Rubinstein's.

The *Fourth Symphony* is remarkable for a display of humour somewhat rare in Tchaikovsky's music. Of all the Russian composers he seems the most deficient in this quality. He has not the keen appreciation of national humour which belongs to Glinka. Still less can he make himself one with the peasantry in their noisy revelry, or in their "levity of despair" as Moussorgsky does. Tchaikovsky's humour, as we see it in the *Casse-Noisette Suite*, and other works of a lighter calibre, is always elegant and restrained; elsewhere it is very fitful, and quickly overcast by the prevailing shadow of his melancholy. But in this symphony it flows more freely, which

seems strange when we remember that he was working at it during a time of great mental depression.
Humour, of a gentler description, peeps out from the
Andante, and becomes more marked and lively in
character in the *Scherzo*, one of the most captivating
movements Tchaikovsky ever wrote. This movement (*Allegro—pizzicato ostinato*) is a rare—if not
unique—instance of a long symphonic movement in
which the strings play pizzicato throughout. The
Finale (*allegro con fuoco*) consists of variations upon
the Russian folk-song, "In the fields there stood a
birch-tree."

The years which followed immediately upon
Tchaikovsky's great domestic trouble were very
fertile in new compositions, and besides those already
mentioned he wrote the music for the *Liturgy of St.
John of Chrysostom* (1878), the *Piano Sonata* (1880),
the *Italian Capriccio* and *Serenade for Strings*, the
Overture 1812, and two sets of songs—all bearing
the dates 1879 and 1880. The *Second Pianoforte
Concerto* also belongs to this period, a work which
presents fewer technical difficulties than the first, but
is still more showy in character.

During the last years of Glinka's life his mind
was very much occupied with national church music,
although his failing health did not permit him to
realise any of the plans he had formed in connection
with these studies. Tchaikovsky was also attracted
by the study of Russian church music, but he wrote
nothing new in this sphere of art. His object was
the same as that of Lvov, who, a few years earlier,

had set himself strenuously to oppose the Italian tendencies which had been introduced by Bortniansky and Berezovsky. In 1875 Tchaikovsky published *A Short Course of Harmony adapted for the Study of Russian Church Music*, which consisted of examples of special difficulties in reading. In 1878 his *Liturgy of St. John of Chrysostom* made its appearance : a service for four voices, in which he keeps rigorously to the old Russian church style, avoiding all western harmonies and forms which are foreign to its spirit. Of the fifteen numbers it contains, the *Credo* is the most remarkable. Berezovsky relates an amusing story connected with this work, which shows the lengths to which Russian officialism can sometimes be carried, even in matters quite unconnected with politics. According to a ukase of Alexander I., all sacred works had to be submitted to the approval of Bortniansky, the intendant of the Imperial Chapel. When Tchaikovsky wrote his Liturgy, Bortniansky had been in his grave for some years. Nevertheless the intendant at that time, Bakhmetiev, refused to take this circumstance into consideration, and confiscated Tchaikovsky's work, on the ground that it had never received Bortniansky's *imprimatur.* Only an order from the chief administration saved the Liturgy from destruction and permitted its publication.

In the spring of 1878 Tchaikovsky returned from abroad, and spent the summer in the country with his relatives. At the close of August—true to his promise—he resumed his duties in Moscow, but not for long. Having enjoyed a whole year of freedom, and known the advantages of unlimited leisure for composition, teaching seemed more irksome than before. Fortunately circumstances now permitted him to resign his classes at the Conservatoire, and early in autumn he went for a short time to Paris. He was, just then, very much preoccupied with the subject of Joan of Arc, and wished to study all that French writers had written about their national heroine.

Meanwhile *Eugene Oniegin* was being studied by the students of the Moscow Conservatoire. "Never was any opera rehearsed with such zeal," says M. Kashkin. Samarin performed wonders in training the pupils, and Nicholas Rubinstein succeeded in putting courage into the hearts of the young singers. A company of experienced artists might have been proud of the results thus achieved. The opera was to be given in March 1879. Tchaikovsky, who had complete confidence in Rubinstein, did not return to Moscow to superintend the rehearsals, but he was expected to be present at the first performance of the work. The actual day of the last rehearsal came, and still the composer had not made his appearance. "I was seated in the amphitheatre," writes M. Kashkin, "the whole theatre being in darkness except for a few candles in the orchestra. Presently I heard some one near to me groping about for a seat, and recognised Tchaikovsky's voice, though he spoke in a whisper. I whispered to him to come and sit near me, and when we met, the

heartiness of our embrace caused some scandal in the
darkened theatre!" All went smoothly, and the
numerous chorus, composed entirely of fresh, young
voices, had a wonderful effect. In the scene in which
Tatiana writes her love-letter to Oniegin, Tchaikovsky
was deeply affected. "How lucky it is dark here,"
he whispered to his friend, "for this touches me so
that I can hardly keep back my tears." No subsequent performance, says M. Kashkin, ever produced
so great an impression upon him as this rehearsal.
When *Eugene Oniegin* was first performed in the
Little Theatre at Moscow, there was an unprece-
dented crush, and among the audience were Laroche
and Anton Rubinstein. The music was of too high
an order to be appreciated at a first hearing, and
Oniegin—like most of Tchaikovsky's works—did
not take the audience by storm. Even the St.
Petersburg critics spoke coldly of the work, and it
was not until five years later that it was heard at
the Marinsky Theatre in that town. Time, however, increased its popularity, and when Jurgenson
published the pianoforte score, it had an immense
sale. Tchaikovsky himself was satisfied with his
work, but did not consider it suitable for performance in a large theatre.

From the year 1879 the relations between M.
Kashkin and Tchaikovsky became naturally of a less
intimate character. Their friendship remained unchanged, but now they only met occasionally, and
both being hard workers, their correspondence was
restricted to what was absolutely indispensable. *The*

Maid of Orleans was written during the winter of 1879-80. It was not wanting in touches of genius, but it was far from being a success. Speaking of this opera a year later, Nicholas Rubinstein said that he considered it a retrograde step from such works as *Vakoula* and *Eugene Oniegin.* He believed that he saw in it a desire to win the public favour, and added that a mediocre talent might succeed in this respect, but Tchaikovsky—never. N. Rubinstein, in spite of his occasionally severe judgments upon Tchaikovsky, both as a man and a musician, worked with untiring energy for the advancement of his fame. Of Tchaikovsky's later works, he produced in Moscow the *First Suite for Orchestra* (op. 43), the *Italian Capriccio* and the *Pianoforte Sonata* (op. 37). With this last work he took immense pains, and it was long before he was sufficiently pleased with his own performance to play it in public. When at last he resolved to produce it at a concert of the Moscow Quartet Society, his rendering was so perfect in every respect that M. Kashkin, unwilling to hear anything more, left the hall and telegraphed in the most enthusiastic terms to Tchaikovsky, who was then living in the country. In the spring of 1880 Nicholas Rubinstein suggested to Tchaikovsky to compose a *pièce d'occasion* for the consecration of the Temple of Christ in Moscow. Besides the church festival, Rubinstein wished to organise a musical one which should embody the history of the building of this temple, that is to say, the events of the year 1812. Tchaikovsky's fantasia or overture was to be performed in the public square before the cathedral by a colossal orchestra, the big drums to be replaced by salvos of artillery. The composition entitled *The Year 1812* was finished at Kamenka in 1880, but M. Kashkin gives no account of this startling performance.

Tchaikovsky never regarded this work as one of his best, as we may see from his objections to having it performed in Berlin during his tour in 1888. But the overture has a certain picturesque brilliancy that raises it above the level of mere sensational music, and has made it very popular, especially in London. Berezovsky says it opens with the subject of a Russian hymn, " God preserve Thy people," and goes on to represent the Battle of Borodino, in which the Marseillaise mingles with the Russian national hymn amid the thunder of artillery. In using these subjects Tchaikovsky is guilty of a double anachronism; for the Marseillaise was probably not in use in the French army as late as 1812, while the Russian hymn was only composed by Lvov in 1863. The cleverest effect in the overture is produced by means of a peal of bells, which very fairly realises the weird sounds heard in the Kremlin on a Russian feast-day.

As to the merits of the opera *Joan of Arc*, there is considerable discrepancy of opinion. Some critics by no means judge it with the severity of Nicholas Rubinstein. Having never seen this opera, I quote the following account of it, condensed from Berezovsky.

The Maid of Orleans—as it was finally named— was produced for the first time on 22nd February, 1880, for the benefit of the conductor of the St. Petersburg opera, Napravnik. The work suffers from a somewhat poor libretto. At times, too, Tchaikovsky seems to be under the influence of Wagner; an influence which is very unsuitable to the particular quality of his genius. As regards the musical presentment of the characters, this opera is far in advance of many others by the same composer. The rôles of Joan, of the King, of Agnes Sorel and Dunois, are all admirably worked out. The remaining characters, such as Joan's parents, Lionel, and the Archbishop, are less developed, but as the interest does not depend upon them, this does not detract from the general effect. But the most prominent feature of the opera is the orchestra, in which Tchaikovsky has centred the chief interest and beauty. He here uses it as the principal medium of expression; sometimes giving life to the masses, sometimes depicting a spiritual condition. He is equally strong in subtile delineation of character and in broad decorative effects, and in no other opera of Tchaikovsky's is the orchestra called upon to illustrate such depths of thought as in *The Maid of Orleans*.

The opera, which is in four acts, opens with an Introduction consisting of two movements. The first depicts the heroine of the opera; the second is based on the subject of the chorus of angels, who appear to Joan in her visions, and ends with a cadenza for flute, in imitation of a shepherd's pipe. The first act takes place in Domrémy, while Joan is still living with her parents. The scene of the fire in Domrémy is exceedingly dramatic. So, too, is the chorus of peasants, " O God, stay Thine anger," in which the anguish of the people in this time of calamity is finely expressed. Bertrand's recitative, describing the unhappy condition of France, is the best piece of declamation in the work, especially when sung with feeling. Joan's scene with the populace is somewhat diffuse. The scene ends with an *ensemble*, "King, of power supreme." One of the best numbers in the act is Joan's farewell to her birthplace, which is full of that lyrical sentiment in which Tchaikovsky is always successful.

The angels now appear to Joan, and incite her to great deeds. This chorus, which is accompanied by harps and bells is exceedingly melodious, and produces a weird effect. The incident of Joan's vision, " Ye host of angels "—the subject of which has already been heard in the Introduction—is a poetical inspiration. The orchestra describes Joan's condition of mind : a sort of mystical ecstasy leading on to inspired action. This scene closes the first act.

The entr'acte which precedes Act II. is not very striking from a musical point of view. The curtain rises upon a room in the palace of Charles VII., where the king is shown in the midst of frivolous gaiety. The beautiful subject of the minstrel's song recalls the style of a Malo-Russian melody. The gipsy dance is effective as regards orchestration, but lacks colour. The ballet which follows—a dance of pages and dwarfs, and a jester's dance—is not specially French in character, but it is splendidly orchestrated.

G

In the duet between the king and " le brave Dunois"
both characters are convincingly portrayed. We
recognise the superficial, effeminate disposition of
the former, and the contrasting energy and virility
of the latter. Towards the close, the duet works up
to an effective crescendo, and ends with an accompaniment of drums in the orchestra. The subject of
Agnes Sorel's air, "If strength be not given thee,"
is slightly Russian in style. The duet between Agnes
and the king is also an excellent piece of character
drawing. The orchestral music which announces the
entrance of Joan is very impressive. Then follows
a fine scene in which she is questioned by the king
and relates her story, beginning, "Holy Father, I
am called Joan." This tale is sincere, naïve, and full
of sentiment, and is the best number of this act.
With the mention of the Holy Virgin, there is a
passage in the orchestra for harps. Only a slight
diffuseness spoils this narrative. The recitative which
precedes the final *ensemble* is poor, but the *ensemble*
itself is grandiose and effective.

The third act is divided into two scenes or tableaux.
The introduction to the first represents a battle.
The love-episode between Joan and Lionel is very
weak. Lionel is altogether lacking in character, and
Joan's recitative—in the Italian style—is not expressive. The duet "Dread Powers" is the best
part of the scene. The arrival of Dunois, whose
personality is always well defined, offers a strong
contrast to what has gone before. The second scene
takes place at Rheims, and musically is the most

effective in the whole opera. It opens with a
Coronation March, repeated three times, and rather
noisy as regards instrumentation. The duet (recitative) between Joan's father and mother is rather
long and monotonous. The father, deaf to his wife's
admonitions and prayers, resolves to denounce his
daughter before the king and the populace. The
scene which follows is highly dramatic. The actual
denunciation is preceded by a short chorus in march
rhythm. Both the king's speech and that of Joan's
father are characteristic. The accompaniments are
somewhat heavy, but throughout the entire act the
orchestra is very prominent. The *Finale* is on a
grand scale, and if given without cuts, would be
almost equal to one-fourth of the whole opera.

The fourth act is preceded by an orchestral
entr'acte, which illustrates Joan's mystical frame of
mind. This instrumental piece reflects all that is
best in Tchaikovsky's genius, and is one of the most
successful things in the work. The first scene opens
with a short recitative for Joan. Lionel then appears,
and there follows a very fine love-scene, ending in
a great duet. In the middle of this duet the choir
of angels is heard, reminding Joan of her duty and
predicting her ruin. But love prevails. Joan does
not heed the warning voices, and disaster is already
at hand. The English soldiers break in upon the
lovers, and after slaying Lionel, take Joan prisoner.

The last scene of the opera—Joan's execution—
opens with a Funeral March, to the strains of which
she is led to the market-place. In a beautiful

recitative she commends her soul to heaven, and is answered by the choir of angels. The maid is then led to the stake, and a great chorus, with most expressive orchestral accompaniment, completes this opera, which, says Berezovsky, is one of the most brilliant creations of Tchaikovsky's genius.

VIII

IN 1880 Nicholas Rubinstein's health was failing rapidly, but almost his last visit to the Conservatoire was made on behalf of his friend. He took a great interest in the *Serenade* (óp. 48), and wishing to get a general idea of the work, ordered the parts to be copied, assembled the students' orchestra, and though he was too ill to stand at the conductor's desk, managed to go through the work in a sitting posture. Shortly after this he went to Paris, where he died on 11th March 1881. The death of this great artist, and devoted friend, was a heavy blow to Tchaikovsky. During the following year he appears to have written only one work—the *Pianoforte Trio in A minor*, dedicated "to the memory of a great artist," and inscribed *Roma*, Gennaio, 1882. The name of Rubinstein was not mentioned in the inscription, because Tchaikovsky desired less to honour his friend than the artist for whom he felt a boundless veneration. As Tchaikovsky had long cherished a prejudice against the combination of piano and stringed instruments, it is interesting to hear his own reasons, as given to M. Kashkin, for his choice on this occasion. In the first place, he said that he would not dream of writing anything in memory of so great a pianist in which the piano did not take a prominent part. Then, again, a concerto or fantasia seemed to him too extravagant and showy a form in which to embody his idea; while the pianoforte alone seemed too monotonous and thin for the purpose. He decided, therefore, in favour of the trio. In the second movement of the work appear the variations in which are embodied Tchaikovsky's memories of Nicholas Rubinstein and his musical characteristics at various periods of his life. " It would be possible," says M. Kashkin, " to label each of these variations with an appropriate title; but I prefer to do this elsewhere."

From 1882-83 Tchaikovsky was chiefly engaged upon the opera *Mazeppa*. The first performances of this work were fixed for almost the same night in both capitals, and Tchaikovsky chose to be present at Moscow rather than at St. Petersburg. All went exceedingly well, and the opera had even a brilliant success, but Tchaikovsky's nervous temperament made rehearsals and " first nights " a torture to him. Every one was pleased but the composer himself, who looked " like a condemned criminal," and seemed on the verge of an hysterical attack. The following evening his *Second Suite for Orchestra* was to be played for the first time at a concert of the Musical Society, but when the audience called loudly for the composer he was not forthcoming, being at that time half-way to Smolensk. Tchaikovsky, unable to endure another ovation, had fled from Moscow, leaving M. Kashkin to make his excuses to the conductor and the public. The libretto of *Mazeppa*, taken from Poushkin's poem *Poltava*, is the joint work of several collaborators, among them the well-known writer Bourenin. The librettists have evidently been anxious to keep as many episodes as possible from the original work, without reference to their fitness for scenic representation. The result is a series of gloomy pictures, prison scenes, executions, deaths, etc., which cannot fail to have a very depressing effect upon the audience. The music of *Mazeppa* is unequal, but, generally speaking, the instrumental parts of the opera are superior to the vocal. The style of the vocal portion is patchy, alternately Russian and Italian, sometimes a little German as regards the recitatives. The scene of the opera is laid chiefly in the Ukraine, and it is remarkable that Tchaikovsky has not been very successful in his use of local colour, for there is nothing distinctively Malo-Russian about the songs and dances of the Cossacks in *Mazeppa*. The hero of the opera is not represented in romantic colours, but appears as an ambitious, sly, and treacherous soldier of fortune. This is Poushkin's presentment of the celebrated hetman of Cossacks, and no doubt, historically, it is the correct one.

The opera opens with an Introduction, and the curtain rises upon the estate of the Cossack chief,

Kochoubey, a wealthy land-owner and judge. Kochoubey's daughter, Marie, is beloved by a young Cossack named Andrew, but she has lost her heart to the great hetman Mazeppa, who is much older than herself. Mazeppa is being entertained by Kochoubey. There is a characteristic chorus of Cossacks, followed by a local dance, the gopak. During the process of the dance, Mazeppa asks for Marie's hand, and is refused. This causes a breach between Kochoubey and the hetman. Marie clings to her lover, and finally goes off with him. In the second scene, which takes place in Kochoubey's house, every one is lamenting the departure of Marie. Her father is heartbroken. But her mother, with true Cossack sternness, bids her husband "cease this grieving," and urges him to action. Kochoubey and his followers decide to denounce Mazeppa to Peter the Great. Andrew is chosen to carry the accusation.

The second act reveals the dungeons of the tower of Bielotsèrkovsky, where Kochoubey, who has been captured by Mazeppa, is languishing in chains and threatened with torture. The scene is exceedingly gloomy, and the actual preparations for the torturing of the prisoner are gruesome; but from a musical point of view the scene has some fine moments. Berezovsky considers that this scene, together with Tatiana's scene in the second act of *Eugene Oniegin*, are Tchaikovsky's *chefs-d'œuvre*, and display his power of psychological analysis at its highest. The second scene of this act opens with a fine monologue for Mazeppa. It is first descriptive of the lovely, soft night of the Ukraine, and then of Mazeppa's inward agitation. Orlik, Mazeppa's follower, now comes in bearing the order for Kochoubey's execution, which the hetman has treacherously secured. Presently Marie comes upon the scene. In the love-duet which follows, Mazeppa reveals something of the treachery at work in his mind, but Marie is absorbed in her love and suspects none of the plots against her father. When Mazeppa leaves her she sings a love-song, which is very Italian in character, but expresses her condition of mind. Her mother breaks in upon her and tells her of Mazeppa's cruelty and falseness towards her father. A military march is heard in the distance. It is Kochoubey being led to execution. The women hear it, and are overcome with despair.

The scene of the execution follows. A crowd has collected in the field, where a scaffold has been erected for Kochoubey and his companion Iskra. The whole scene is gloomy and unpleasantly realistic, especially the chorus of drunken Cossacks, "Ho, get along." The farewell of the condemned men to the populace and their prayer are very dramatic. The latter, says Berezovsky, is based on church tones. The loud chord in the orchestra which announces that the prisoners' heads have fallen is a piece of sensationalism which has its parallel in Richard Strauss's symphonic poem *Till Eulenspiegel*, where a hideous discord informs the audience that "the drop" has been rightly judged and "death was instantaneous," as the reporters say.

Marie and her mother arrive at the foot of the scaffold too late to save Kochoubey or say a last farewell. The last scene is ushered in by a descriptive orchestral number entitled "The Battle of Poltava." Two subjects are employed: one the melody of a national song, "Glory" ("Slavsia"); the other a march of the period of Peter the Great. The action returns to Kochoubey's estate, now ruined and deserted. Andrew, who has been wandering in search of Mazeppa with the intention of killing him, comes back to the homestead. In the orchestra some phrases of the first duet, between Andrew and Marie, recall the happy days of prosperity before Mazeppa appeared on the scene. Presently the hetman and his follower Orlik come on. Andrew throws himself upon Mazeppa, but the latter draws his pistol and fires upon the young Cossack. Marie now appears. Her grief has unhinged her mind. She sings a duet with Mazeppa which is not particularly expressive, but the orchestral accompaniment, in which the theme of the love-duet in the second act is ingeniously brought in, supplements the dramatic feeling and reminds us of her past love for the treacherous hetman. When Mazeppa and Orlik have gone away, abandoning the poor crazy girl to her fate, one of the most pathetic and dramatic scenes in the opera is enacted. Marie is now left alone with Andrew. Her duet with the dying Cossack is full of sentiment, but the supreme touch of pathos is felt when she unconsciously lulls her former lover into the sleep of death with her graceful, innocent slumber-song. The chorus of the people, with which the opera concludes, comes as an anticlimax after this very moving incident.

Tchaikovsky's *Third Orchestral Suite* was finished in July 1884, and during the second half of the summer, while on a visit to the beautiful estate of Plestcheevo, he began to work upon the fantasia for orchestra, *Manfred*. The subject had been suggested to him by Balakirev, but it did not suit his particular genius as well as *Romeo and Juliet*. He never seems to have been possessed by his subject, and the composition was only achieved by dint of strenuous efforts. "*Manfred* cost me a whole year of my life," he once said to M. Kashkin; and even in the opinion of his friend it does not compare at all favourably with Schumann's treatment of the same subject.

Manfred is described as "a symphony in four scenes," and its programme is based on Byron's poem, with this difference, that Tchaikovsky's Manfred does not die a haughty but sublime rebel, like Byron's hero, but is finally reconciled to Heaven. The programme of the symphony stands as follows:—

First movement or scene. "Manfred wandering amid the Alpine heights. Worn out with fruitless questioning of Fate, torn by tortures of despair and the memory of his guilty past, he endures intolerable anguish of soul. Manfred has penetrated deeply into the mysteries of witchcraft, and associated with the powers of evil; but neither they, nor anything else in the world, can give him the boon of forgetfulness which he is always vainly seeking and imploring. The remembrance of the dead Astarte, once so passionately loved, gnaws at his heart, and there is no limit or end to Manfred's despair." This movement affords great scope for varied emotional treatment. Manfred is alternately racked with anguish, or lost in the memory of his past love. Throughout the scene we hear the love-subject, detached like a shimmering streak of moonlight upon a black and fathomless pool.

The second scene may be considered in the light of a *scherzo*, and has the following title: "The spirit of the Alps appears to Manfred in the rainbow over the waterfall." The third scene is described as "A picture of the simple but prosperous life of the mountaineers." It is pastoral in character, but amid the joyous and peaceful strains of the shepherds' pipes we hear the sinister subject which represents Manfred.

The final tableau is entitled, "The subterranean palace of Arimane. Orgy of evil spirits. Manfred appears at the bacchanalian revels. The invocation and apparition of the spirit of Astarte. She predicts the end of his sufferings on earth. Manfred's death." The orgy is not particularly impressive. The subject is more suited to a Berlioz or a Moussorgsky than to the more delicate lyricism of Tchaikovsky. The death of Manfred brings a reference to the *Dies Irae* of the Greek Church. At the close of the movement there is a return to the first subject of the *Finale* in D (with organ accompaniment). This probably represents the redemption of Manfred.

Composed at a somewhat later date than *Manfred*, and allied to it, if not in musical structure at least as regards its psychological basis, is the fantasia-overture *Hamlet*. The music of *Hamlet* is chiefly based on three themes: the sombre one, appropriate to the hero; a contrasting theme, pathetic and graceful, associated with Ophelia; and one which has the character of a march. The subject ought to have been congenial to Tchaikovsky's temperament, and yet it is impossible to look upon this work as one of his greatest successes. It seems as though he had set himself to realise too minutely the interminable agitations and misgivings which beset the prince. He has approached the play from the psychological rather than the dramatic side, and the result is a work of inordinate length, with few salient emotional crises and much that is vague and impossible to realise convincingly in music. That *Hamlet* exercised a fascination upon Tchaikovsky seems evident from the fact that before composing this fantasia-overture he had already written incidental music to the play, consisting in all of fifteen numbers. Of these the Overture, Elegy, three scenes for Ophelia, and the Gravedigger's Song are the most interesting.

IX

TCHAIKOVSKY was now able to realise his ideal of a quiet life, spent chiefly in the country. In 1885 he took a house in the village of Maidanovo, not far from the little town of Klin. Maidanovo was a pretty village, close to a luxuriant park, with a good bathing-place and many rural attractions. It had, unfortunately, one supreme drawback. In summer-time the neighbouring houses were let to families from the city, who brought with them the inevitable piano, and soon the sounds of scales and exercises reached the unfortunate composer at his work. In consequence of this, Tchaikovsky moved into another house outside the park, enclosed in its own grounds and beyond reach of his neighbours' music. Here he would spend months together without visiting the town. His intimate friends were welcome at Maidanovo, but they respected the solitude of " The Hermit of Klin," as they called him. From time to time, as a work was finished, or Tchaikovsky felt the need of a rest, he would invite a party of musical friends from Moscow for a night or two. M. Kashkin was often privileged to stay on by himself for a longer visit at Maidanovo. Very simple, strictly regulated, and calm was this country life. The two friends breakfasted at eight. At nine they separated for the morning, which was spent in work. At one o'clock came a simple, early dinner of two courses (Tchaikovsky kept a good man-cook, and could entertain his guests lavishly enough when he thought it necessary), and then followed a long country walk, which the composer never missed in any weather. Sometimes Tchaikovsky would announce at dinner his intention of going out alone, and then his friend understood that he was meditating some new creation, for many of his works were planned and his themes invented during these long solitary rambles across country. After tea he went back to his work until supper was served at eight o'clock. After supper the servant put a bottle of wine on the table, and was told that he was free until the next morning. "Left to ourselves we immediately went to the piano," writes M. Kashkin, "and began to play arrangements for four hands, of which Tchaikovsky had a large store. Often we played Brahms, whom he esteemed very highly for his seriousness and sincerity, and his contempt for superficial success; but at the same time he had not much sympathy with his music, finding it cold and dry." Even after repeatedly playing Brahms's works his first impression was not greatly modified. Occasionally the occupation was varied by M. Kashkin's reading aloud some of

Tchaikovsky's favourite Russian authors; or the composer would write up his diary, of which he possessed many bound volumes, the contents of which were never revealed even to his closest friends. That it contained many intimate things as regards himself, besides the secrets of others, there can be no doubt. Once, he told M. Kashkin, he was spending the evening quite alone at his country house. As his eye fell upon the volumes of his diary he was assailed by a sudden terror lest he might die with no friends at hand, and that some one should pry into these life-secrets. Under the influence of this feeling, he immediately ordered his fire to be lit, and burnt every volume before he went to bed. There was much in it which he regretted, but on the whole he believed that he had acted wisely.

Tchaikovsky had very little idea of the value of money. On one occasion a friend inquired: "Peter Ilich, where do you invest your capital?" Tchaikovsky stared at him in astonishment, and then burst out laughing. It had never occurred to him that there was any possible investment of capital otherwise than in personal expenditure and presents to friends. Breathless with laughter, he explained to his friend that his last investment of capital had been in the hotel where he had stayed at Moscow; "and where my next investment may be, I am sure I cannot tell you at present."

In the country he spoilt all the peasant children by giving them coppers. Taneiev and Kashkin reproached him for this bad habit, saying that it demoralised the children, and using other virtuous arguments. The next time they went for a walk, Tchaikovsky resolved to make an heroic effort to escape from the youthful beggars whose morals were corrupted by his kopecks. They started for the bridge which crosses the river on the road to Klin. Tchaikovsky's hour for walking was known to every child in the neighbourhood, and feeling sure that he would be waylaid on leaving the park, he tried to deceive his persecutors. Leaving Taneiev and Kashkin on the path, he descended to the river-bank and crept under the thick sallow-bushes, while Taneiev, from the upper road, watched his furtive movements, and recited with mock pathos, " Behold the worthy fruits of evil-doing," etc. Tchaikovsky's innocent ruse availed him nothing. The children, who had studied the character of their victim to some purpose, had posted sentries in ambush, and by the time Tchaikovsky reached the bridge a party of boys were awaiting him. His friends came up just in time to hear the joyful laughter of the victorious enemy as they moved off laden with booty. Tchaikovsky, blushing with confusion, hastened to explain that he really could not help it, that he had given the children the merest trifle, etc. M. Kashkin did not quite believe in this extenuating circumstance. On one occasion Tchaikovsky had given away at least fourteen shillings in an afternoon's walk, and, in addition, had borrowed all that his friend had with him at the moment.

The chief works of 1886 and 1887 comprise an

H

opera, *Charodaïka* (" The Sorceress "), *Dumka*, a rural scene for orchestra, a number of songs, the *Fourth Orchestral Suite* (" Mozartiana "), a *Pezzo Capriccioso* for violoncello and orchestra, and the *Fifth Symphony*.

It will be a matter of surprise to many to find that Berezovsky ranks the last-named work lower than the *Fourth Symphony*, whereas in England many critics have pronounced it to be almost, if not quite, equal to " The Pathetic." But Berezovsky's account of the work, in spite of his critical judgment upon it, is so interesting that I give it here in full. " The *Fifth Symphony*," he writes, " is the weakest of all Tchaikovsky's symphonies; nevertheless it is a striking work, and takes a prominent place not only among Tchaikovsky's compositions, but among Russian musical works in general. The symphony is divided into the usual four movements. The first—*Andante, Allegro con anima*—opens with an introduction in which we hear the exposition of the chief subject of the symphony. This subject runs like a dark thread through the whole tissue of the work. The introduction is conceived in that mood of sadness so common to Tchaikovsky. The *Allegro* has two subjects : one melancholy in character, the other full of brightness and vitality. Both are developed with much brilliance and animation. Then, suddenly, the chief subject reappears and the music grows sombre once more. As this theme dies away on the bassoons, the movement comes to an end. The second movement—*Andante cantabile con alcuna licenza*—takes the form of a romance.

The subject given out by a solo horn passes over to the violoncello, and is afterwards assigned to the strings. Here again the chief theme of the symphony breaks in in a fragmentary, almost unexpected, manner, casting momentary shadows over the radiant mood which pervades the movement. The third movement consists of a poetical, graceful valse. As in the preceding movement, the chief theme returns occasionally in a fitful way; but later on, in the *Finale*, it is displayed in its fullest power. The introduction to the *Finale—Andante maestoso—*is entirely based upon it, and is penetrated with religious feeling. The *Finale* itself (*Allegro vivace*) grows gradually clearer as it proceeds, as though the heart had cast off a load of suffering and God's world shone out bright once more. An episode in the *Finale* has a subject which is quite Russian in character. The entire symphony seems to set forth some dark spiritual experience, some heavy condition of a mind torn by importunate memories which have poisoned existence. Only at the close the clouds lift, the sky clears, and we see the blue stretching pure and clear beyond."

When Tchaikovsky left Maidanovo, he moved to the old manor-house of Frovolo, which was also situated in the neighbourhood of Klin. Here Kashkin was an occasional visitor. On the completion of his opera *The Queen of Spades*, the composer invited a large party of friends, chiefly from the Moscow Conservatoire, to hear the new work. The subject of the opera was borrowed from a tale by Poushkin, and a great part of it was composed during a visit to Italy. On the occasion of the trial of *The Queen of Spades* at Frovolo, Siloti took the piano part. The libretto was prepared by the composer's brother, Modeste Ilich Tchaikovsky, and differs considerably from Poushkin's original story.

Herman, a needy young lieutenant, a moody hero of the Byronic school, falls in love with Lisa, a beautiful orphan who lives with her grandmother. The old Countess has been celebrated in her day as "The Venus of Moscow," and equally noted as an inveterate card-player. Herman is also passionately fond of gaming, so much so that he hardly knows which fascinates him most—his love of Lisa or his love of the cards. Lisa is very much attracted by the young man's interesting melancholy, but she is affianced to Prince Yeletsky, a richer and more desirable match. Herman wishes to make a fortune at cards in order to win the woman of his heart. There is an ugly story to the effect that the Countess owes her luck at cards to some supernatural agency. Herman sets himself to fathom this mystery, but manages so clumsily that the old lady dies of fright without having revealed her secret. After death she revenges herself. Her ghost appears to Herman, and whispers the names of three cards which he imagines to be her lucky ones. On these cards he stakes his all, is ruined, and stabs himself.

The subject of *The Queen of Spades* has some points of resemblance with that of *Eugene Oniegin*, but the music has not the freshness, the lyrical charm, or the pathos of Tchaikovsky's earlier opera. It was originally written for another libretto, based upon Poushkin's story "The Captain's Daughter"; but after working at this subject for some time, Tchaikovsky, for some unexplained reason, changed his mind, and used up his material for *The Queen of Spades.*

Tchaikovsky's last effort in dramatic music was the one-act opera *Iolanthe*, on the subject of Herz's drama, "King Réné's Daughter." It is generally considered to be the weakest of his operatic works.

Very superior, in its own way, is the music of a ballet, in thirty numbers, *The Sleeping Beauty*. This charming new setting of an old story is one of Tchaikovsky's most delicate and graceful inspirations. The music, though not deeper than the subject demands, is melodious in the best sense of the word, fantastic, brightly coloured; while it never descends to the commonplace level of the ordinary ballet music. Another work of this description which appeared in 1892 has won extraordinary popularity in this country—the *Casse-Noisette*. This was originally written as a fairy ballet in fifteen numbers, from which Tchaikovsky afterwards arranged the Suite which is so often heard at the Queen's Hall and elsewhere, and of which the English public never seems to have had enough.

Among Tchaikovsky's last works was the *Sextet for Strings* ("Souvenir de Florence"), dedicated to the St. Petersburg Chamber Music Society. M. Kashkin, who was staying with Tchaikovsky while he was engaged upon this, says that at first the composer found it extremely difficult, but after a few days he declared he had quite solved the mysterious art of writing for this special combination of instruments—two violins, two alti, and two violoncellos. But the result showed that even a very experienced musician may sometimes fail to realise the effect of what he has put on paper. Kashkin writes: "The first movement of the sextet, with its second theme —in character resembling a broad Italian *cantilena*— did not present any special difficulties, as it approached more nearly to symphonic form than to chamber music. In the remaining movements the composer endeavoured to keep strictly to chamber-music form, and had recourse to contrapuntal combinations, which gave each instrument its full independence and equality with the others." When the two musicians tried it on the piano for four hands they were delighted with the effect; especially with the two fugues for six voices, which seemed to them entirely successful. Tchaikovsky determined to hear the work played by stringed instruments before sending it to the publisher, and dispatched it to Albrecht, in Petersburg, to have the parts copied. Albrecht was very enthusiastic, and declared it would rank among the first works of its kind. For some time M. Kashkin heard no more of the sextet, and on inquiring what had become of it, Tchaikovsky informed him that at the trial much of it had proved quite impracticable, especially the fugues which had pleased them so much. The crossing of the parts with instruments of uniform *timbre* made it impossible

to follow the independent movement of the voices in .
the counterpoint, and produced some very ugly
harmonies. The sextet in its present amended form
was not published until 1892.

To those who understood Tchaikovsky's sensitive
shrinking from publicity, the alacrity with which,
during the last years of his life, he accepted engage-
ments to conduct his own works, was a problem
beyond solution. According to his own account, he
took no pleasure in conducting, and was always
relieved when the task was over. When responsible
for the works of others, Kashkin says his anxiety was
so acute that his face wore " an expression of physical
pain." His renown as a composer gave him some
weight as a conductor, which he was unable to profit
by to any great extent. On his tours abroad he
was occasionally very successful with his own works,
but he had not the temperament which finds pleasure
in applause. There seems to be little doubt that
many of his compositions suffered from his resolve to
conduct the first performance of them himself. This
was the case with his *Fifth Symphony*, written in
1888, and published the following year. For some
years after its first production the symphony was
scarcely heard a second time, and Tchaikovsky was
so discouraged by the coldness of the public and the
critics, that, had it not been already published, it
would undoubtedly have shared the fate of his earlier
works *Undine* and *Fatum*. It was revived by Nikisch
with brilliant success in 1895. The same cause—
his rather easy-going and inanimate style of conduct-

ing—brought about the failure of his orchestral ballade *The Voievoda*, which composition he actually did burn on the night of its first performance.

M. Kashkin gives an amusing account of the meeting between Brahms and Tchaikovsky at Hamburg, where the latter had gone to conduct his *Fifth Symphony*. They had met two years earlier in Leipzig, but Brahms journeyed to Hamburg on purpose to hear the new symphony. After the concert he invited the Russian composer to dine with him, and after entertaining him most hospitably, he confided to him with quiet sincerity that he did not like the symphony at all. He spoke so simply that Tchaikovsky did not feel in the least hurt, only he was encouraged to speak out with the same uncompromising sincerity his own convictions about the work of the great German master. They parted excellent friends; but never had another opportunity of meeting.

Tchaikovsky, although he gave no impression of great physical strength, was wiry and not easily fatigued. He had lived simply, and hardened himself by taking outdoor exercise at all seasons of the year. Nevertheless, at fifty he began to show some signs of the troubles he had suffered and the hard mental work he had accomplished. He could no longer give himself up so entirely to composition; he needed more rest and distraction, and unfortunately his sight began to be affected. He could no longer read with comfort, and thus he was deprived of one of his chief sources of occupation during the long evenings which he spent alone in his country house. He had left the manor-house of Frovolo and taken up his residence nearer to Klin itself. Four years before his death he was appointed one of the directors of the Moscow Musical Society, and considered it his duty to remain in the city during the concert season. But town life, with its constant succession of visitors, and other encroachments upon his time, was very distasteful to him, and he was relieved when his conscience allowed him to give up his rooms there and return to the solitude of Klin. That he preferred it to any other life seems beyond a doubt, but there is something rather pathetic in M. Kashkin's picture of the "Hermit of Klin," touched—however lightly —with the infirmities of age and of a strenuous existence, sitting by his solitary fire, longing, as he sometimes said, "for my three rubbers" which he could not get, and consoling himself with a game of patience, or with the score of some new work which had awakened his interest. To have made friends with his neighbours would have been to surrender his complete liberty and lay himself open to interruption at inconvenient times. His art demanded the sacrifice of the social life.

The *Sixth Symphony*, to which, after its first performance, Tchaikovsky gave the title of "The Pathetic," was sketched out early in 1893, and finished a few months later, on his return from his last tour abroad. It bears the date of 31st August 1893. The work is so well known, and has been so frequently analysed, that it is superfluous to go into further details about it here. But a few words may be said as to the circumstances under which it was written, and the feelings that inspired it. Each of Tchaikovsky's symphonies has a definite colouring which shows the prevailing influence under which it was written. The Second shows us the composer still strongly dominated by national tendencies. The Third is tinctured throughout by his increasing eclecticism in general, and in particular by his newly awakened enthusiasm for Schumann. The Fourth is remarkable for its brighter qualities, and especially for its unwonted display of humour. The Fifth has touches of religious feeling which are absent from all the rest. In the Sixth, Tchaikovsky seems to have concentrated the brooding melancholy which is the most characteristic and recurrent of all his emotional phases. Throughout the whole of his music we are never far away from this shadow. Sometimes this mood seems real enough; sometimes it strikes us as merely artificial and rhetorical. But melancholy in some form constitutes the peculiar quality of his genius, and nowhere does it brood more heavily or with more tragic intensity than in the last movement of this symphony.

There is no doubt that one of the reasons of the extraordinary popularity of this work lies in the fact that it has been invested with an autobiographical interest for which there is no real warranty. It is said that in some vague and mysterious way it foreshadowed the composer's approaching end. Perhaps it is also with the idea of supporting this theory that sensationalists have discovered that Tchaikovsky shortly afterwards committed suicide. The idea is picturesque, but neither in Russia nor abroad have I discovered any substantial ground for the report. At the time of writing the *Sixth Symphony*, Tchaikovsky had passed through his dark hour and won his way back to the light. M. Kashkin distinctly explodes "the pathetic fallacy," if I may so far distort the meaning of Ruskin's phrase. He shows that the work was not composed under the influence of a morbid pre-occupation with death. Tchaikovsky had some idea of writing out the programme of the symphony, but never did so, chiefly because no sooner was it finished than he became absorbed in new plans, of which the remodelling of *The Oprichnik* was one. Had he done so, the world would not have found that the symphony was a kind of legacy to the living from one who was filled with a presentiment of his own approaching end. It seems, then, more reasonable to interpret both the overwhelming energy of the third movement, and the abysmal sorrow of the *Finale*, in the broader light of a national or historical signifi-cance, rather than to narrow them to the expression of an individual experience. If the last movement is intended to be predictive, it is surely of things vaster, and issues more fatal, than are contained in a mere personal apprehension of death. It speaks rather of a "*lamentation large et souffrance inconnue*," and seems to set the seal of finality on all human hopes. Even if we eliminate the purely subjective interest, this autumnal inspiration of Tchaikovsky's, in which we hear "the groundwhirl of the perished leaves of hope," still remains the most profoundly stirring of his works. Less artistically perfect than those glowing summer blossoms of his genius *Romeo and Juliet* and *Francesca di Rimini*, the *Sixth Symphony*, with its strange combination of the mediocre and the sublime, is profoundly human. Few works have awakened such an immediate echo in the heart of the public. It is interesting to know that he himself had no misgivings about the first three movements of the symphony, but thought it not improbable that, after its first performance in St. Petersburg, he might have to rewrite the *Finale*.[1]

During the spring and summer of 1893 Kashkin and Tchaikovsky never met; but on 7th October the latter returned to Moscow, partly in order to attend the funeral of a very dear friend—Zoeriev. On the 9th, Tchaikovsky attended the Conservatoire to hear a vocal quartet of Mozart's for which he had written the words, and in the evening he invited M. Kashkin to dine with him at the Moscow Hotel. Pollini, the conductor of the Hamburg opera, and Safonov were of the party. During dinner the talk was of a business character, Pollini being anxious to make a tour through Russia with a German orchestra, engaging Tchaikovsky and Safonov as conductors.

[1] I have the best authority for stating that this symphony was not specially commissioned by any musical society in Russia or abroad. Tchaikovsky had a great objection to composing to order, a custom which was not in agreement with his artistic views. The *Sixth Symphony* is dedicated to his favourite nephew M. V. Davidov.

After dinner M. Kashkin was left alone with his friend. They had much to talk about after their long separation. Tchaikovsky told of his visit to Cambridge, when he received his doctor's degree, and spoke in kindly remembrance of the hospitality offered to him there, and particularly of the Professor who had taken him into his own house. He also spoke of Arrigo Boïto, who had charmed him with his wit and culture. Then they took up a sadder theme—the death of their intimate friends, Albrecht and Zoeriev. Their particular circle was growing narrow. Who would be the next to go? M. Kashkin, half joking, said that Tchaikovsky would be the last; and he answered in the same tone that it was not unlikely, for he had never felt better or happier in his life. Tchaikovsky had to catch the night mail to St. Petersburg, where he was going to conduct his *Sixth Symphony*, and so the friends parted, without the least presentiment that it was for the last time.

There was a concert of the Musical Society fixed for 12th October, and Tchaikovsky intended to return to Moscow in time for it, and invited M. Kashkin to dine with him in the evening to meet the singer, Eugene Oudin. At the concert M. Kashkin looked for his friend, and he then heard, for the first time, that a telegram had been received announcing Tchaikovsky's illness, but stating that the danger was over. The telegram was hardly understood by his friends, who, not being sure of his address, decided to telegraph to the St. Petersburg

Conservatoire. But it was Sunday, so the message lay unanswered until the next day, when the announcement of Tchaikovsky's death appeared in the Moscow *Viedomosti.* M. Kashkin at once left for St. Petersburg, but there he learnt the sad circumstances of the case. Tchaikovsky had died of cholera; the preparations for the funeral were made in haste, and he had not even the sad consolation of seeing his friend's face again.

M. Kashkin concludes his book with the following somewhat enigmatical passage, which probably refers to the unhappy circumstances of Tchaikovsky's marriage:—

"I have now finished my reminiscences. Of course they might be supplemented by a few more events, but I shall add nothing at present, and perhaps I shall never do so. One document I shall leave in a sealed packet, and if thirty years hence it still has any interest for the world, the seal may be broken; this packet I shall leave to the care of the Moscow Conservatoire. It will contain the history of one episode in Tchaikovsky's life upon which I have only touched in my book."

Upon this episode I am not able to throw any further light. When the authorised life and correspondence of the composer appears, his relatives may possibly clear up the mystery which surrounds it. On the other hand, it is more than probable that they will not take the public into their confidence upon a subject about which Tchaikovsky himself preserved an almost unbroken reticence.

TCHAIKOVSKY AS A MUSICAL CRITIC

THERE are certain books which owe their prestige more to the personality of their authors than to their intrinsic literary value. To this class belongs *The Collected Writings of Tchaikovsky*, edited, with a preface, by his friend and colleague G. A. Laroche. Such books, although devoted to special subjects, generally command a wide public. For though it may be true, as Tchaikovsky himself says, that great composers are rarely gifted with an infallible critical instinct, the majority will always pause to hear a great artist speaking of his own art rather than listen to the voice of the professional critic, prose he never so wisely.

Tchaikovsky's career as a musical writer was brief. He undertook the work rather from necessity than from inclination, and, regarding it as an unwelcome interruption in his busy, creative life, he gladly laid aside his pen when circumstances permitted him to do so. His literary legacy cannot be

compared in importance and interest with those of
Schumann, Liszt, or Berlioz. It is chiefly valuable
because it throws a narrow shaft of light upon his
personal tastes and the tendencies which influenced
his music; subjects which Tchaikovsky generally
kept in modest obscurity. It is evident that his own
ideal in criticism was something strictly impersonal
and objective, "a system founded on rational and
philosophical principles. But this kind of critical
utterance is rarely associated with the subjective,
creative temperament. Tchaikovsky, with all his
reserve, cannot always hold up the mask of im-
personality between himself and his readers. Thus,
in what is often a dry record of musical events, we
come upon oases of purely personal appreciation.
And what positive good sense, what lucidity and
soberness of judgment, what liberal-minded eclecticism
we find in these pages! They are "appreciations"
in the intellectual rather than the emotional sense;
for Tchaikovsky—to borrow a phrase from Mr.
Hadow—never condescends to substitute mere auto-
biography for criticism. We who in England know
Tchaikovsky so well—so much too well—by his
Sixth Symphony, are disposed to interpret the whole
trend of his character by this one dark-toned work,
which may reflect—for all we know—as much the
tragic historical destinies of his country as the
shadow of a purely personal sorrow. This work
has now come to be regarded as the expression
of Tchaikovsky's creed—or want of creed; and,
according to the more or less morbid temperament

of its commentators, "The Pathetic" is made to represent him as something between a fallen angel weeping "ever through vasts forgotten of the sun," and a whimpering agnostic prig. For my part, I think we shall never appreciate the true greatness of Tchaikovsky until we have forgotten, for a time, the over-wrought emotion of the *Sixth Symphony* and the fascinating triviality of its musical antithesis, the *Casse-Noisette Suite*. Then perhaps we shall turn with pleasure to the wholesome vigour and dramatic interest of *The Tempest;* to the poetic sentiment, the intense passion, the poignant—but controlled—melancholy of *Francesca di Rimini*, one of the most beautiful examples of programme music ever written; and the numerous other interesting works of his best and most robust period. Meanwhile it is good to see Tchaikovsky in a sober, business-like capacity, sane and clear-headed, exercising his critical faculties with a discretion and reserve that goes far to correct any false impressions of his extreme morbid subjectivity.

Tchaikovsky's first musical article, a message of consolation and encouragement to Rimsky-Korsakov, appeared in the *Sovremennaya Lietopis* in 1868. It was not, however, until 1872 that, yielding to the pressure of circumstances, he resolved to add to his income by regular journalistic work. During the next four years he wrote for the Moscow papers; first for the *Sovremennaya Lietopis* and afterwards for the *Russky Vestnik*. In 1876, disgusted by the polemics which he considered had been unjustly

I

fastened upon him, he resigned his post as musical
critic.   On the opening of the Bayreuth Theatre, however, he was induced to act once more as correspondent
for the *Russky Vestnik*, and recorded in five long
articles his impressions of the *Nibelungen King.*
Twelve years later he again took up the pen and
published, in a series of twelve articles, portions of a
journal kept during his tour of 1888.

Tchaikovsky's journalistic work, says Laroche,
"made no impression upon his subsequent development, and left hardly any visible trace upon his life."
At the close of the sixties and during the seventies,
Tchaikovsky's genius was abnormally active.   One
work after another took shape in his brain with a
feverish and exhausting rapidity; and to a man thus
preoccupied by the things of the imagination the
weekly letter to the *Russky Vestnik* was a tax.   He
was oppressed by an almost fateful realisation of the
shortness of his working days.   To him *ars longa,*
vita brevis, was no mere copybook phrase.   He
was haunted with a fear lest he should "die with all
his music in him," and more than once in his life he
paid the penalty for his feverish activity in periods of
enforced idleness and depression.   The lust of finishing left its mark upon his work.   "He wrote, wrote,
wrote in haste," says Laroche, "using up bales of
music paper; not finishing his work at once, or
rather—to be quite accurate—finishing it as regards
externals, and conscientiously attending to technical
details, but frequently in his eagerness losing sight of
the plan and proportions of the whole."   This accounts

for the destruction of so many of his earlier works and the constant rewriting and modification of others.

The collected criticisms of Tchaikovsky must not be taken as more than a partial indication of his thoughts on music, for it will be evident that the concerts of the Musical Society at Moscow, and the performances at the Opera, gave only a limited field in which to express his views.

What, then, were Tchaikovsky's musical ideals in his youth and maturity, and how far did they influence his individual development? He himself would have repudiated the use of the word "ideals." He had the positive Russian temperament that feels intensely, and instinctively avoids gush. Was it not a Russian who remarked that a piece of bread and cheese was worth all the poems of Poushkin put together? In a similarly practical manner Tchaikovsky answered those who questioned him about his inner consciousness.

"What are your musical ideals?" Serov's daughter inquired of Tchaikovsky as he sat at the piano during one of her father's musical evenings in Petersburg.

"My ideals?" he answered: "is it absolutely necessary to have ideals in music? I have never given a thought to them." Then, after a few moments' reflection: "I never possessed any ideals."

To another lady who put the same question he replied: "My ideal is to become a good composer."

I

MOZART AND HAYDN

TCHAIKOVSKY, says Laroche, was constant in his leading ideas, but very variable in the shades of his opinion. The chief deity of his musical Olympus was Mozart. In this he differed from the majority of his countrymen, who, preferring fire to light, and intensity of emotion to "sweet reasonableness," have rarely appreciated Mozart at his immeasurable worth. Glinka thought *Don Juan* "a fine opera, but not a model one." Tchaikovsky writes of it : —

"Every work of art, however much it may transcend the artistic level of the day and the society in which its author lived and moved, must still inevitably bear the stamp of its period. No matter how strong and profound the creative gift of an artist, he cannot escape certain characteristics, certain purely external peculiarities of form which, in the hands of second-rate talent, degenerate into mere tricks of routine and finally assume a sort of archæological importance. Therefore it is not surprising that even in the loftiest spheres of art the works of human genius should grow obsolete. In the creations of Raphael, Shakespeare, and Mozart, despite all their depth of conception, we find certain external features which do not answer to the tastes of younger generations. But it does not follow that the hand of time has power to touch the essential substance of a work of art; and so—notwithstanding its eighty years— the opera of *Don Juan*, in which are enshrined the powerful and incorruptible relics of Mozart's genius, is only old-fashioned as regards technical details. It awakes in us the same enthusiasm, it touches our feelings as effectively as in the days of our fathers and grandfathers before us. Compared with that of Berlioz, Mozart's orchestration is, of course, slight; his arias are somewhat diffuse, and sometimes err by pandering to the caprices and virtuosity of his singers. His style is laid out to please the affectations of the court-circle of his day. Nevertheless, all his operas, and *Don Juan* above all, are full of beauties of the highest order and of strong dramatic situations. His melody is wonderfully beautiful, his harmony rich and interesting. But Mozart was pre-eminently a master of dramatic music, and no other composer ever created such well-sustained or realistically conceived musical types as Don Juan, Donna Anna, Leporello, Zerlina, etc.

"As I have remarked, Mozart's weak side lies in his lengthy concert arias, which, purposely designed that the singer might show off his or her skill, are not invariably of great musical value. But in the concerted parts, in the scenes which depict dramatic movement, he has left us a long series of masterpieces. The scenes in which Donna Anna takes part are especially strong in this intense dramatic power. Her heart-rending cries over the body of her murdered father, her horror and thirst for vengeance when she meets the author of her misfortunes, all this is realised by Mozart with such convincing power that its effect can only be compared with some of Shakespeare's best scenes.

"I would point out as the best things in the opera the *Finale* of the first act; the scene at the grave of the Commandant; the sextet in the second act (when the rest of the characters mistake Leporello for Don Juan), so remarkable for its humorous contrast to the rest of the work; and, finally, the last scene between Don Juan and the Statue.

"To what simple—I might almost say poor—means Mozart had recourse in this scene in order to express the horror of the impenitent libertine before this awful apparition! Contemporary composers would have let loose upon us the full tornado of trombones, trumpets, cymbals, and drums; whereas Mozart attains an infinitely stronger effect by the actual strength of his genius alone."

To this love for Mozart, Tchaikovsky remained faithful during his whole life. He studied the composer from every side of his genius, and left two memorials of his affection for him: his "Mozartiana" Suite for Orchestra (op. 61), and the vocal quartet

"Night," the music adapted from Mozart's *Fantasia* No. 4 (1893).

A few days before his death Tchaikovsky conducted the dances from *Idomeneo*. "His admiration for the composer of *The Magic Flute*," says Laroche, "extended in a certain degree to his whole period, and he was delighted with one of Sarti's operas." In his own opera *La Dame de Pique*, there is a scene which might almost pass for the work of a contemporary of Mozart. But it cannot be said that he paid his favourite the flattering homage of imitation. In spite of his consistent admiration for Mozart, Tchaikovsky's genius has nothing in common with him, and Laroche explains this attraction by the theory of "unlike to unlike."

For Haydn, Tchaikovsky had a sincere, if conventional respect, and a due sense of his importance in the historical development of music. He thought his music valuable for educational purposes, and declared that a Haydn quartet was preferable to many chamber works of the modern German school. In 1873 he writes:—

"I have a very high regard for the respectable and even *great* services rendered to music by this venerable man. Haydn has immortalised himself, if not by his inventive powers, at least by what he did towards perfecting those two ideal forms—the Symphony and the Sonata—afterwards carried to the utmost degree of beauty and finished workmanship by Mozart and Beethoven. Haydn is an indispensable link in the chain of symphonic music; without him

Mozart and Beethoven could hardly have existed; at least the development of these two dominant figures in the world of music would have been very different. They would have sprung from a less cultivated soil, and must have met with greater obstacles to the growth of their genius. But without in any way detracting from Haydn's invaluable services, we cannot fail to see that his inspiration did not soar very high; that he never got beyond the 'miniature' and the 'pretty,' and never once touches those secret heart-strings from which later composers have drawn such soul-stirring, deeply pathetic tunes. This is not a suitable place for entering into the historical conditions under which Haydn's genius was developed. Would he have shown more depth, more tragic force, more passion if he had been born at some other period? Does not his music owe its artificial atmosphere of elegant coldness to the customs and surroundings in which he chanced to develop? Is not this the reason why he has no power to move us deeply, to draw our tears or to carry us away by strong emotions? May not this be the reason why he has survived from the last century with difficulty, through a period torn by doubt and exhausted by the irresponsible sufferings of the romantic school which followed him? These deep and interesting questions may be discussed by lovers of musical æsthetics. I have said that Haydn belongs entirely to the sphere of the 'pretty' in art. In all his symphonies you may find the same playful episodes, a sort of medley, or kaleidoscopic play of sounds which involuntarily charms the ear. By this

I do not for a moment mean to suggest that Haydn should be irrevocably excluded from the concert-room.   In Russia, especially, his works form a necessary stepping-stone by means of which we can lead on the mass of our public until it attains to the level of Beethoven and learns to appreciate him. Only it is desirable to contrast with his slightness and superficiality of form and idea some great work by one of the later masters."

II

HANDEL—CHOPIN—BEETHOVEN

TCHAIKOVSKY did not share the revived interest in
Bach which made itself felt in Russia, as elsewhere,
towards the middle and close of the fifties, and spoke
of his great choral works as "real classical bores";
while Handel he found intolerable.

If his preference for Mozart, who is in many
respects his musical antithesis, is somewhat unaccount-
able, so, at first sight, his want of sympathy for Chopin
has its element of mystery. For many years he felt
no enthusiasm whatsoever for the works of the Polish
master, and would only grudgingly admit that there
was a certain "charm" in the *Barcarolle* and the
F minor Fantasia. Yet there is undoubtedly some
affinity between Chopin and Tchaikovsky in temperament and, in a much less degree, in style. Both have
the tendency to alternate between profound melancholy and fiery energy characteristic of the Slav;
both have the same rather morbid preference for
the minor, the same chromatic colouring; the same

restless agitation in the middle parts. Tchaikovsky seems to have been aware of this likeness, and to have turned from Chopin as from a reflection of his own weaknesses. In later days, Nicholas Rubinstein partially converted Tchaikovsky from this prejudice against Chopin's works.

It is not easy to arrive at a clear view of Tchaikovsky's attitude towards Beethoven. "Generally speaking," says Laroche, "he cherished a sentiment of *veneration* for Beethoven, quite distinct from the enthusiastic *affection* and true worship which he felt for Mozart." There are indications in his articles that he sometimes resented the general tendency to an indiscriminate Beethoven worship. But Tchaikovsky is often so reserved in his writings, so averse from rashly running counter to opinions which have been consecrated by authority, that his views on Beethoven seem rather colourless. In conversation he was less reticent, but there seems always to have been an element of doubt as to his real feelings on this subject. "In 1867," writes Laroche, "I showed him a MS. (part of my article on Glinka) treating of the exaggerated fanaticism with which Beethoven was regarded. He then praised me for my manliness, in what certainly did not sound like empty phrases; but when eighteen years later I developed the same idea in various articles, and at greater length, he showed himself very reserved, and merely remarked that I was unjust to the *Finale* of the *Ninth Symphony*." Tchaikovsky started life as a great admirer of Glinka, and, like all young Russian composers, was proud of the independent views upon Western art which were part of the master's legacy to the school he had founded. Glinka certainly venerated Beethoven, but just as he shocked all cultivated Russia by his criticisms of Bellini and other Italian idols of his day, so his disciples went a step further and scandalised a later generation of formalists by repudiating their obligation to traditions which their nation had in no way helped to build up. It may have begun as a rebellion; it ended in the constitutional protest of a foreign-ridden people. Tchaikovsky was not a stranger to this movement; but a period of eighteen years works changes in a malleable nature. In his maturity he grew more eclectic, more tolerant of tradition; and it is easy to conceive that he mistrusted the two-edged blade of Laroche's criticism, which, while striking a blow at venerable traditions, was often equally hostile to the music of the New School. From numerous criticisms I have endeavoured to collect the passages about Beethoven in which the personal note seems to be of some value. In 1871 I find the following paragraph : —

"I am not disposed to proclaim the infallibility of Beethoven's principles, and, without in any way denying his historical importance, I protest against the insincerity of an equal and indiscriminate laudation of all his works. But undoubtedly in certain of his symphonies Beethoven reached a height to which scarcely any of his contemporaries could attain."

In the list of Beethoven's "unrivalled works" he places the *Eighth Symphony*, and a year after writing the above paragraph he drew the following comparison between the *Eighth* and the *Ninth Symphonies*, which is, I think, one of the most subjective of his criticisms : —

"Beethoven's *Eighth Symphony* is distinguished from its predecessors and from the one which followed it—the great *Choral Symphony*—by an unusual conciseness of form and by its unbroken joyfulness and festal character. It is the last bright smile, the last response given by the poet of human sorrow and hopeless despair to the voice of gladness. In the *Ninth Symphony* Beethoven concludes his colossal work by a Hymn to Joy, which represents the eternal and universal chorus of humanity, united in brotherly love and chanting in one voice an ecstatic dithyrambus to Nature and the Creator. But such joy is not of this earth. It is something ideal and unrealisable; it has nothing in common with this life, but it is only a momentary aspiration of humanity towards the holiness which exists only in the world of art and beauty; afterwards, this vale of earth, with its endless sorrow, its agony of doubt and unsatisfied hopes, seems still more gloomy and without issue. In the *Ninth Symphony* we hear the despairing cry of a great genius who, having irrevocably lost faith in happiness, escapes for a time into the world of unrealisable hopes, into the realm of broken-winged ideals. The *Eighth Symphony*, on the contrary, is filled with a spirit of serene content and unrestrained joy. It depicts the gentle earthly delights of humanity, before the soul is distracted by evil, doubt, and despair.

"Both subjects of the first movement are full of grace and elegance, their exposition is simple and concise, with a delicate accompaniment and transparent harmony. The second subject is exceedingly original by reason of its unexpected modulations and capricious changes of tonality. The second movement (*Andante scherzando*) shares popular favour with the famous *Allegretto* of the *Seventh Symphony*. Its originality lies chiefly in the employment of the wind instruments which, contrary to the customary laws of instrumentation, are used by Beethoven as an accompaniment, while the violins keep up a lively —almost humorous—melody, and the basses reply heavily in a similar phrase. All this is unexpected, fresh, and piquant. The third movement, in the form and tempo of a minuet, recalls, by its style and by the unpretentious simplicity of its leading idea, the minuets of Haydn. In the *Finale*—one of Beethoven's symphonic *chefs-d'œuvre*—we meet with an endless series of humorous and unexpected episodes; of contrasts in harmony, varied modulations, and ingenious orchestral effects. I must indicate the striking unison effect of the whole orchestra cn C♯ which breaks in so unexpectedly upon the remote key of C major, just after the *diminuendo* where Beethoven recalls the first subject in different registers of the various instruments; and again, the very humorous effect—twice repeated—which he gets by the combination of drums and bassoons on the note F, in succeeding octaves, struck at regular intervals, staccato. The *Finale* abounds in such interesting details."

His account of the *Seventh Symphony* seems also worth quoting : —

"Beethoven's *Seventh Symphony*, thanks to its well-known *Allegretto*,[1] is a great favourite with the public. Among the works of the great symphonist, this *Allegretto* plays something of the same part as what is known as the *air favori* in a popular opera. Very often such an air is only distinguished from the numbers that precede or follow it because the melody is more vulgar, the harmony coarser and less poetical. To fine gradations of artistic colouring the majority is always blind. Bright tints, florid outlines, and strong colouring—effects which catch the eye—these alone can attract their attention. Tender half-tones, finished details, elegant roundness of form, all this escapes the notice of these unfortunate victims of blindness. A long time must elapse before details, at first unobserved and misunderstood, begin to detach themselves from the background of the picture. The more a musical work becomes the property of the public, the more they begin to observe with astonishment all the beauties they failed to appreciate at first hearing. At the same time they grow disenchanted with their *air favori*, discover that it is commonplace, and finally turn it into the streets, where it becomes the property

[1] Tchaikovsky invariably speaks of this movement as an *Andante*.

of the grateful organ-grinder who caters for a public that never outgrows the *air favori*.

"But there exist some rare compositions which possess the power of pleasing alike the educated and uneducated public. Their beauty is immutable; the oftener we hear them the more we love them. Their power and originality is such that it is impossible to analyse them; but they can never become ephemeral because they are inaccessible to imitation and plagiarism. To this class of music belongs the *Allegretto* of the *Seventh Symphony*, which—for over sixty years—has been a fertile source of delight to the whole civilised world. The first and last movements of this wonderful work, which shine with the same radiance as when they astonished all Europe in 1812—when Beethoven first took them from his portfolio—are not inferior to the *Allegretto;* but the latter, I repeat, has the privilege of popularity, thanks partly to its fascinating melody and partly to material beauty of sound—its admirable instrumentation.

"The first movement of the symphony opens with a broad, bold Introduction, and is remarkable for the gradual increase of interest with which Beethoven develops it, by means of what is known in technical terms as the 'elaboration' of a simple, short theme of an energetic character. The orchestral effect at the opening of this Introduction is very original, and is frequently repeated in that which follows. The whole mass of instruments give out loud staccato chords from which is formed the theme

of the Introduction, at first imperceptibly, but afterwards announced and sustained by the oboe. The
first subject of the *Allegro*, a melody of a naïve,
pastoral character, served the purists of Beethoven's
day as a pretext for accusing him of a want of discrimination in his choice of symphonic themes: as
though an artist who painted the sublime in Alpine
scenes or tempests at sea might not be equally
successful in representing a simple rural landscape.

" The rhythm of this theme, with its original
accent on the third beat of the bar, is maintained
with wonderful skill throughout the entire movement.[1] Modulations, modifications of the themes,
strikingly new and bold harmonies, succeed each
other with ever-increasing interest, but the fundamental rhythm, which holds the first place, remains
unchanged throughout. It is impossible to translate
into words the astounding effect of this infinite
variety in unity; only a colossal genius such as
Beethoven could bring such a task to a successful
issue without wearying the attention of his audience,
or allowing them for a moment to feel anything
but pleasure in the importunate reiteration of the
first rhythmic figure. Among other details of this
wonderful work I would point out the *stretto* at the
close of the first movement, where the bassi, 'celli,
and alti repeat twenty times in succession a little
two-bar phrase, while the higher registers of the
orchestra move in a progressive development of the

[1] I have printed this sentence as it appears in the Russian,
but I consider *third* evidently a misprint for *first*

K

tonic-chord. This original method of procedure, like the inaugural chord of the Introduction, has served as a model for numerous imitators, among them Berlioz, who makes use of a similar effect at the end of the first movement of his *Romeo and Juliet* symphony.

" The *Allegretto* consists of the development of a rhythmic figure unusually simple in conception, and this simple leading idea lends to the movement that undeniable charm to which it owes its great popularity. This figure is first heard in the lower registers, from the alti, 'celli, and bassi. When it passes to the violins, it becomes associated in the 'celli with a sad, complaining phrase of contrapuntal character in the minor. Gradually the leading subject grows and becomes more and more prominent, until at last it is given out by the full power of the orchestra. Afterwards follows a contrasting melody, serene and joyful, suggestive of hope in some as yet remote happiness. Meanwhile the original rhythm, like a whispered foreboding, a gloomy *momento mori*, is heard in the bassi. When the leading subject returns, it is completely transformed, and receives its final development in a *fugato* form. Then it dies away, to reappear in a fragmentary way as though it still had something to say, and finally ceases altogether on a vague chord. If we, after all these years, are still astonished by the novelty and freshness, the power shown both in the design and execution of this marvellous work, what must our forefathers have felt when Beethoven by the magic power of his genius first raised the curtain which hid this ideal world of eternal beauty and harmony from human eyes?

"The *Scherzo* is full of life and joyous movement, and in the middle episode Beethoven gives it a character of triumphal, solemn joy. In this movement occurs another striking and novel effect—exceedingly original for the period at which it was written—I refer to the pedal-point on the dominant, in contrast to the upper parts and the accent on the appoggiatura.

"If in contrast to the serious character of the *Allegretto* the *Scherzo* is remarkable for its joyful mood, the *Finale* is almost bacchanalian, and depicts a whole series of scenes replete with unconstrained gladness and contentment with life. Hearing this superb last movement, we do not know which to admire most: the creative imagination of Beethoven, or the perfection of form, his astounding skill in handling all musical means, both in the development of the themes and in the fulness and luxuriance of his orchestration."

III

SCHUMANN—ITALIAN MUSIC—BRAHMS

I HAVE said that in spite of his great love for Mozart, Tchaikovsky was not directly influenced by him, but as regards Schumann the case is completely reversed. In 1862 he was already a student of Schumann's works, and constantly played the symphonies and overtures arranged for four hands with his friend Laroche. Tchaikovsky's *opinion* of Schumann was variable, and rarely rose to wholehearted approbation; but Schumann's *influence* is traceable throughout the whole of his career, though gradually weakening as time progressed. One of his earliest criticisms of Schumann is that of the *Fourth Symphony*, in 1871 :—

"It may be said with truth that in the future history of the art the music of the second half of this century will be known to coming generations as 'Schumannesque.' Schumann's music, which is organically allied to Beethoven's, while at the same time sharply differentiated from it, reveals a whole world of new musical forms, and touches heart-cords which have never yet vibrated at the bidding of his predecessors. In it we seem to catch an echo of those profound, mysterious stirrings of our spiritual life, of the doubt, the despair, the yearning towards the Ideal, which agitate the hearts of the men and women of to-day. History has not yet taken cognisance of Schumann; only in the distant future will it be possible to make an objective critical evaluation of his work. But it is an undisputed fact that this composer is the brightest star among recent musicians; for hardly any good concert is now given which does not include at least one of Schumann's multitudinous works, in which his creative power is proportionate to his wonderful productiveness.

"At a recent concert, given by the Musical Society, we heard Schumann's *Fourth Symphony* (D minor) and the little piece for piano, *Abends*, which, in spite of its brevity, is full of charm and true genius. I am even inclined to give the palm to this exquisitely poetical trifle rather than to the greater symphonic work. The *Fourth Symphony* is the last[1] of the series, and at the same time the least in value. It has not that overwhelming power, that searching pathos, which strikes us in the first two symphonies. The sum-total of its beauties cannot unfortunately redeem that great fault which prevails in all works of Schumann, considered especially

---

[1] It is really the second in order of production, a fact which Tchaikovsky seems to have overlooked.

as a symphonic writer. This fault would be called by painters a lack of colour; it is a pallor, a dryness—I may almost say harshness—of orchestration. Without entering into technical details, I may explain to my readers that the art of instrumentation (*i.e.* the distribution of a work among the various instruments) consists in understanding how to employ alternately the individual groups of instruments; how to blend them appropriately; how to economise strong effects, and also in the intelligent use of colouring—that is to say, the application of *timbre* to musical ideas. This knowledge Schumann has not acquired. His orchestra works continuously; all the instruments take part in the exposition and development of his ideas. They are not used in detachments; there is no contrast between them (and contrasting effects are inexhaustible in orchestration); most of the time they mingle in a continuous roar, often spoiling the best parts of the work. As regards instrumentation, Schumann not only stands on a lower level than such masters as Berlioz, Mendelssohn, Meyerbeer, and Wagner, but he cannot even be compared with many second-rate composers who have borrowed his best inspirations."

Tchaikovsky regards Schumann's *Second* and *Third Symphonies* as the culminating points of his orchestral work; especially the *Second*, in which "the depth of thought, beauty of form, and breadth of plastic conception take us by surprise." But it is to the *First Symphony* that he has devoted the longest and most careful analysis, and for which he seems to feel a warm personal appreciation, which does not, however, disarm his critical attitude. Writing in the *Russky Viedomosti* in 1872, he says:—"Schumann's *First Symphony* was written in 1841, and was his earliest attempt in that species of composition. Beginning to compose at twenty, and having produced a number of fine pianoforte works and a quantity of songs, Schumann waited until his thirty-first year to approach orchestral music. The very fact that this master took up symphonic music so late seems to prove that he had no strong inclination towards the orchestra. A great connoisseur of all the qualities and most subtle resources of his favourite instrument —the piano—he is an inimitable master in the art of drawing out the rich, luxuriant sonority of this miniature orchestra. But apparently Schumann could never call forth the inexhaustible treasures of the modern orchestra. All his later works reveal his lack of a sense of colour, of genial design. He disdained colour, and preferred the pen and pencil to the brush. The most enthusiastic admirers of Schumann's music—which is invariably rich in invention and pale in colouration—are agreed that his orchestral works actually gain in being transcribed for the piano. Schumann had not the art of clothing his wealth of ideas in beautiful sounds; his orchestration is always opaque and heavy, and lacks brilliance and transparency. This characteristic negative feature of Schumann's genius is not often present in his *First Symphony*. It is said that he wrote this work under the strong influence and personal guidance of

Mendelssohn. The traces of this influence are not, however, apparent. Schumann, in his *First Symphony*, with all its positive and negative qualities, shows more strength and capability and greater individuality than Mendelssohn. On the one hand, wealth of imagination, simplicity of design, the plasticity of a Beethoven in its fundamental form; on the other, a lack of colour, obscurity, and a disregard of attractive details in orchestration—this is what we find in Schumann's first essay in symphonic writing.

" The work opens with an Introduction in which the leading idea is announced in a slow *tempo* by a few of the brass instruments and is repeated by the whole orchestra. This is, as it were, the signal which heralds the sumptuous, motley pageant which unfolds itself as the work proceeds. The triumphant joy of the first subject gives place to an episode of a contrasting character which—in spite of all contrast —has a close connection with that which precedes it. It is evident that these are twin themes and originated simultaneously in Schumann's mind; their union is not marred by that unsightly join which always shows in the works of inferior composers with their superficial habit of pasting their thoughts together. In working out this subject, Schumann, without departing from classical forms, as laid down by Mozart and Beethoven, introduces entirely new methods of procedure, and displays an independence completely free from the influence of the earlier masters. The whole of this first movement proves that new, romantic, and original ideas can be united to the established traditions of form; it is, as it were, the link which connects the classical school, ending with Beethoven, to the new movement in which Schumann joined with Chopin and Berlioz. The rest of the symphony bears also the stamp of this eclecticism. In the *Andante*, a beautiful melody of an elegiac character, accompanied by brilliant variations, produces a fascinating effect, especially when it passes to the 'celli in the key of the subdominant. In the third movement, the rhythm of which recalls a minuet rather than a scherzo such as we find in Beethoven's symphonies, the first trio is specially remarkable for the ingenious chords which seem to call to each other alternately from the string and wind instruments, and also for its concluding coda with its rushing syncopated rhythm and highly original harmony. The *Finale*, bold, brilliant, and finished in form, rich in beautiful modulations and in varied rhythm and harmony, serves as an admirable close to this exquisite work."

Another interesting example of Tchaikovsky's views upon Schumann is the following account of the *Pianoforte Quintet* (op. 44) : —

" It is a fact that Schumann, with his colossal creative gifts, yet lacked the particular instinct which might have enabled him to express his thoughts through the medium of orchestral or chamber music. In this he resembled Chopin, the pianist composer *par excellence*. . . . In spite of the luxuriant beauty scattered throughout his symphonic works, as regards form, structure, and finish, the first place must be given to Schumann's purely pianoforte works and to the chamber music in which the piano plays the chief part. To this class belongs the fine *Quintet in E flat*.

"The first movement is based on two very simple but striking and beautiful subjects, of contrasting character. The *Andante*, in the style and rhythm of a funeral march, depicts on a small scale a whole sombre tragedy. After the exposition of the wonderful leading subject, Schumann passes on to tributary ideas which have a solemn religious colouring, and seem to express faith and self-renunciation, a gentle submission to Providence, and a willingness to bow before the inevitable decrees of Fate. Then the gloomy theme of the funeral march returns, to be suddenly interrupted by a stormy episode which echoes the voice of a passionate soul agitated and rebellious at the tragic loss of some beloved being. But the notes of the funeral march break once more upon this music, like the lamentations of a broken heart. Gradually, a tender religious sentiment conquers all other emotions; the agitated spirit grows calm, and strives to become reconciled to the oppression of earthly life by looking forward to the beauty of heaven. The *Andante* comes to an ethereal close on the transparent major tonic chord, given out in harmonics by violins and viola in their highest flute-like register. The *Scherzo* is full of virile energy and inspired impetuosity. The *Finale* carries the listener back to the joyous mood of the first movement; and here, by starting the leading subjects of the first and last movements on 'pedal-points,' Schumann displays his inimitable technical skill in the polyphonic development of his themes. This is one of the inexplicable musical phenomena of genius before which musical specialists can only bow down in respect."

In his youth Tchaikovsky was a devotee of Italian opera, especially of Rossini's more serious works, *Semiramide, Otello,* and *Tell.* His appreciation of the *Barber of Seville* was of later growth. Tchaikovsky, though rarely stooping to direct imitation, was extremely susceptible to external influences. Italian opera was, moreover, associated in his case with a love episode which—though ephemeral in character—left a lingering sentimental impression in his memory. For Donizetti he felt no sympathy, but comparatively late in life—when the current of fashion had set in quite other directions—Tchaikovsky began to value the works of Bellini. But it was the glamour and warmth of the South, so forcibly expressed by Rossini's brilliant dramatic power, which exercised the strongest fascination for the Russian composer. He shared with the Italian school the cult of graceful and sensuous melody, and was strongly influenced by Rossini in this respect. We cannot doubt it, when we recall, for instance, some of the solos in his opera *The Oprichnik,* or the second subject of the first movement of the *Sixth Symphony.* The lovely things of art are preserved to reappear in unexpected disguises, and just as the gracious beauty of Italian melody seemed doomed to pass away under a new dispensation, it was reincarnated in the works of this northern composer. Such cases of musical atavism are by no means rare, and would make an interesting study in themselves. Tchaikovsky's views on Italian music, written at a time when all critics who wished to be taken seriously were condemning Italian opera, in the words of Dr. Johnson, as "an exotic and irrational entertainment," were admirable in their tone of unbiassed reserve. His attitude was that of negative rather than of positive defence. He refused to exalt Wagner and Schumann at the expense of Rossini and Meyerbeer, and succeeds in keeping an open mind and an individual opinion throughout the period of heated polemics during which he acted as a musical critic.

The note of decision which is sometimes lacking in Tchaikovsky's defence of Italian opera is fully heard, however, on the question of classical music, in the narrower sense of the word—that is to say, the great period at the close of the eighteenth and beginning of the nineteenth centuries. While he gives Schumann one of the highest places in modern music, he scarcely veils his contempt for the rank and file of the new romantic school of Germany. Nor could he bring himself—even after conscientious efforts— to accept Brahms as one of the Immortals. In the seventies, the period during which Tchaikovsky was engaged in musical criticism, Brahms's works were so seldom given in Moscow that his name rarely appears in the first part of this volume. The first important record of Tchaikovsky's opinion on this subject occurs in November 1872, when Brahms's *Sextet in B flat* was given at one of the chamber concerts of the Musical Society. He then writes : —

"All Germany has looked with unction upon this composer,—who is still young,—thinking to find in him the man destined to lead his art into unexplored paths, and capable, by the power of his creative gift, not only of equalling, but even of surpassing, his great predecessors. The rumours circulated throughout the German musical world on the appearance of Brahms's first compositions owed their origin to Schumann. It is a well-known fact that great composers are rarely endowed with infallible critical instincts, and are generally remarkable for their leniency to their fellow-artists. Schumann is a striking example of this critical indulgence. All his life he bowed down to Mendelssohn, Chopin, and Berlioz, and even to such musical nobodies as Henselt, Hiller, etc. He went into sincere ecstasies over every fresh manifestation of genius, and only depreciated his own value. Towards the end of his career, Schumann, through the medium of his musical journal, published in Leipzig, began to prophesy the advent of a musical Messiah, who was destined to illuminate the whole world of music and to fill the place left vacant by Beethoven. When Brahms's first sonatas appeared, Schumann, in one laconic phrase, 'He has come,' announced the advent of the expected genius, whom he proclaimed in the person of young Brahms. Time has proved, however, that Schumann's unexpected proclamation was a mistake into which the indulgent and amiable composer was easily led. Brahms has not fulfilled the obligations which Schumann laid upon him and upon all musical Germany personified in him. He is merely one of those *routinier* composers in which the German school has been so rich. He writes fluently, skilfully, correctly, but without a spark of independent genius; contenting himself with endless trifling with empty musical ideas, long since become stale, and borrowed chiefly from Mendelssohn; while he also strives to imitate certain external mannerisms of Schumann's. Brahms, however, is not devoid of talent; therefore he stands a whole head above his contemporaries. But there is now no question of the fulfilment of impossible hopes in his genius."

Sixteen years later Tchaikovsky's views upon Brahms were less crude, and tempered by a sentiment of personal respect, but they remained essentially unchanged. During this period he had more frequent opportunities of hearing the works of the German master, and Kashkin says that during the long, quiet evenings of Tchaikovsky's life at Klin, he would often take one of Brahms's scores from his shelves and try to work himself up to a flickering enthusiasm for the contents. But there is no doubt that these two great musicians found no common meeting-ground, and Brahms on his part was too sincere to pretend to any appreciation of Tchaikovsky's works. The unsympathetic attitude of the Russian composer towards Brahms's music is regarded by many in the light of a grievance, or even of an impertinence. Is it not really a blessing in

disguise? An artist may admire his great predecessors to the extent of being influenced by them,
but no more; whereas a whole-hearted admiration
for a contemporary seems invariably to lead to more
or less direct imitation of his methods. The Brahms
cult has immolated too many rising talents as it is;
for even those who have the most genuine admiration for the splendid qualities of the master cannot
deny that his disciples form the dullest school in
contemporary music. In the independence of the
Russian school—with its many imperfections—there
is at least the charm of freshness and sincerity.

IV

BERLIOZ—SAINT-SAËNS—WAGNER

COLD as was Tchaikovsky's attitude to Wagner's music in his early days, it is somewhat singular to find that the works of the Arch-Wagnerian Serov moved him to enthusiastic praise. *Judith*[1] was one of his favourite operas, and remained so through his whole life. But Serov left no traces of influence upon Tchaikovsky's own works, which show a close acquaintance with the dramatic compositions of Glinka and Meyerbeer, and later of Bizet and the modern French school. In connection with this school it may be said that, at first, Tchaikovsky was very little impressed by Gounod's *Faust*, which achieved such immense success in Petersburg. At a later date his favourite singer, Madame Artot, in the part of Margaret, partially dispelled this indifference. He had a great admiration for the orchestration of Berlioz, but he was not influenced

Judith, an early opera of Serov's, was written in 1862, and performed in Petersburg in May 1863.

by him in the same degree as many of his compatriots: Moussorgsky, for instance, as regards sentiment, and Rimsky-Korsakov as regards style and technique. In March 1873, on the occasion of a performance of the overture to *Les Francs Juges*, he gives his opinion of Berlioz at considerable length : —

"Berlioz is both a brilliant and exceptional phenomenon in the history of music. In certain spheres of his art he has reached ideal heights to which few other artists have ever attained. He has not composed a single work which does not equally display all-round technical perfection and depth of thought, joined to beauty of form, which are essential properties of all great works of art. In many respects he has struck out in new lines, yet it cannot be said that he actually belongs to the new school; nor has he left any direct disciples. Throughout his career he aroused great interest, but never possessed such warm partisans and patrons of his music as Mozart or Beethoven did, and—in our day —Wagner. The enthusiastic welcome accorded to him almost everywhere in Germany—with the exception of the stubborn attitude of the Leipzig Conservatoire—and also in Russia, was due not so much to a universal sympathy for his music as to a certain side impulses. Germany and Russia honoured in the person of Berlioz his disinterested labours, his passionate love of art, his energetic and noble efforts to fight against the obtuseness, conventionality, ignorance, and intrigue of that brutal collection of

L

units which poets call 'the crowd.' No matter
how remarkable some sides of Berlioz's genius may
be, no matter how prominently his sympathetic
personality may stand out among the great musicians
of our time, I still maintain that his music has never
touched the masses in the same sense as that of
Mozart, Beethoven, Schumann, Schubert, Mendelssohn, or Meyerbeer, or as that of Wagner must
assuredly do in the future. That Berlioz was the
victim of the misunderstanding of the French nation,
led on by French musicians; that he was never
appreciated in that country; that he was worthy of
a better and happier fate than that which commonly
falls to the lot of a persevering, hard-working artist—
all this cannot be denied. But his isolated position
among his contemporaries in art, his want of success,
the coldness of the public and of musicians, these
things are due to certain peculiarities of his exceptional musical temperament, and the incompleteness,
in many respects, of his natural creative endowment.

"In composition we must distinguish two separate
factors : a purely inventive faculty, and imagination.
The history of music furnishes examples of composers
who have possessed astonishing powers of the first
order; their minds have been inexhaustibly pro-
ductive of beautiful melodic ideas and exquisite
harmonies, which were not the outcome of any effort
or labour, but of inherent instinct and tendency.
But they lacked a rich, luminous imagination. In
this connection we may instance Schubert, Chopin
to a certain extent, and our Russian composer

Dargomijsky. Other composers, endowed with the second factor of the creative mind, but possessing relatively poor inventive faculties, know how to extract all the contents of a musical germ; and by variety in the contrasts of colour, and by special attention to external beauty, they make the most of the situation. Such are Mendelssohn, Liszt, and Balakirev. An equal proportion of inventive power in melody, rhythm, and harmony, joined to wealth of imagination, is only to be found in the wake of the very greatest masters, such as Mozart and Beethoven. As regards Berlioz, he belongs undoubtedly to the second category of composers. The preponderance of fiery poetical imagination over absolute musical creative power is all the more apparent in him, because he is entirely lacking in the art of harmony, which is so indispensable to the development of leading ideas. His harmony is distorted, and sometimes intolerable to a finely organised ear. We hear in it an insane incoherence, the absence of any natural feeling, and an inconsequence in the management of the parts which prevents his works from appealing directly to the musical emotions of his audience. Berlioz works upon the imagination. He knows how to engage and interest; but he can rarely move us. Poor in melodic inspiration, lacking a fine feeling for harmony, but endowed with a marvellous gift of exciting the imagination of his hearers, Berlioz applied all his creative powers to the externals of musical beauty. The results of this tendency are shown in that marvellous orchestration, that inimitable beauty of sonority, that picturesque musical presentment of the natural and fantastic world, which proclaim him the subtle and inspired poet, the unapproachably great master. We recall all the poetic glamour with which he depicts the supernatural world in his *Faust*, or the tiny fairy-folk in the scherzo 'Queen Mab,' from the *Romeo and Juliet* symphony. Here the music gives such a realistic picture of a fantastic subject that the imagination is carried away, as in a beautiful dream, to the unknown region where lies the valley of eternal and ideal happiness."

Tchaikovsky had a great respect for Monsieur Saint-Saëns as an all-round artist who combines a remarkable creative gift with refined and brilliant executive power. In 1875 the French musician visited St. Petersburg in the threefold capacity of composer, pianist, and conductor. In November he played his *Pianoforte Concerto in D flat* at a concert of the Musical Society, and Tchaikovsky then writes of him: "Monsieur Saint-Saëns belongs in his own country to a small circle which represents the progressive element in music. In this advanced set, which consists of the most talented of contemporary French composers—Massenet, Dubois, and Paladihle (also Bizet, a composer of extraordinary endowments who died last year at thirty years of age)—Monsieur Saint-Saëns occupies a very prominent position." He then gives a brief biographical sketch of the composer, and goes on to speak of the general features of his work: "All the most sympathetic characteristics of his nationality, cordial sincerity, warmth of feeling, intellect, make themselves felt in every note of our guest's compositions. They are further illuminated by his artistic interpretation of them, which shows such distinction, such thoughtful and careful phrasing, without a trace of affectation." Elsewhere, he dwells upon the union of strictly classical methods with modern sentiments which is so characteristic of Saint-Saëns. "If I am not mistaken," he says, "the originality of the French master's creative methods lies in the fact that he combines most successfully the style of Sebastian Bach—for whom he has an evident affection—with the national French elements, of which the characteristically piquant rhythm makes itself clearly felt."

As regards Wagner, it may be said that his influence is not at all evident in Tchaikovsky's early works, and only to a very limited extent in those of his maturity. Laroche, however, considers that Wagner's influence had perceptibly increased during the last years of Tchaikovsky's life, though more in the direction of technique than of sentiment. In 1862, all that Tchaikovsky knew of Wagner's music were the selections given at the concerts of the Russian Musical Society, and by Strauss at the Pavlovsky. "It might be supposed," says Laroche, "that the impressionable young composer would have fallen under Wagner's influence after the Easter concerts of 1863. But it was not so. Even the prelude to *Lohengrin*, which excited so much enthusiasm in the public, especially among the students of the Conservatoire, was received by Tchaikovsky in a cold, sceptical spirit."

His early views of Wagner are set forth in a criticism of the *Faust Overture*, written in 1872. "At the present moment," he writes, "Wagner is undoubtedly the most striking personality on the horizon of the musical world. His works are still far from being understood by the general public, either in Germany or abroad; nevertheless, by means of his rabid polemic against all constituted authority and by the vastness of the problems he has set himself to solve, he has succeeded in attracting to himself the attention of the whole musical world, and even in arousing the interest of those to whom music is not a matter of everyday life. Some regard Wagner as a musical light, second only to Beethoven; to others he appears a charlatan in the style of our 'Abyssinian maestro'; but in any case, if we may believe—not without justification—that Wagner desired to win celebrity at any price, his aim is now attained. He has ardent worshippers and equally furious enemies who make it their business to write about all his utterances, and his words are awaited in a spirit of admiration, antagonism, or simple curiosity, by the public of both hemispheres.

"Among those who labour at art or science we may clearly distinguish two types. The one consists of those who, in obedience to their vocation, select the path which seems best suited to their powers and most in conformity with their idiosyncrasies and lot in life. They do not adopt any fashionable idea as their device. They do not seek to clear their road by overthrowing authority; nor do they constitute themselves the instruments of Providence whose duty it is to open the eyes of blind humanity. They labour, study, observe, and perfect themselves; then they create, by virtue of their natural qualities and the circumstances of time and place in which they have developed. They work out their own problem, and, quitting the arena of life, leave the fruits of their labour for the pleasure and profit of future generations. To this type of 'artist-workers' belong Bach, Haydn, Mozart, Beethoven, Mendelssohn, Schumann, Glinka. Others, consumed by un-measured ambition, in order to attain more rapidly to a prominent position, push noisily through the crowd, dispersing right and left all whom they meet on their road, and striving to attract universal attention to themselves. Such artists are ready to pose as the representatives of every new—and sometimes false—idea, and strive, not for the realisation of their genius, but only to astonish the world by their Don Quixot-ism. To this type belong Wagner and Serov."

Wagner's personal vanity and chauvinistic tactics were hateful to the "Hermit of Klin." Moreover, Tchaikovsky—at least during the earlier years of his career—sincerely believed that Wagner was a sym-phonist *manqué*. An intimate friend of Wagner's once repeated to Tchaikovsky a remark which the com-poser of *Parsifal* had made to him in a moment of friendly conversation: "Even if I had desired to occupy myself with the composition of chamber music and symphonies it would have been impossible, since my duty lies within the limits of opera." "Do not these words of Wagner's"—comments Tchaikovsky—"show to what a degree a preconceived theory prejudiced the mind of this obstinate, richly-endowed, but narrow-minded German?"

His views were practically unchanged when, four years later, in 1876, he went to hear the *Nibelungen Ring* at Bayreuth. Laroche, who was also there in the capacity of musical critic, says that Tchaikovsky did not conceal from him the fact that the *Ring* did not afford him any pleasure. "But," adds Laroche, "the company among which he found himself at Bayreuth made it exceedingly difficult to say anything against Wagner. He had as an inseparable companion one of the professors of the Moscow University, Klindworth, who united an 'adoration' for Tchaikovsky with Wagnerism of the first water and of a most rabid description. In our hearts we Moscovites were all a little afraid of Klindworth, but Peter Ilich was particularly in, awe of him, for he was by nature far more deferential and gentle than courageous." The result was that before others Tchaikovsky was either silent about Wagner's music or only spoke in praise of those particular features which happened to please him. But though both in 1863 and 1876 Tchaikovsky passed unmoved through these Wagnerian experiences, there came a moment when he was carried away by a sudden enthusiasm. This was in 1886, when he first saw the pianoforte score of *Parsifal*, and was delighted with the close of the last scene of the first act. From that time Laroche thinks that he began to look upon Wagner with different eyes, although he still kept to the laws of opera as formulated by Gluck, and was never attracted by the innovations of the Music Drama.

V

RUSSIAN MUSIC—GLINKA—DARGOMIJSKY

IN order to understand Tchaikovsky's attitude towards the composers of his native land, it is necessary to know something of the rival schools of criticism which have divided musical opinion in Russia from the time of Glinka to the present hour. The chief Russian critics were at first unanimous in recognising in Glinka not only the leader of a national movement, but a composer worthy to be ranked with the great composers of all time. It was not until the appearance of his second opera, *Russlan and Ludmilla*, that the schism arose which led to endless controversy and extreme bitterness on the part of the representatives of both sides. On the one hand was Serov, who, taking his stand upon the Wagnerism principle "Opera must be music drama," endeavoured, in a series of articles entitled "Russlan and the Russlanists," to prove that whatever might be the intrinsic value of the work as regards music, it could not claim to be considered an opera. "*Russlan*," argues Serov, "has no dramatic interest; its libretto is a thing of shreds and patches. It lacks historical significance, vitality, and the savour of real life. *A Life for the Tsar*, despite the literary weakness of its book, teems with human interest and has a definite dramatic development; therefore it is legitimate opera. But *Russlan*, at the best, can only be considered as a series of delightful musical illustrations to fantastic scenes; at the worst, as the interesting failure of a great, but wrong-headed, composer." On the opposite side we find an equally capable and fervent advocate in the person of M. Vladimir Stassov, the friend and biographer of Glinka. He is prepared to maintain that Glinka shows far greater creative power in *Russlan* than in his earlier works. He has thrown off the fetters of conventionality that impeded the free play of his genius in *A Life for the Tsar*, and reveals himself in his full maturity. *Russlan*, he thinks, must not be considered as an aberration of wilful genius, but as the deliberate work of a man who knows quite well the goal for which he is striving, but prefers to reach it by paths of his own.

A precisely similar difference of opinion exists with regard to the two great operas of Glinka's contemporary, Dargomijsky. His earlier effort, the fantastic opera of *The Russalka* (*Water Sprite*), was generally accepted as a work of great merit; while the critics split upon the subject of *The Stone Guest*, some regarding it as the logical outcome of his artistic theories, and others as the last eccentricity of a warped and incoherent imagination.

Tchaikovsky had not the vigorous critical "mailed-fist" of Serov, nor his obstinate dogmatism and blind adherence to the Wagnerian creed. Neither had he the generous, comprehensive sympathy, nor the fine literary gift of Stassov. His views of Russian music were on the whole slightly coloured by those of Serov, but his remarks upon his compatriots have, generally speaking, a characteristic note of reserve which naturally failed to satisfy the leaders of either party. Writing about these differences of opinion, he says:—

"It is impossible not to see that Serov's criticism is the more rational. Looking at the question from a specific musical point of view, he never denies the merits of *Russlan* as regards musical material, or, indeed, any of its best qualities. But it is a well-known fact that great works of art are valued less for the undoubted creative force of their authors than for the perfection of form into which this force is moulded, and also for their symmetry and for the successful fusion of the idea and its external expression. Is not this the reason why Beethoven is considered the first of composers, although every musician knows that Mozart, and even Schubert, possessed as great—if not a greater—volume of musical inspiration? If we wished to indicate Glinka's place in the pantheon of musicians, for sheer strength of creative genius, we might place him among the greatest representatives of his art. But it is a fact that fate did not set Glinka in such an environment as was necessary to the full development of his gift. He was a

lion in the sheepskin of dilettantism. . . . Like the
rich young man in the parable, he possessed a fund
of power which he did not realise, and never understood how to give it the direction it deserved.
Although the character of his musical nature was
pre-eminently lyric and symphonic, Glinka has
left hardly any purely symphonic works. Yet,
judging from certain episodes in his operas, he might
have given us inimitable examples in this style.
Deprived of a highly-cultured musical environment,
and not having found the support he deserved,
Glinka sought an outlet for his inspiration, and was
carried away by the first subject that presented itself.
He embraced it with ardour, never pausing to consider if it was suitable for a successful and serious
work of art.   For instance, *A Life for the Tsar* shows
that Glinka was fascinated in this way by the
contrasting effects of the mazurka-rhythm and the
melancholy of the Russian songs. *Russlan* was
written for the sake of a few fantastic scenes which
had actually excited his musical inspiration—his
symphonic rather than his *dramatic* instincts. Thus it
follows that *A Life for the Tsar*, composed to an
accidentally successful plot, turned out a fine opera;
while *Russlan*, consisting of disconnected fantastic
scenes, put together at different times by different
people, cannot be considered a model opera, because
of its inorganic structure and total lack of dramatic
interest. It is a fairy spectacle joined to most
distinguished music."

Here we have a fairly clear statement of Tchaikovsky's opinion of Glinka as an operatic composer. It is my immediate design merely to show Tchaikovsky as a musical critic, and not to discuss or refute his opinions. But because our whole view of Russian music will be true, or distorted, according to our judgment of Glinka as the source from which it flowed, it seems only just to say that—viewed in the light of biographical facts—this idea of Glinka, as a gifted but irresponsible amateur, requires considerable modification. It is true that he was denied the doubtful blessing of academic training, but when we remember his sojourn in Italy, his visit to Paris, where he listened to and learned from the music of Berlioz, his musical tour in Spain, and his brief but severe course of study under one of the first theorists of his day, it is absurd to imagine that he entered upon his operatic tasks with less preparation than the average Conservatoire student. Can we believe that Glinka, who for thirty years had meditated the creation of a national opera, was induced to compose *A Life for the Tsar* merely for the sake of contrasting Russian and Polish rhythms? Equally the whole history of his musical development contradicts the theory that *Russlan* owes its existence to purely fortuitous circumstances.

As Tchaikovsky looks upon Glinka as a great symphonic composer, led astray by the tastes of the society in which he lived, it is interesting to read what he has to say about his finest effort in this sphere of art. The incidental music to the tragedy *Prince Kholmsky* is a most remarkable work, and contains, besides the instrumental entr'actes, at least two of Glinka's finest songs. But the work has never been appreciated by the Russian public, and is still unaccountably neglected in this country, where Russian music is often better received than it is in Petersburg and Moscow. "In this composition," says Tchaikovsky, "Glinka shows himself one of the greatest symphonic composers of his day. Many touches in *Prince Kholmsky* recall the brush of Beethoven. There is the same moderation in the means employed and total absence of all striving after mere external effects; the same sober beauty and clear exposition of ideas that are not laboured, but inspired; the same plasticity of form and mould. Finally, there is the same inimitable instrumentation, so remote from all that is affected or far-fetched; strong, but never noisy; solid, and free from all flimsiness or vagueness of harmonic design. Every entr'acte which follows the overture is a little picture, drawn by a master-hand. They are symphonic marvels which would suffice a second-rate composer for a whole series of long symphonies."

Tchaikovsky has not much insight into the character of Dargomijsky's genius. He himself was so invariably preoccupied with the purely musical beauty of his vocal works that he frequently sacrifices truth of expression to a love of graceful *cantilena*. How then should he be in sympathy with Dargomijsky, to whom expressive realism was the chief aim of vocal art, and a fine literary text an object of veneration?

He admits that *The Russalka*, by reason of its
melodic charm, sincerity of inspiration, and elegance
of *cantilena* and recitative, must be ranked next to
the operas of Glinka. But he does not believe in his
further development. The same unfavourable circumstances—the lack of academic training—which
impeded the artistic evolution of Glinka, were, according to Tchaikovsky, equally prejudicial to Dargomijsky's career. He says: "It was only by means
of his surprisingly delicate instinct, and his strong
individuality, that Dargomijsky managed to attain,
in certain aspects of opera, to a degree of perfection
reached by only a few of the elect. His strength lay
exclusively in his wonderful realism and in his emin-
ently vocal recitative; qualities which lend to his
splendid opera the charm of inimitable originality.
The composer recognised the dominant quality of
his gift; but this knowledge, which unfortunately
was not supported by a sober, critical instinct, led him
to the strange notion of composing an opera consisting entirely of recitative. With this intention, Dargomijsky selected the text of 'The Stone Guest' by
Poushkin, and without altering a single letter of it,
without adapting it to the practical demands of opera
—he fitted recitative to every line of the lengthy
text. We know that recitative has no definite
rhythm, no clearly defined melody or musical form—
it is merely the cement which unites the various parts
of a musical edifice. It is indispensable, on the one
hand, because of the ordinary conditions of scenic
development; and on the other, because it forms a

contrast to the lyrical situations in the opera. What an aberration of a daring mind, unguided by any sober conception of æsthetic development! To write an opera without music—is not this the same as writing a drama without words or action?"

M

VI

ALTHOUGH Tchaikovsky was sometimes influenced by Serov as a critic, and was entirely carried away by his enthusiasm for his early opera *Judith*, yet he was able to gauge with perfect accuracy the artificial causes of this composer's success. Writing of one of his later works, *Rogneda*, he says: "The continued success of this opera, and the firm place it has won in the Russian repertory, is due not so much to its intrinsic beauty as to the subtle calculation of effects which guided its composer. Beginning to write at a time of life when other and more strongly gifted composers are already on the wane, he worked less from inward impulse than because, having for years made a critical study of music in all its branches, he saw that he could take up the work rapidly and with ease. Undoubtedly a talented musician of such remarkable intellect, and possessed of such stores of varied erudition as Serov, had every chance of winning popular sympathy. The public of all nations are not particularly exacting in matters of æsthetics; they delight in external and sensational effects and violent contrasts, and are quite indifferent to deep and original works of art if their *mise en scène* are not highly coloured, showy, and brilliant. Thus it was with Serov. He knew how to catch the public; and if his opera suffers from poverty of melodic inspiration, from want of organic sequence, from weak recitative and de-clamation, and from harmony and instrumentation which are crude and merely decorative in effect—yet what sensational effects the composer succeeds in piling up! Mummers who turn into geese and bears, real horses and dogs, the touching episode of Ruald's death, the Prince's dream made actually visible to our eyes, the Chinese gongs made very audible to our ears, all this—the outcome of a recognised poverty of inspiration—literally crackles with startling effects. Serov, as I have said, had only a mediocre gift, united to great experience, remarkable intellect, and extensive erudition; therefore it is not surprising to find in *Rogneda* numbers—like rare oases in a desert—in which the music is excellent. Such are the Chorus of Idolaters in the second act; Iziaslav's charming little song : Rogneda's ballad ; and the fine hymn with which the opera winds up. As to those numbers which are the special favourites of the public, as is so frequently the case, their real value proves to be in inverse proportion to the success they have won. For instance, the duet between Ruald and the Traveller is neither better nor worse than a dozen Italian operatic duets. The celebrated third act owes

its success, on the one hand, to the beautiful chorus
à capella, and, on the other, to the touching sentiment
of faith and love—in the Christian sense of the word
—which is awakened by the episode of Ruald's
death."

With those members of the Russian school who
were his more immediate contemporaries Tchaikovsky
was rarely in complete sympathy. Naturally he could
never be in touch with the talent of Moussorgsky, the
fervent disciple of Dargomijsky's later doctrines of
realism and declamatory science. For Balakirev he
seems to have felt the respect due from one great
craftsman to another. Here, at least, there could be
no question of faulty training or amateur pretensions.
He admired Balakirev as a conductor, and regretted
that his counsels of perfection led to such a small
output as regards composition.

I have mentioned that his first article was written
to call public attention to an early work by Rimsky-
Korsakov. As time went on, Tchaikovsky was more
frequently brought into personal rivalry with Korsakov
than with any other member of the New Russian
school. More than once they were engaged in actual
public competition, and on several occasions chose the
same subjects for their works. This in no way
impaired their friendly relations, but the note of
characteristic difference between them was accentuated
with advancing years. Tchaikovsky himself, so frankly
passionate in expression, was unable to understand the
emotional reticence of Rimsky-Korsakov any more
than that of Brahms. In both cases he attributes it

to constitutional coldness and a lack of inspiration.
The following paragraphs show how Tchaikovsky
regarded the artistic development of Rimsky-
Korsakov, who, as a lyric and symphonic composer,
stood nearer to him, in some respects, than any other
among his compatriots.

"The general impression of the symphony,"[1] he
says, "may be resumed as follows : the predominance
of technical skill over the quality of the ideas, and a
lack of inspiration and fire. In place of these, we have
an elaborate design, with a superfluity of elegant details.
This symphony seems to have been petted and
coaxed into existence with the kind of maternal love
which believes that all education consists in warming,
feeding, and coddling the child. Rimsky-Korsakov
is apparently in a transition stage. He is still seeking
a point of support, still wavering between what is
modern and a secret sympathy for old and archaic
musical forms, which may be traced in him from the
beginning. This Philistine—a conservative at heart
—has been enticed into the arena of the free-thinkers,
and is timidly making his abjuration of faith. As a
result of this want of sincerity, Rimsky-Korsakov's
recent works have become dry, cold, and formless; a
condition of things not always concealed by his elegant
workmanship and minute stippling. For this reason
we cannot be surprised that the public do not receive
his symphony with particular enthusiasm.

"Connoisseurs cannot fail to be delighted with the
charming details and a play of sound-combinations so

[1] This criticism probably refers to the *Third Symphony* (op. 32.)

flattering to the ear. Through the two masks of the Philistine and the innovator, which the composer alternately dons without being able to decide frankly to which side he belongs, we get constant glimpses of a strong, highly gifted, elegantly plastic individuality. When he has gone through this process of moral fermentation, which apparently proceeds from his inherent musical disposition, and has reached some definite stage in his development, Rimsky-Korsakov will certainly turn out one of the first symphonists of the day. But he will join the classical school to which his musical nature inclines, rather than the formless romantic school of Berlioz and Liszt. Then he will be a musical eclectic in the best sense of the word— as Glinka was—uniting in himself strict classical forms and methods with that dazzling beauty of modern exposition, wherein lies the imprescriptible quality of the new school."

Rimsky-Korsakov has not fulfilled Tchaikovsky's prediction that he would eventually revert to classicism. Starting with a knowledge of, and reverence for, formal tradition, unique among the Russian composers, he has nevertheless consistently followed the path which attracted him most, the musical illustration of national legend and national landscape. Indeed the accusation of wavering faith and want of sincerity comes strangely from Tchaikovsky, who, from the beginning to the end of his career, gave no signs of definite adherence to the old forms or the new. A glance at the list of his works will show how, starting with a programme symphony of a not very advanced type, he modified

his modern tendencies in the *Second Symphony* only
to revert to them in *The Tempest*. Again, having
written his *Third Symphony* under clearly conventional influences, he shows us in *Francesca di Rimini*
that programme music still has its fascinations for
his genius; and so on, throughout the whole list of
his opus numbers—*Manfred* following the *Fourth
Symphony*, and *Hamlet* the *Fifth*. The same un-
certainty characterises his use of national colour.
Like so many of his fellow-countrymen, sometimes
he uses foreign idioms with the fluency of a cosmopolitan, sometimes he speaks in a way that only
Russians can understand. In this complex dual
attitude lies much of Tchaikovsky's charm; and much
of his weakness—

> Oui, mon malheur irréparable,
> C'est de pendre aux deux éléments.

DIARY OF MY TOUR IN 1888

TRANSLATED FROM THE RUSSIAN

I

In 1886 it was proposed to produce my opera
Cherevichek ("Two little Shoes") at the Great
Theatre of Moscow. The scenery, elaborately designed by K. Valtz, was quite ready; all the superb
mounting, upon which, during the previous year,
I. A. Vsievolovsky had decided to expend a considerable sum, was complete, and the music was also
finished. Meanwhile I—who was then residing in
the country near Klin—lived in daily expectation of
a summons to attend the first rehearsal in Moscow.
But the season drew to its close, a few weeks only
remained before Easter, and still the expected
summons did not come. During that winter the
business of the opera-house had been almost brought
to a standstill in consequence of the prolonged
illness of the conductor, I. K. Altani. At the beginning of December 1885 it was confidently believed
that this respected artist, who was making a slow
recovery to health, would soon return to his desk,

where his place was filled by the chorus-master, Avranek, who had almost broken down under the strain of double work. But Altani's illness was variable, and the period of convalescence was obstinately prolonged. Just as I began to realise that *Cherevichek* was not likely to be offered to the judgment of the Moscow public during the season of 1885-86, and had concluded that the performance must be postponed for some future season, an unexpected offer was made to the directors by a young musician in Moscow, who professed his readiness to take Altani's place and produce my complicated score at some date in the immediate future. The offer was at once communicated to me, and M. P. M. Pchelnikov, then the head of the theatrical administration, begged me to say if I had sufficient confidence in this substitute to entrust him with the rehearsing and conducting of *Cherevichek*. As I set a high value on Altani's friendliness to me as a composer, and also esteemed his remarkable talent and experience, I promptly declined the proposal of this young musician to take the place of my respected friend at the conductor's desk. At the same time, as I did not wish to put any obstacle in the way of the directors, if it seemed to their advantage to give an immediate performance of my opera, I adopted the heroic measure of offering my own services as conductor. They thanked me cordially, and accepted my proposal. But finally a combination of different circumstances made the performance impossible during the season of 1885-86.

The following season, when the staging of *Chere-*

vichek came once more under consideration, Altani
had completely regained his health, and there appeared
no need whatever for me to attempt to act as
conductor. Nevertheless the chiefs of the theatrical
administration, and Altani himself, as well as my
numerous friends in Moscow, still wished me to
conduct the rehearsal and the first public performance
of my opera in person. It had long been the pre-
valent opinion that I had no gift whatever for
conducting; and I myself clung obstinately to the
belief that I was completely incapable—so much so,
that my timid efforts, on two separate occasions, to
conquer my morbid nervousness and appear before
the public had ended most disastrously in my entire
discomfiture. If, however, my well-wishers, including Altani, desired, in spite of this, to make me
overcome my diffidence, and were anxious that I
should make one more effort, in my declining years,
to become a conductor, they were doubtless guided
by sincere affection and by a strong conviction that
my lack of talent as a conductor was a great hindrance
to the spread of my works, and believed that if I
once conquered myself and succeeded in conducting—
if only tolerably—some of my compositions, the result
would be a great impulse to the popularising of my
music and a rapid increase of my fame as a composer.

Fortified by the warm sympathy of my friends,
and the invaluable advice and guidance of Altani,
as well as by my entire confidence in the indulgence
of the Moscow public, who had encouraged my
first efforts as a composer, and, since that time, had

invariably shown me the most cordial sympathy—on
19th January 1887, at 8 P.M., I took the conductor's
place in the orchestra of the Great Opera House, and
successfully conducted the first performance of *Cherevichek*. I was then forty-seven years of age. At this
time of life a real, inborn conductor has plenty of
capacity, in proportion to his natural gifts and length
of experience; when it is borne in mind that such
was not the case with me, my *début* may be considered exceedingly successful. I still think that I have
no positive gift for conducting. I am aware that I
do not possess that combination of moral and physical
qualities which make an ordinary musician a conductor of the first rank; but this attempt—and all
subsequent ones—proved that I could more or less
successfully direct the performance of my works, and
this was all that was necessary for my future success.
I have considered it important to relate in detail
the story of my first attempt at conducting, because
among the many good results which it led to was
the three months' concert tour which I made through
Western Europe. Of the success which attended
this tour I cannot fail to be proud, and I afterwards
resolved to relate the details to the Russian public;
for, with the exception of Glinka, who gave but
one concert in Paris, and Rubinstein, who, thanks to
his gifts as a virtuoso, won laurels on all the platforms
of the world, I was the first Russian to introduce my
works personally abroad. I venture to think that
there are a considerable number of Russians to whom
this account will be of interest.

II

Six weeks after the events related above, when experience had proved me to possess sufficient capability to conduct opera, I made a similar attempt on the concert platform. On 4th March 1887 I conducted a concert given in the Salle de la Noblesse, St. Petersburg, by the Philharmonic Society, the programme of which consisted entirely of my compositions. The experiment was crowned with success. To my great astonishment, I heard from those in whose judgment I have the fullest confidence such flattering opinions of my conducting that my heart beat for joy, and I could not help feeling proud of having won a victory over myself, and over that desperate, cruel, tyrannical, moral ailment against which I had contended all my life—namely, nervousness. Only one well-known musical critic showed no moderation in his judgment of me. He had hailed my *début* as a composer in the following words: "M. Tchaikovsky is very poor; he has not a spark of talent." This is very severe; but he equally distorted the truth when he said I was an "admirable" conductor. However, I did not believe him on this occasion any more than I believed his earlier statement as to my absolute want of talent. Men who first take up the conductor's baton at forty-seven cannot possibly be "admirable" conductors; indeed it is useless to hope that they will become such, even if they have the necessary natural endowment; and I am perfectly aware that innate nervousness, weakness of character, and want of self-confidence will always prevent me from competing with such conductors as Wagner, Bülow, and Napravnik. Only one thing, I repeat, was of importance to me: to be able to conduct my own works no worse than any other mediocre conductor would have done. I foresaw that, thanks to this victory over my incapacity, it would now be possible for me to make my music known at home and abroad, and very soon my premonition became actual fact.

In June I received an invitation from the Hamburg Philharmonic Society to conduct some of my works in the following January. Afterwards I received similar invitations from Vienna, Dresden, Copenhagen, Prague, Leipzig, Berlin, and London. As regards Paris, Felix Mackar—a great enthusiast for my music—had already promised that I should appear there as conductor at a concert which he wished to organise during the winter season.

A very natural ambition to extend as far as possible the circle of my fame as a composer did not prevent me from cherishing a hope that I might also succeed in serving the cause of Russian art, and popularise the works of other Russian composers on my travels. Imagining that I possessed sufficient funds to risk giving a Russian concert in Paris on my own account, at which should figure the names of Glinka, Dargomijsky, Serov, Rubinstein, Balakirev, Rimsky-Korsakov, Glazounov, Liadov, and Arensky, I firmly resolved to follow up the concert arranged by Felix Mackar, at which only my music was to be performed, by another consisting of the works of these stars. It was extremely flattering and agreeable to think that I might be the one to interpret these gems of Russian music to a French public imbued and inspired with sympathy for everything Russian. The evening before my departure, I spent some hours in the society of three of my most valued musical friends, Rimsky-Korsakov, Liadov, and Glazounov, with whom I worked out in every detail the programme of the enterprise I meditated carrying out. Thus, in quitting Petersburg I had three ends in view—to conduct my own works in Leipzig and other foreign towns, and to conduct two concerts in Paris, one of which was to be devoted to my own works, and the other to be organised at my own risk.

For two months preceding my departure I had also been in correspondence with a certain Herr N., a concert-agent abroad, who showed himself most zealous in the propagation of my works out of Russia, going so far as to consider it practicable for me to visit a whole series of second-rate towns in Germany and Austria, because he had formed a very exaggerated estimate of the interest which my music awakened in these neighbouring empires. But, realising with consternation that Herr N. was going too far in his zeal, I declined to accept—whether he liked it or not—his proposal for a personal interview which was to take place in Germany. When later on it actually did take place, it seemed to me that I had to do with a very peculiar and eccentric man, and from that moment to this I have never really understood him. Whether from inexperience or misapprehension, or from a natural want of practical ability and tact, or simply from some abnormal, morbid condition of mind, in any case Herr N. was very unreliable, and being apparently my devoted friend, his actions were sometimes those of an enemy. He did me many important services, for which I shall never cease to be grateful, but he was also the cause of several serious unpleasantnesses and annoyances that befell me during my tour. Thus, even now, I cannot form any just opinion upon this singular man, who remains altogether an enigma to me. I was equally puzzled as to his nationality—he called himself Russian, but spoke the language atrociously—his position in the world, and more especially as to the motive which guided his conduct towards me, now persecuting me with hostile proceedings, now rendering me the most valuable service. In any case, I must acknowledge that it was entirely due to his initiative that I owed my invitations to Leipzig, Prague, and Copenhagen. This last city I did not succeed in visiting, because I had not time; while the concert at Dresden never even came off, in consequence of Herr N.'s strange and unpractical management. Nor was it my luck to make the Viennese acquainted with my music, because the day fixed for the concert in Vienna was identical with the date on which I had to be in Paris. Finally, the incomprehensible and eccentric fancy of Herr N.'s to compel me to wander through a series of little German towns, conducting a miniature orchestra which was quite incapable of rendering my difficult and complicated scores, was, needless to say, never realised. The Russian concert I meditated giving in Paris proved a childishly impossible dream, about which I will speak more fully elsewhere. Thus it happened that I only visited Leipzig, Hamburg, Berlin, Prague, Paris, and London. I now return to my story.

III

I LEFT St. Petersburg on 15th (27th) December, and
arrived in Berlin on the 17th (29th). Here I wished
to interview the director (Vorsteher) of the Berlin
Philharmonic Society, Herr Schneider, who had been
corresponding with me about the concert in February,
which was to consist entirely of my works, and at
which I was to act as conductor. A personal interview was necessary in order to discuss the details of
the programme, and the matter presented some
difficulties, for Schneider, who desired for my own
interests to please the Berlin public, did not altogether
agree with my selection of works. He wished to
include some that I did not care for, and at the same
time to omit those of which I was most proud, and
by which the splendid Berlin orchestra might have
shown me at my best. However, this time I did not
succeed in seeing Herr Schneider, for the following
reason. In the newspaper which the waiter brought
with my tea I read, with horror, the following lines
about my arrival: "To-day, 29th January, the Russian composer Tchaikovsky arrives in Berlin. His
numerous friends (?) and admirers (?) will assemble

N

to celebrate his arrival by a *Fruhschapp* (breakfast) at —— Restaurant, in such-and-such a street, at —— o'clock." I must explain that Herr N. had already spoken of this *Fruhschapp* in a letter to me at Petersburg, and had even sent me a copy of the circular which he had distributed through Berlin, in which all music-lovers, artists, and fellow-countrymen of mine living in the town were invited to assemble at a certain hour in one of the best-known restaurants, because Herr N. informed them that I was exceedingly modest, and wished the welcome to be of quite a friendly and intimate character. On receiving this letter I telegraphed immediately to Herr N. that I distinctly declined to take part in this festivity, and that I would not on any account appear at this friendly *Fruhschapp*. Therefore I was beyond measure incensed when I now saw in the paper that he had not dropped the matter, but even published this on the day of my arrival. Luckily Herr N. did not know where I was staying, and I decided not to let him know of my arrival until the next day. I think it will be clear to most of my readers why this proceeding on the part of Herr N.—who sincerely wished to render me a service, but had a most singular notion of how to do it—covered me with confusion, horror, and fright. But to such of my readers as know little or nothing of the attitude of the foreign public towards Russian composers, I will merely say that not only had I very few admirers in Berlin, but that previously to this my music was almost unknown there. A few of my orchestral works had been occasionally heard, it is true. Bilze, at his National Concerts, had often played the *Andante* from my Quartet; but the whole acquaintance of the Berliners with my music was limited to these few bars; and as to my "numerous friends and admirers," I was a complete stranger in Berlin. With the exceptions of the head of the firm of Bote and Bock, Herr Hugo Bock, I had not a single acquaintance. Moreover there could be no question of admirers, for the few things of mine which had hitherto been performed in Berlin had had no particular success, and the Press had not been unanimous in its praise. This puffery of Herr N.'s, this idea of honouring me in Berlin by means of a *Fruhschapp*, is the best example of his queer, unmethodical, flighty way of acting on my behalf. Yet he was, to all appearances, really well-intentioned, and with incredible zeal, energy, and eccentricity, devoted all his time and thought to making my name familiar to the German public. The result of all this was that I felt almost ashamed of myself. It seemed to me that all the musical world of Berlin would be laughing at me, and thinking perhaps that *I* wanted, through the medium of Herr N., to get up this festive reception which I did not merit. I felt no further desire to see any one in the German capital, and the next day, having seen and tried to explain to Herr N., and after visiting K. V. Davidov—who was then passing through Berlin, and whom it was a great pleasure to meet again—I started for Leipzig, from whence I began my tour through Western Europe.

IV

IN Leipzig I met three compatriots and one German critic. My fellow-countrymen were: Brodsky, Siloti, and Arthur Friedheim. The two first are very well known to the Russian public, especially in Moscow. I had long been on intimate terms with Brodsky, who was for some time a professor at the Moscow Conservatoire when I took the theory class there. In 1877 Brodsky left Moscow, spent one season at Kiev as director of the Musical Society, and, after travelling about for a considerable time, was finally appointed to the honourable post of Professor of the Violin at the Leipzig Conservatoire, where he won universal affection and esteem both as a man and as an artist. In speaking of this admirable master, I must take this opportunity of expressing in public the sincere gratitude which I shall feel for him till my dying day. The reason is as follows. In 1877 I wrote a violin concerto which I dedicated to Auer. I do not know whether my dedication was flattering to Herr Auer, but, in spite of his genuine friendship, he never tried to conquer the difficulties of this concerto. He pronounced it impossible to play, and this verdict, coming from such an authority as the Petersburg virtuoso, had the effect of casting this unfortunate child of my imagination for many years to come into the limbo of hopelessly forgotten things. Five years later, however, I was staying in Rome, and going into a café, chanced to pick up a number of the *Neue Freie Presse* containing a criticism, by the celebrated Hanslick, of a concert given by the Vienna Philharmonic Society, the programme of which included my unlucky concerto, which Auer's verdict had doomed to extinction. Hanslick found fault with the player (who was none other than Brodsky himself) for his unfortunate selection, and cut up my poor concerto unmercifully, not sparing the pearls of his caustic humour, nor the poisoned arrows of his sarcasm. "We know," he writes, "that certain works have recently appeared in contemporary literature, the authors of which delight in reproducing certain revolting physiological phenomena, as, for example, disgusting smells. Such literature may be well termed—stinking. Tchaikovsky's concerto appears to us to belong to the category of 'stinking music.'" On reading this notice by the celebrated and influential critic, I called up a lively picture of all the energy and pains that Brodsky must have expended in carrying out this performance of my "stinking" concerto, and thought how annoying and unpleasant he would find this kind criticism upon a friend and compatriot. I hastened, therefore, to express my warmest gratitude to Brodsky, and learnt from the letter he wrote in reply what difficulties and trials he had gone through in order to accomplish his aim—the resuscitation of my concerto from the depths of oblivion. Afterwards Brodsky played the "stinking concerto" everywhere, and everywhere the critics abused him in the same style as Hanslick. But the deed was done; my concerto was saved, and is now frequently played in Western Europe, especially since there came to Brodsky's assistance another fine violinist, young Halir, of whom I shall often have occasion to speak. It will now be evident how pleased I was to meet Brodsky in Leipzig, where I was a stranger without friends, and to look forward, amid the fears and agitations which beset me, to the moral support of his long-standing and intimate friendship.

Not less glad was I to see once more that young, but already celebrated pianist, Siloti. I had known him when a mere boy, a pupil of the Moscow Conservatoire, where he went through some finishing courses in composition under my guidance. Since then Siloti, who had studied the piano under Nicholas Rubinstein, and after his death under Liszt, had won a great name in Russia and Germany, especially in Leipzig, where he had been living for several years, visiting other German and Russian cities from time to time. This young artist, like Brodsky, rendered me many a friendly service, and did a great deal towards making my works known in Germany. Thanks to him, I found in Leipzig a circle of musicians who did me the honour of showing great interest in my music. This was of great importance to me, for I entered Leipzig—a town renowned for its violent conservatism in general and its rabid anti-Russian feeling in particular—as into a hostile camp, with the sense of attracting all its insolence and derision to myself. Of course there was some exaggeration in this feeling, for, as the reader will presently see, the Germans as a rule do not hate us so outrageously as many think. But it is a fact that I suffered a great deal from the consciousness of this fancied enmity in Leipzig, and that it was very consoling to find some amateurs among its inhabitants who knew my music and felt a genuine sympathy for it—and for its composer.

The third fellow-countryman whom I met in Leipzig was Arthur Friedheim, a talented pianist and pupil of Liszt's, a native of Petersburg, who had been living for some time in Leipzig. As regards the German who came to the station in order to receive me, he was Martin Krause, the influential critic of the Leipzig *Tageblatt*, an intimate friend of Siloti's, who took a very gratifying interest in my music.

I found, on my arrival at Leipzig, the same really severe winter weather as in Russia. Snow lay thick in the streets, and I went almost straight from the station—in a little sledge very ingeniously contrived —to a Christmas Tree at Brodsky's. I found him established in thoroughly Russian surroundings, and these were further graced by the presence of two very sympathetic Russian ladies, the wife and sister-in-law of my host. During recent years I had hardly ever left home, and being quite unaccustomed to stay away from my country for long together, I felt restless and homesick; therefore no words will describe the comfort I derived, both that evening and subsequently, during my three different visits to Leipzig, whenever I had occasion to spend a few hours in Mr. Brodsky's family. I was also very pleased to visit Siloti, who had not long since married a young lady whom I had known almost as a child in Moscow, and with whom I had long been on terms of intimate friendship.

V

THE next day I made two very interesting acquaintances. Going to Brodsky's for the one o'clock
dinner, I heard sounds of the piano, violin, and
'cello. They were rehearsing for the next day's
performance of Brahms's new Pianoforte Trio (op.
100), and the composer himself was at the piano.
Thus it chanced that I saw the famous German
musician for the first time. Brahms is rather a short
man, suggests a sort of amplitude, and possesses
a very sympathetic appearance. His fine head,
almost that of an old man, recalls the type of a
handsome, benign, elderly Russian priest. His
features are certainly not characteristic of Russian
good looks, and I cannot conceive why some learned
ethnographer (Brahms himself told me this after I
had spoken of the impression his appearance made
upon me) chose to reproduce his head on the first
page of one of his books as being highly characteristic of German features. A certain softness of
outline, pleasing curves, rather long and slightly
grizzled hair, kind grey eyes, and a thick beard

freely sprinkled with white—all this recalled at once
the type of pure-bred Great Russian, so frequently
met with among our clergy.

Brahms's manner is very simple, free from vanity,
his humour jovial, and the few hours spent in his
society left me with a very agreeable recollection.
Unfortunately I was forced to confess that, in spite
of a somewhat prolonged stay among them in
Leipzig, I had not got on very well with the most
prominent representatives of modern German music.
The reason was as follows. Like all my Russian
musical friends, without exception, I only respected
in Brahms an honourable, energetic musician of
strong convictions; but, in spite of all efforts to the
contrary, I never could, and never can, admire his
music. Brahmsism is very widespread throughout
Germany; there are a number of authoritative people
and an entire musical institution specially consecrated
to the Brahms cult, and he is considered a great man,
almost the equal of Beethoven. But there are anti-
Brahmsites in Germany and everywhere beyond the
German frontier, with the exception, perhaps, of
London, where, thanks to the energetic propaganda
of Joachim, who is very popular in England, the
greatness of Brahms is recognised to a certain extent.
Everywhere else, as I say, there reigns complete
ignorance and ignoring of Brahms. But nowhere,
perhaps, has he made less way than in Russia.
There is something dry, cold, vague, and nebulous in
the music of this master which is repellent to Russian
hearts. From our Russian point of view Brahms

does not possess melodic invention. His musical ideas never speak to the point; hardly have we heard an allusion to some tangible melodic phrase than it disappears in a whirlpool of almost unmeaning harmonic progressions and modulations, as though the composer's special aim was to be incomprehensible and obscure. Thus he excites and irritates our musical perceptions, as it were, yet is unwilling to satisfy their demands; he seems ashamed, to put it plainly, to speak clearly and reach the heart. Hearing his music, we ask ourselves: Is Brahms deep, or does he only desire to have the semblance of depth in order to mask the poverty of his imagination? This question is never satisfactorily answered.

It is impossible in listening to Brahms's music to say that it is weak or unremarkable. His style is always elevated. Unlike all our contemporary musicians, he never has recourse to purely external effects; he never attempts to astonish us, to strike us by some new and brilliant orchestral combination; nor do we meet in his music with anything trivial or directly imitative. It is all very serious, very distinguished, apparently even original, but in spite of all this the chief thing is lacking—beauty! This is my view of Brahms, and as far as I know it is shared by all Russian composers and all the musical public of Russia. A few years ago, when I frankly expressed my opinion of Brahms to Hans von Bülow, he replied: "Wait awhile, the time will come when you will enter into the depth and beauty of Brahms.

Like you, it was long before I understood him, but gradually I was blessed by the revelation of his genius. It will be the same with you." And still I wait; but the revelation tarries. I deeply revere the artistic personality of Brahms. I bow to the actual purity of his musical tendencies, and admire his firm and proud renunciation of all the tricks which solemnise the Wagnerian cult, and in a much less degree the worship of Liszt, but I do not care for his music.

My readers will see that this fact prevented my seeking for an intimate acquaintance with the very attractive personality of Brahms. I met him in the society of devoted partisans (of whom Brodsky is one), and it appeared to me unseemly—seeing that I was a stranger and did not share in the worship of their idol—to bring any discordant element into the complete harmony of these intensely devout believers in this musical dogma. Brahms himself, as though he distinctly understood, or was actually aware of, the fact that I did not belong to his camp, made no effort to become intimate. He was quite simple and polite to me as to every one else, but nothing more. Meanwhile, all that I have heard of Brahms as a man has made me doubly regret that the "revelation" predicted by von Bülow has not been vouchsafed to me. He is an unusually pleasing and attractive man, and all who have come in contact with him are inspired by a warm affection and devotion. The celebrated Czechist composer Dvorak used to speak with tears in his eyes of the warm interest Brahms showed him at a time when his compositions found neither publishers nor performers, and what powerful support he gave him, and what energy he showed in sounding the depths of unknown genius of his Slavonic brother in art! Brodsky also related instances which revealed the sympathetic side of Brahms's character, especially his rare and pleasing modesty. It is well known that Wagner treated his contemporaries with the greatest animosity, and always showed himself particularly caustic to Brahms's works. Once, when some one reported to the latter some fresh sarcasm which Wagner had levelled at him, he exclaimed: "Good heavens! Wagner, honoured and triumphant, takes up most of the high-road. How can I, going my own modest way, be any hindrance or annoyance to him? Why cannot he leave me in peace, since we are never likely to clash?"

VI

AT this same dinner at Brodsky's I made another acquaintance, not less interesting, but deeper and less fleeting than the first, and destined soon to be transformed into a genuine friendship, based upon the undoubted affinity of two musical natures, though neither of us was well acquainted with the other's works. During the rehearsal of Brahms's new trio, as I was taking the liberty of making some remarks as to the skill and execution of the relative *tempo* 2-3—remarks which were very good-naturedly received by the composer—there entered the room a very short, middle-aged man, exceedingly fragile in appearance, with shoulders of unequal height, fair hair brushed back from his forehead, and a very slight, almost boyish, beard and moustache. There was nothing very striking about the features of this man, whose exterior at once attracted my sympathy, for it would be impossible to call them handsome or regular; but he had an uncommon charm, and blue eyes, not very large, but irresistibly fascinating, recalling the glance of a charming and candid child.

I rejoiced in the depths of my heart when we were mutually introduced to each other, and it turned out that this personality which was so inexplicably sympathetic to me belonged to a musician whose warmly emotional music had long ago won my heart. He proved to be the Norwegian composer Edward Grieg, who twenty years earlier had gained great popularity in Russia and the Scandinavian Peninsula, and together with Svendsen had acquired the highest respect and a great name. I think I am right in saying that just as Brahms was undeservedly disliked by the Russian musicians and general public, so Grieg had known how to win over Russian hearts once and for all. In his music there prevails that fascinating melancholy which seems to reflect in itself all the beauty of Norwegian scenery, now grandiose and sublime in its vast expanse, now grey and dull, but always full of charm to the hearts of Northmen, and having something akin to ourselves, quickly finds its way to our hearts, and evokes a warm and sympathetic response.

Grieg is probably not by any means so great a master as Brahms; his range is not so extensive, his aims and tendencies are not so wide, and apparently in Grieg the inclination towards obscurity is entirely absent; nevertheless he stands nearer to us, he seems more approachable and intelligible because of his deep humanity. Hearing the music of Grieg, we instinctively recognise that it was written by a man impelled by an irresistible impulse to give vent by means of sounds to a flood of poetical emotion, which obeys no theory or principle, is stamped with no impress but that of a vigorous and sincere artistic feeling. Perfection of form, strict and irreproachable logic in the development of his themes, are not perseveringly sought after by the celebrated Norwegian. But what charm, what inimitable and rich musical imagery! What warmth and passion in his melodic phrases, what teeming vitality in his harmony, what originality and beauty in the turn of his piquant and ingenious modulations and rhythms, and in all the rest what interest, novelty, and independence! If we add to all this that rarest of qualities, a perfect simplicity, far removed from all affectation and pretence to obscurity and far-fetched novelty (and many contemporary composers, including some Russians, are striving with a morbid tendency to break into new ways without possessing the least vocation or natural gift), it is not surprising that every one should delight in Grieg, that he should be popular everywhere—in Paris, London, and Moscow—that his name should appear in all concert programmes, and that visitors to Bergen should deem it a pleasant duty to make a pilgrimage to the charming though remote haven among the rocks of the shore, where Grieg retires to work and where he spends most of his life.

I trust it will not appear like self-glorification that my dithyramb in praise of Grieg precedes the statement that our natures are closely allied. Speaking of Grieg's high qualities, I do not at all wish to impress my readers with the notion that I am

endowed with an equal share of them. I leave it
to others to decide how far I am lacking in all that
Grieg possesses in such abundance, but I cannot help
stating the fact that he exercises and has exercised
some measure of that attractive force which always
drew me towards the gifted Norwegian. Later on
I shall have occasion to prove this; meanwhile I will
only say that I value Grieg's sympathy very highly,
and thank my lucky star for this meeting and
opportunity of personal acquaintance with him.

Together with Grieg, there entered the room
where we were assembled a lady who was growing
slightly grey and resembled him very closely in
appearance, being just as small, fragile, and sympathetic. She was his wife, and also his cousin, which
accounts for their resemblance. Subsequently I was
able to appreciate the many and precious qualities
possessed by Madame Grieg. In the first place she
proved to be an excellent, though not very finished,
singer; secondly, I have never met a better-informed
or more highly-cultivated woman, and she is, among
other things, an excellent judge of our literature, in
which Grieg himself was also deeply interested;
thirdly, I was soon convinced that Madame Grieg
was as amiable, as gentle, as childishly simple and
without guile as her celebrated husband.

There was another lady at this party about whom
I should like to say a few words. After the Christmas
Tree, while we were all sitting round the tea-table at
Brodsky's, a beautiful dog of the setter breed came
bounding into the room and began to frisk round

O

the host and his little nephew, who welcomed his arrival. "This means that Miss Smyth will appear directly," everybody exclaimed at once, and in a few minutes a tall Englishwoman, not handsome, but having what people call an "expressive" or "intelligent" face, walked into the room, and I was introduced to her at once as a fellow-composer. Miss Smyth is one of the comparatively few women composers who may be seriously reckoned among the workers in this sphere of music. She had come to Leipzig a few years before and studied theory and composition very thoroughly; she had composed several interesting works (the best of which, a violin sonata, I heard excellently played by the composer herself and Mr. Brodsky), and gave promise in the future of a serious and talented career. Since no Englishwoman is without her originalities and eccentricities, Miss Smyth had hers, which were: the beautiful dog, which was quite inseparable from this lonely woman, and invariably announced her arrival, not only on this occasion, but at other times when I met her again; a passion for hunting, on account of which Miss Smyth occasionally returned to England for a time; and, finally, an incomprehensible and almost passionate worship for the intangible musical genius of Brahms. From her point of view Brahms stood on the supreme pinnacle of all music, and all that had gone before him served merely as a preparation for the incarnation of absolute musical beauty in the creations of the Viennese master. And in this case, as invariably,

when I came in contact with rabid Brahmsites, I
tormented myself with the question: Are they all
wrong and imagine what does not exist, or have I
so offended God and Nature that the "revelation"
predicted by Bülow will never condescend to bless
me?

The first day of 1888 (New Style) fell at this
period, so full of varied impressions, and that day
I was present at an extra concert at the Gewandhaus, at which a new work by Brahms—his *Double
Concerto for Violin and 'Cello*—was played for the
first time. Joachim played the violin, the 'cello
was taken by the celebrated Berlin virtuoso Hauss-
mann, and Brahms himself conducted the orchestra.
The concerto, notwithstanding its excellent rendering, produced no impression upon me whatever. I
was struck by the absolute perfection with which the
famous choir of the Thomaskirche—consisting of
men's and boys' voices—sang a number of choruses
à capella, among them a motet by J. S. Bach. I
never heard anything like it at home, and I confess
that I was unpleasantly surprised, for I had hitherto
believed that some of our first-rate choirs were the
very best in the world. The performance of Beethoven's *Fifth Symphony* by the splendid Gewandhaus orchestra would have quite sent me into
ecstasies if it had not been that the respected conductor, Herr Reinecke, took the *tempi* too slow, as
I thought. Perhaps he was justified by the true
traditions; if so, it is better not to keep them too
strictly, for I am firmly persuaded that this inspired

symphony is better and more charming when taken quicker, as with us. The hall of the new Gewandhaus is very fine, and holds a large audience; it is lit by electric light, is comfortable, beautiful, elegant, and, most important of all, possesses exemplary acoustic arrangements. In the large box belonging to the directors, in which I sat, were many distinguished members of the Leipzig musical world, with all of whom I was acquainted, and among them Reinecke, who was very attentive to me. The head of the Concert Society of the Gewandhaus, Herr Linburger, informed me that my first rehearsal would take place the following morning at ten o'clock.

VII

THE famous Gewandhaus concerts, given in connection with the little town of Leipzig, which is one of the first musical centres of Germany, are celebrated for the excellence of the symphony orchestra, and distinguished by their conservative and classical programmes, in which—apart from the three great classical composers, Haydn, Mozart, Beethoven, and their contemporaries—only Mendelssohn and Schumann are recognised. The works of Wagner, Berlioz, and Liszt are rarely performed there. It is only very recently that the directors of this musical institution have begun to make some timid advances in the spirit of the times, and one of these moves was my unexpected invitation to Leipzig in order to conduct one of my own works. Both in Germany and at home this invitation excited considerable surprise; but especially in the former country, where many people, without any real foundation, regard me as a representative of the ultra-revolutionary party in music, just as in Russia I am often placed, equally without grounds, in the ranks of the retrogrades. Probably the event would never have come off but for the kind intercession of Mr. Brodsky, who has great influence in Leipzig; but the initiative in this instance is due to Herr N., of whom I have already spoken. In any case I recognise the fact, in all sincerity, that the choice of a work of mine in the Gewandhaus programmes was very flattering to my vanity as a composer, and that I was exceedingly glad to be starting my tour from Leipzig, because this incident was sure to lend greater weight to my name throughout Germany. But the prouder I felt of this attention from the Direction of the Gewandhaus, the more anxious I was to prove a worthy representative of Russian music abroad, and the more indescribably was I agitated by my inherent shyness and the fear " lest I should do something to blush for." After a night of misery, disturbed by every possible apprehension, and particularly by the dread lest my nervousness should prevent my doing myself justice as a passable conductor, I started for the rehearsal, accompanied by Siloti. As we approached the Gewandhaus, we met, at the entrance, the respected Capellmeister, Reinecke, who was hurrying in to the rehearsal in order to introduce me to the orchestra. In Germany and throughout Europe, Reinecke enjoys the reputation of being an excellent musician and a talented composer of the school of Mendelssohn. He is a skilful conductor of the Gewandhaus concerts; that is to say, he conducts them in a worthy manner, but not with that especial brilliance which has made them so famous throughout the world.

I say "not with especial brilliance," because many Germans deny that Reinecke possesses talent as a conductor, and would like to see his place filled by a musician of a more impassioned temperament, of stronger and more decided character. At any rate he is one of the most prominent and influential members of the German musical world, and if there are not a few Wagnerians, Lisztites, Brahmsites, and other progressists of all shades who do not love Reinecke, none refuse to respect him as a capable and conscientious musician. Such a respect I, too, had long since felt for Reinecke, and now the unusual attention and kindness which he hastened to show, both at the extra concert at the Gewandhaus and during my entire visit to Leipzig, were of the greatest value to me.

When the Capelldiener announced that all the musicians were assembled, we went from the artists' room to the platform; Reinecke took me to the conductor's desk, tapped with the baton, spoke a few words of introduction, to which the musicians replied by clapping and rapping on their desks with their bows, and handed me the baton. I then stepped into the conductor's place, spoke a few complimentary words, probably in very bad German, and the rehearsal began, Reinecke now quitting the room. We played my *First Suite*, in five movements, of which the first (Introduction and Fugue) is considered one of my most successful efforts. The first quarter of an hour of this rehearsal, before I had had time to take in all the strange faces in the orchestra, was very trying and agitating, at least for such a nervous and inexperienced conductor as myself. Only after the first break, when I had to set right some misunderstandings, I was able to look more closely at the members of the orchestra,—then the nervousness passed off, and there remained only my anxiety to make the business go as well as possible. After the first movement of the *Suite*, I could see by their looks and smiles that many of the players were already friendly towards me. At this the last traces of shyness vanished, the whole rehearsal went off very pleasantly, and I came away with the conviction that I had to deal with an orchestra of extraordinary capability. Both Reinecke and Brahms were present at the rehearsal. On meeting Brahms, he made no encouraging remarks; I was told he was very pleased with the first movement, but did not praise the rest, especially the " Marche Miniature."

The next rehearsal was a general one. It is the custom in Leipzig to admit the public to this final rehearsal, and this audience consists chiefly of young students, who are very warm and generous in the expression of their feelings, while the audience at the concerts themselves is exceedingly cold, critical, and chary of its praise. At the rehearsal my *Suite* and its composer were honoured by a storm of applause and by repeated recalls. But this was perhaps entirely owing to the presence of a great number of Russian students in philology, who were not sparing in the loud expression of their feelings for a fellow-countryman. In any case I was very pleased with my success, and on returning home I was to experience a still greater pleasure. This took the form of a card which Grieg had left for me on his way back from the rehearsal, with a few written words in which the impression the *Suite* had made upon him was expressed with such warmth and enthusiasm that I scruple to repeat them to my readers. A sincere compliment from such a gifted *confrère* as Grieg is the highest and most precious joy that can fall to an artist's lot.

The next day the concert itself took place. Mr. Brodsky had previously prepared me for a chilly reception by the audience, therefore I was neither surprised nor annoyed when on mounting to the conductor's desk there was not a single clap, and the sole response to my bow was a sepulchral silence. But after the first movement followed lively applause, more or less repeated after each succeeding movement of the *Suite*, and at the end I was twice recalled, which, at the Gewandhaus, may be interpreted as the proof of a great success. After the concert I went to supper with Reinecke. He and his family all did their best to be kind and polite; and Herr Reinecke, who among other things is an excellent French scholar, proved exceedingly agreeable and charming in conversation. In his youth he had been intimate with Schumann, and related many incidents in the life of the great German master. Schumann was really melancholy, and it might have been predicted from the first that this inherent depression would lead to hypochondria and insanity, as it eventually did. He was surprisingly silent; it seemed as though every word cost him an extraordinary effort. What was peculiarly striking in his musical organisation was his complete lack of power as a conductor, and Reinecke told me of an instance which made it evident that he could not even distinguish accurately the various *timbres* of orchestral instruments, and that he was entirely wanting in a natural feeling for rhythm, so indispensable for a conductor. How difficult to realise such an anomaly in a musician who, judging from his works, was so especially inventive as regards rhythm !

At Reinecke's I made the acquaintance of the French composer Gouvies, who always spent the winter in Leipzig. Monsieur Gouvies was completely Teutonised, spoke German perfectly, was rather hostile towards his own country (that is as regards music), and on the whole gave me the unpleasant impression of a man who thinks himself disillusioned and injured, and not being appreciated by his own countrymen, is consequently disposed to exaggerate the virtues and value of foreigners. It is quite probable that Monsieur Gouvies had some good cause for railing against musical France; but it was painful to me to hear him extol everything German at the expense of France. I had never met such a type of Frenchman before.

VIII

ANOTHER day (Christmas Day itself, according to Russian style) I was present at a concert given by the Liszt-Verein in the room of the old Gewandhaus. Just in proportion as the new concert-room is beautiful, sumptuous, roomy, and elegant, the old one is small, uncomfortable, and even rather dirty. But this room, and especially the little artists' room attached to it, has sacred memories in German art, and a thrill of awe passed through me when, seated there, I thought how its walls had often looked upon Mendelssohn, Schumann, and many other great musicians who had appeared, through many decades, upon the platform of the Gewandhaus.

The concert took place in the morning, and consisted exclusively of my works. The society which bears the name of Liszt, contrary to the Gewandhaus, devotes all its energies to the production of modern music. It has only been in existence two years, but already it has its own public, a fairly large one, which on this occasion filled the hall to the last seat. Among the directors of this society are many admirers of

Liszt, mostly young people of energy and talent, and it seems as though, in time, it might become a serious rival to the Gewandhaus. Among those who are particularly delighted with the success of the society, I must mention the talented musical critics Martin Krause and Fritsch, the gifted conductor of the Leipzig Opera (a native of Vienna), and our fellow-countryman Siloti.

The leader of the Grand Ducal orchestra of Weimar came from that town on purpose to hear this concert. The young violinist Halir, of whom I had heard so much from his admirer Siloti, and whose acquaintance I was all the more pleased to make because in recent years he had made a special study of my violin concerto—the one I have already alluded to in connection with Brodsky—took part in the concert. Halir had played my concerto everywhere, enduring the sneers and censure of the most influential critics upon his queer taste, and striving, in spite of all this, to make my much-abused creation one of the show-pieces at symphony concerts in Germany. On this occasion Herr Halir, together with Siloti and that excellent 'cellist Schroeder (who has since had a great success in Moscow), played my Trio dedicated to the memory of Nicholas Rubinstein. The rendering was quite exemplary. Herr Petri's quartet (he is the leader of the Gewandhaus orchestra) played my first quartet very finely, and, besides these, one or two smaller compositions of mine were performed. The audience of the Liszt-Verein are enthusiastic and very generous in their applause. I could not complain of any lack of warmth. The society presented me with a wreath. During the whole performance I sat on the platform in full view of the audience, having Grieg and his wife as neighbours. Afterwards a friendly critic—Fritsch—told me that he saw a lady point out the Griegs and myself to her daughter, saying, "Look, dear, there sits Tchaikovsky, and by his side his children." This was said quite seriously, and is not so very surprising, because I am quite grey and elderly, while Grieg, who is forty-five, and his wife, look extraordinarily young and small at a distance.

After the concert I spent some very pleasant hours with Siloti and some friends of his, directors of the Liszt-Verein. We talked a great deal about Russian music, and I was very much gratified to find that these gifted young musicians were well acquainted with our music, and very sympathetically disposed towards Glinka, Balakirev, Rimsky-Korsakov, Borodin, and Glazounov. They were particularly fond of Balakirev's *Islamey*, and considered this work, on account of its originality, quite unique of its kind. On this memorable day I first heard Halir play my concerto. It appeared to me that this artist, who is endowed with wonderful beauty of tone, prodigious technique, passion, brilliancy, and power, must soon take one of the first places among the violinists of our time.

IX

AFTER these two great days in my life I spent a whole week in Leipzig, and afterwards I twice returned there for a few days at a time. That I may not have to take up the subject of Leipzig again, I will now mention some interesting acquaintances whom I made there, and other facts of interest.

The Opera of Leipzig is proud of its gifted young conductor, Nikisch, who is a specialist as regards the later Wagner dramas. There I heard *Rheingold* —the first of the famous tetralogy—and *Meistersinger*. The orchestra of the Opera is the same as that of the Gewandhaus, and consequently first-rate; but as their playing at the concerts under Reinecke is not beyond reproach, it is evident that we can only form some idea of the perfection to which they can attain under a talented conductor by hearing their rendering of Wagner's elaborate scores when conducted by such an astonishing master of his business as Nikisch. His conducting has nothing in common with the effective and, in its way, inimitable conducting of Hans von Bülow. In proportion as the latter was mobile, restless, and showy in his style of conducting, which appealed to the eye, Herr Nikisch is elegantly calm, sparing of superfluous movements, yet at the same time wonderfully strong and self-possessed. He does not seem to conduct, but rather to exercise some mysterious spell; he hardly makes a sign, and never tries to call attention to himself, yet we feel that the great orchestra, like an instrument in the hands of a wonderful master, is completely and irresponsibly under the control of its chief. And this chief is a somewhat short, pale, young man, about thirty years of age, with beautiful bright eyes, and gifted—it must surely be—with some magic power which makes the orchestra resound like a thousand trumpets of Jericho, or coo like a dove, or die away in a mysterious whisper. And all this is done in such a way that the audience do not notice the little conductor who is quietly ruling his obedient slave—the orchestra.

Nikisch is a Germanised Hungarian; I imagine this is not a unique example. But certainly, among musicians at least, I never met but one who, having been born in Florence and spent his youth there, had so entirely lost the characteristic southern features (I speak from a musical point of view) of his native land, and had so completely borrowed from the Germans their language, customs, and above all their musical style, as the talented Ferrucio Busoni, with whom I became somewhat intimately acquainted. Busoni was still young when he came to live in Germany, where he attended a good music school

and became a pianist of marvellous technique. I
heard a quartet which Busoni had recently composed
excellently played by Herr Petri's quartet. This work
proved that Busoni has a decided gift for composition
and also serious tendencies; and as I have reason to
believe, from personal knowledge, that the young
composer has strength of character, brilliant intellect,
and lofty ambitions, I have no doubt that he will
soon be much talked of. For my part I listened to
this quartet, and while delighting in the exceedingly
original rhythmic and harmonic combinations, I could
not but regret that Busoni in every way did violence
to his nature, and strove, apparently, to be German
at any price. Something similar may be observed
in another Italian of the new generation, Sgambati.
Both of them seem ashamed of being Italian; they
seem to fear lest their compositions should show a
shadow of melody, and desire to make them obscure,
in the German style. A sad phenomenon indeed!
That inspired old man Verdi opened out a new path
to Italian composers in *Aïda* and *Otello*, without in
the least imitating the German style (although some
suppose, quite wrongly, that Verdi is following in
Wagner's footsteps); while those of his young compatriots who tend towards Germany are striving to
win their laurels in the land of Beethoven and
Schumann at the price of doing violence to their
nature. They strive to be like Brahms, deep,
obscure, even wearisome, if only they may not be
confounded with that host of Italian composers who,
even in these days, still continue dishing up in every

style the old operatic commonplaces of Bellini and
Donizetti. But they forget that the sheep remains
a sheep in spite of the lion's skin; and if the lion is
endowed by nature with his share of beauty and
strength, the sheep, too, is gentle, and has his
wonderful warm fleece, as well as other virtues which
should be cultivated, perfected, and valued no less
highly than the opposite qualities and merits of the
lion. I am firmly convinced that Italian music will
only enter on a new period of prosperity when, instead of quarrelling with their national tendencies
and joining the ranks of the Wagnerians, Lisztites,
Brahmsites, etc., they begin to draw fresh musical
elements from the bosom of their national genius,
and, discarding the trivialities of the thirties, create
new forms in the spirit of their nationality and in
conformity with their surroundings and gorgeous
southern scenery. For the brilliant natural characteristics of the Italians, their richness of melody,
and the facile external beauty which belong to the
genius of Italian music are not perhaps incompatible
with a certain depth, though of a different kind to
that of the Germans. Busoni is an excellent pianist,
and it is very desirable that he should visit us in the
immediate future; in any case he is a striking and
interesting personality.

To complete my impressions and experiences
of Leipzig, I will relate one interesting episode
which tends to prove that politics do not influence
music, and that Mars and Apollo, being gods, are
not jealous of each other. Since Bismarck made

his celebrated inflammatory speech in February, all Germany has been enveloped in a flame of fierce Russophobism. However, early one morning I was awakened by a noise and bustle in the corridor of my hotel, which was soon followed by a knock at my door. Somewhat alarmed, I jumped out of bed, opened the door, and learned from the waiter who was knocking that an aubade was about to begin under my window, and that politeness demanded that I should appear there, in spite of the unusual severity of the frost. The waiter then handed me a programme, elegantly designed, consisting of eight numbers of very varied music. At this moment the strains of our National Hymn resounded from below. As soon as I was dressed I opened the window and beheld in the small courtyard of the hotel, stationed immediately under my windows, a full military band, in the midst of which stood the band-master in a uniform as resplendent as that of a field-marshal. All eyes were turned towards me. I bowed, and remained standing bareheaded in the bitter frost of this early February morning. It was the band of one of the regiments then stationed in Leipzig; an excellent one too, and they played their programme very well, which was the more surprising, because the cold was enough to paralyse the fingers of the poor musicians, who endured the cruel winter frost for over an hour. The conductor, Herr Jahrow, did me the honour of being particularly fond of my music, and, thanks to this, a body of Germans, in full uniform, had been compelled to flatter my ears that

morning. After the serenade was finished, the conductor came up to see me, gave me a cordial greeting,
and then hastened away to his military duties.
Needless to say, I was very much touched by this
expression of sentiment. I do not know if the other
visitors in the hotel were equally gratified at being
roused from their beds at such an early hour by the
strains of trumpets and trombones; but at least their
curiosity must have been aroused. From all the
windows people in various stages of costume looked
out to see what was going on.

X

THERE are two distinct symphony societies in Hamburg. One is old-established, possesses large funds and a very celebrated orchestra. The other has been started quite recently by a well-known Hamburg concert-agent, Pollini. It has no orchestra of its own, but employs the band of the Opera, which consists of second-rate artists, who are, moreover, overworked to the last degree by their service at the theatre. Both societies give a series of symphony concerts, and the Philharmonic has long since been conducted by Dr. Bernuth, an excellent and experienced conductor, who is generally respected in Hamburg both as a musician and as a very amiable and charming man. The orchestra of the other society is conducted by Hans von Bülow. As invariably happens, there exists between these two musical enterprises a deep enmity, a mutual antagonism and desire to outdo each other in receipts, success, and fame. I had been invited to conduct three of my works at one of the concerts of the Philharmonic Society, and thus fell into the camp which was opposed to Hans von Bülow, who, it seemed to me, cherished no great friendship for the Philharmonic. I felt that I was placed in an awkward position. Hans von Bülow had, in time past, done me invaluable service, and I considered myself for ever in his debt. Therefore, realising the situation of musical affairs in Hamburg, I was grieved to think that I might cause him any annoyance. But my anxiety was quite unnecessary. Hans von Bülow, being a born gentleman, took my appearance at the concert of the opposition society in a most gentlemanly way. In spite of ill-health, and extreme fatigue caused by the constant travelling from Hamburg to Bremen, Bremen to Berlin, and back again to Hamburg, which he continued to do all through the three years during which he conducted the Subscription Symphony Concerts, von Bülow accorded me a most hearty welcome. He came to call upon me, and what still more attracted the attention of all the Hamburgers, he remained from beginning to end of the concert in which I took part.

As at the first rehearsal at the Gewandhaus, I felt exceedingly nervous when on the 17th of January I attended the rehearsal at Covent Garden, the room in which the concerts of the Hamburg Philharmonic Society take place. My method of procedure with the orchestra was just the same as at Leipzig. I began with the *Finale* of my *Third Suite* (Theme and Variations). The faces of the players at the moment of my first beat expressed nothing further than a rather cool curiosity, but soon some of them began to smile and nod to each other as much as to say,

" This Russian bear is not really so very bad." A bond
of sympathy was established between us, and all my
agitation and diffidence vanished as though at the touch
of some magic wand. The subsequent rehearsals and
the concert itself brought me nothing but pleasure.
Such anxiety is only unbearable when an artist is not
sufficiently at home in his business, and feels himself
a stranger in an entirely new sphere. These fears
and agitations which every one goes through—
especially a nervous man—before appearing in public,
will cease to trouble him if he can believe in the
sympathy of his colleagues and those around him. At
the second rehearsal I experienced a rare delight at
the success which fell to the lot of our young compatriot Sapellnikov. This young artist had been
invited at the recommendation of Madame Sophie
Menter (in whose class he had finished his course at
the Conservatoire of St. Petersburg) to play, under
my conductorship, my difficult *Pianoforte Concerto*,
No. 1.

On the eve of my departure from Petersburg I had
occasion to hear Sapellnikov's playing; and although
I had been able to form some slight appreciation of its
fine quality, yet—owing, perhaps, to the bustle and
haste which precedes a long journey—I did not at
the time observe all the rare qualities possessed by this
sympathetic young pianist. Now, at the rehearsal,
as Sapellnikov surmounted one after another the
inconceivable difficulties of my concerto, and gradually
revealed all the power and distinctiveness of his colossal
gift, my enthusiasm increased, and, what was still more

agreeable, it was shared by the whole orchestra, who applauded him warmly between each break, and particularly at the end. A rare force, beauty, and brilliancy of tone; inspired warmth of rendering; a wonderful power of self-restraint; finish of detail, musical sensibility, and complete self-confidence—these are the distinguishing characteristics of Sapellnikov's playing. *Famos, unglaublich, kolossal!* were the expressions which escaped from the musicians as soon as they had finished their ovation. I need not say how I rejoiced at this genuine and hearty outburst of enthusiasm called forth from these German artists by our future great pianist. There are so many mediocre pianists; it is so hard to distinguish oneself in this career; and to be able thus suddenly to astound and carry away a body of strange musicians is a thing to be proud of!

The following morning the rehearsal, as at the Gewandhaus, was a public one, and the concert took place the same evening. Of my three works, the *Serenade for Strings and Orchestra* pleased the Hamburg public most, and evoked a storm of applause. My *Pianoforte Concerto* did not please much in itself, but Sapellnikov's rendering was appreciated for its own merits, and the highly-gifted pianist was very enthusiastically received. The *Finale* of my *Third Suite* did not seem to suit the public taste. Too noisy and restless in its orchestral effects, this movement puzzled the audience of the Hamburg Philharmonic Society, who are not accustomed to the modern symphonic style. It was explained to me afterwards that this audience is exceedingly conservative, and of living composers only willingly acknowledges Brahms.

After the concert there was a large supper-party at Dr. Bernuth's house. Very complimentary things were said about Russian music in general and the writer of this journal in particular. I replied in a German speech, to the many mistakes in which the company showed themselves kindly indulgent. When the party was over, some of my new friends carried off Sapellnikov and myself to a *Bier-Kneipe*, where we talked and drank beer until two in the morning. But this was not the end; we were then persuaded to go on to one of the Viennese cafés which, in Hamburg, remain open all night, and there we sat a long time, making libations to Bacchus. It seems to me that in Hamburg people do not live so quietly and decorously as in other German towns. All my friends there, even those who were serious-minded and occupied solid positions in the world, loved to "dissipate"; and nowhere else did I "dissipate" so often and so much as in this lovely, gay, and charming town.

Another day the Tonkunstlerverein (a society of musicians) gave an evening in my honour. Only my music was performed. A young lady—a Fräulein Nathan—sang some of my songs, and Sapellnikov played three of my pieces.

As in Leipzig I had enjoyed my intimacy in the family circles of Brodsky and Siloti, so in Hamburg I was made quite at home by the firm of Blüthner— well known throughout the musical world—and by the amiable Herr D. Rather, whose family have long been living in this town—ever since the death of a dear son in Petersburg, and the consequent anxiety as to the health of his remaining children, induced Herr Rather to separate himself from his family, whom he visits occasionally for three months at a time. I spent many pleasant hours with Rather, his wife, and his charming children, of whom, unfortunately, only the eldest knows a few words of Russian, although they were born in Russia. I should like to take this opportunity of declaring my deep gratitude to Herr Rather for his unceasing kindness and the friendly part he played on my behalf; for to his initiative I owe my invitation to Hamburg, and from Hamburg date all the flattering invitations which reached me, one after another, from various places in Germany.

XI

In Hamburg, as in Leipzig, I made some very interesting acquaintances. First of all I must mention the head of the committee of the Philharmonic Society, a very old gentleman, Herr Ave-Lallement. This venerable old man of over eighty paid me great attention, and gave me the flattering reception of a compatriot. In spite of his age, his infirmity, and the great distance at which he lived, Herr Lallement attended two rehearsals, the concert, and the party at Dr. Bernuth's. He carried his amiability so far as to desire to possess my photograph, taken by the best photographer in Hamburg; came to see me in person in order to ask about it, and himself arranged the hour of the sitting and the size and style of the picture. I visited the kindly old gentleman, who, as the reader can see for himself, was quite free from the prejudices of old age against all that is modern, and I had a long and very interesting chat with him. Herr Lallement candidly confessed that many of my works which had been performed in Hamburg were not at all to his mind; that he could not endure my noisy instrumentation, and disliked some of the orchestral effects to which I had recourse, especially my use of the instruments of percussion; but, for all that, he thought I had in me the making of a really good German composer. Almost with tears in his eyes he besought me to leave Russia and settle permanently in Germany, where classical conventions and the traditions of high culture could not fail to correct my faults, which were easily explicable to his mind by the fact of my having been born and educated in a country so unenlightened and, as regards progress, so far behind Germany. It was evident that he did cherish a deep prejudice against Russia, and I strove my best to overcome his hostility towards our national sentiments, of which, moreover, he was ignorant, or only knew them through the speeches of the Russophobist section. We parted good friends.

I also met with equal courtesy and amiable frankness from the leading Hamburg critic, Herr Sithardt. He attended all the rehearsals, made a close study of such of my scores as were performed, and wrote a long and detailed article, in which he censured in decisive terms the tendencies which I upheld, and found fault with my symphonic style, describing it as rough, patchy, barbarous, and suggestive of Nihilism. Herr Sithardt frankly repeated these reproaches to me in person; but at the same time his words rang with such genuine feeling, and gave evidence of such careful study and friendliness, that I preserved a very pleasant recollection of my short acquaintance with him.

Several other musicians, and people not professionally engaged in music but deeply interested in it, paid me flattering attentions, and understood how to express a cordial sympathy, leaving an ineffaceable impression upon my memory. Such were Dr. Riemann, who has devoted himself to the study of musical theory, and is not unknown to us in Russia; that witty old man Gurlitt, the composer of a number of well-known piano fantasias and transcriptions; the talented violinist Willy Burmeister; the conductor Laube, appointed to the Pavlovsk concerts in the summer of 1888; the violinists Morvege and Behr; Armbrust the organist, and many others.

From my conversation with all these, I gathered that nowhere was the Brahms cult more extensive than in Hamburg. The question of this composer's position, which was always troubling me, met with the same response here as elsewhere. Only in Hamburg I finally realised how an artist's work may sometimes be valued not for its intrinsic worth, for itself alone, but for some fortuitous reason. As our Russian proverb admirably expresses it: "When there is no fish the crayfish passes for one." The fact is that Wagner and Wagnerism does not suffice the entire German public, as many believe. No doubt there are fully convinced, energetic, and powerful advocates of Wagner, who strive in every way to establish his creed in Germany and to further the progress of his music; but the great mass of the German public are intensely conservative and ready to protest against every kind of musical innovation. If, to a certain extent, they are reconciled to Wagner's triumph in the domain of opera, yet in the concert-room they stand firmly by classical tradition. The school of Liszt, which would like to monopolise the concert platforms, meets with incredible obstacles and has no success. Musical Germans who are not infected with Wagnerism, and hold aloof from his exclusiveness, possess a certain modesty and a nice ear which makes them turn in disgust from all violent effects, from all that is decided, eccentric, piquant, brilliant, singular; in a word, from everything that scintillates in the new symphonic music of all the European schools. So strong is the need of a musician who will devote himself to symphony in the classical style, to the sober and recognised traditions of the great masters, that for the lack of a new genius capable of leading the German school in the path indicated by Haydn, Mozart, Beethoven, Mendelssohn, and Schumann, and their compeers, the Germans—at least the majority of them—have concentrated their hopes on Brahms, who, if he cannot be Beethoven, is at least inspired by a noble ambition to follow in his steps.

XII

THE Berlin Philharmonic Society, or I should rather say the society of instrumentalists who hire the room known as the "Philharmonia," invited me to attend an extra concert consisting entirely of my own compositions. I have already stated that the arrangement of the programme was attended with some difficulties, because Herr Schneider, the president of the society, was anxious to perform something which would bring me into favour with the Berlin public. I considered, and still consider, my *Overture 1812* quite mediocre, having only a patriotic and local significance which made it unsuitable for any but Russian concert-rooms. But it was precisely this overture that Herr Schneider wished to include in the programme, saying that it had been performed several times in Berlin with success. On the other hand, I thought that my *Romeo and Juliet* fantasia ought to be the chief item on the programme, and Herr Schneider, who is a very charming and amiable man, finally agreed to this, but very unwillingly. He thought it would be a great risk to perform such a difficult work, which, in his opinion, was not likely to please. I decided to consult Hans von Bülow, who was well acquainted with my music as well as with the tastes of the Berlin public, and to my great surprise he sided with Herr Schneider. I then gave in.

The orchestra of the Berlin Philharmonic Society is very fine, and has what I must call the quality of elasticity, the power of stretching itself to the dimensions of a Berlioz or Liszt orchestra, and of rendering to perfection the capricious effects of Berlioz, or the massive, sonorous tones of Liszt's orchestra; while, on the other hand, it can contract to the requirements of a Haydn. In this respect the Berlin orchestra reminds me very much of those of our capital towns. This probably is due to the fact that in Berlin, as with us, a decided eclecticism dominates the concert programmes. Here, as in Petersburg or Moscow, you may hear at one concert Haydn and Glazounov, Beethoven and Bizet, Glinka and Brahms, and thus everything is executed with the same loving care, brilliancy and *ensemble*. The musicians who are members of the Philharmonic Society are not employed at the Opera; consequently they are not tired out. Besides which, they form an association, the members of which are on an equal footing, and play for their own benefit and not for that of an agent, who pays a very small salary. This is the reason why their performances are strong and full of expression. From the very first rehearsal I was encouraged by the gentlemen of the orchestra, and by their attention and affability, and everything went off well. The rehearsal was attended by many prominent musical people, who expressed their interest in every possible way. Among them I must mention Grieg, who had purposely come from Leipzig to be at my concert, Moritz Moskovsky, Professor Ehrlich, and Hans von Bülow himself, who, in spite of extreme fatigue, appeared at the first rehearsal and was most kind to me. In spite of very unfavourable weather, the concert attracted a large audience and went off very brilliantly. Siloti played my concerto very finely, and had a great success; Sapellnikov was so good and amiable that he undertook to accompany the singer Friede, who sang several of my songs. Of the symphonic works, the *Overture 1812* and the Introduction and Fugue from my *First Suite* pleased best. I was received with loud applause.

My reader will perhaps observe that I speak less willingly and give fewer details of my visit to Berlin than might be expected, seeing its importance as the capital of Germany, but I have a reason, which I will explain. The fact is that it is difficult and painful to speak of Berlin. In my heart I still have a lively recollection of the irreparable loss which befell me in the death of the late J. I. Koteka, my pupil, and afterwards my most intimate friend, who lived in Berlin for eight years, and held a high position in the town. Every day I came in contact with people among whom the dead man had lived; many of them, like myself, were attached to him by ties of friendship; every moment I was discussing circumstances and events which keenly reminded me of my departed friend, and reopened a wound that was scarcely healed. Time alone can soften such a blow; and it needs a long, long time to reconcile us to the death of a gifted young man full of strength and energy. . . .

Among those who were especially friendly to me in Berlin I will mention the well-known concert-agent Wolff; the fine violinist Emil Sauret; the celebrated Moritz Moskovsky, whose personality seemed to me as interesting as his creative gift; the publisher and charming man Hugo Bock; and finally Madame Artôt—so well remembered by the Moscow public. This talented singer had been living for some time in Berlin, where she was particularly appreciated and loved by the Court and the public, and where she sang with great success and also gave lessons. I was invited, together with Grieg, to spend an evening at Madame Artôt's house, the memory of which will never be effaced. Both the personality and the art of this singer are as irresistibly fascinating as ever.

THE
RELATION OF TCHAIKOVSKY
TO ART-QUESTIONS OF TO-DAY

I

TCHAIKOVSKY AND INSTRUMENTATION

THE gentle and sincere nature of Tchaikovsky, whilst rendering his view of debatable subjects always interesting, sometimes confers upon expressions simple in themselves an element of value to the student in composition; requiring only a more extended form of expression for its practical application. My observation of this having often been associated, not only with regret that the master did not condescend to enlarge more upon his themes, but also with the feeling that the sense might easily be amplified without risk, I here venture to offer a few suggestions which occur to me in consequence of the disfavour with which he regarded the instrumentation of Schumann.

Tchaikovsky, like Berlioz, greatly relied upon his instrumentation. But, unlike Berlioz, he was superbly endowed with the gift of melody; and the extra charm thus imparted to his work gives an added value to whatever he has to say about the orchestra; for the excellent reason that the figures which he clothed orchestrally were always so graceful in themselves. The student either knows or should know that in composition the best work is always done very rapidly; and, though speed is not in itself desirable, the means of speed should be well provided, in order that rapid expression of the musical idea may not be impeded when occasion requires.

There are those who contend that, as orchestral works should be conceived in score, so they should also be drafted. There are also those who, though they do not confess it, really write for the piano; and orchestrate afterwards. Let us, by all means, give the latter credit for " thinking orchestra " as they go; for I am not dealing with their intentions but only with their mode of procedure. Both these extremes are wrong; and I therefore welcome Tchaikovsky's definition of instrumentation; as "the *distribution* of a work among the various instruments."

Now as we can only distribute what already exists it is reasonable to infer that Tchaikovsky's method must have been something of a middle course. This is not only an inference from his definition, but also from his manner of detailing the habits desirable to be acquired in the study of the art.

That which he places first in order is the habit of

"employing alternately the individual groups of instruments." It might, of course, be contended that
the use of a full draft-score would offer no impedi-
ment to this. But his next desideratum is that the
student should know "how to *blend* the groups appropriately." This blending of groups being equi-
valent to the creation of new groups of composite
character, exhibits at once the inconvenience of the
draft full-score system; as such composite groups
would be so scattered in appearance as greatly to
impede the act of composition. Then, he advises that
"strong effects should be economised"; which I presume not only means that they should be used
sparingly, but also that the contrast of their entry
should be an especial object of care; as we always
find it to be in his own works. But this latter proceeding is also one which renders handy manipulation
desirable; so that on the whole he certainly favours
a mode of sketch something between the two extremes.

But the question is—"What is that *something*"?
No doubt this is a matter in which we are all entitled
to be guided by our own individual preferences; and
I am far from supposing that mine are likely to be
better than those of my readers. On the present occasion, therefore, if I am emboldened to make a suggestion, it is because my plan appears to be in accord
with Tchaikovsky's advice;—so far, that is, as I may
be safe in taking the latter (which is expressed only
in general terms) as the basis of a detailed *modus
operandi*.

The plan, therefore, which seems most advisable is

to work to a score of *seven* staves. Roughly speaking, each stave should represent a group; and (as in
the case of the three trombones on a single line) there
should be no difficulty in this. The main idea is to
insert only essentials; and, to this end, two real parts
will nearly always be sufficient to indicate a group.
From the moment that more appear to be necessary
it will be time for the student to suspect his composition of an overdose of polyphony; and to act
accordingly.

Next, let him divide the wood-wind into flutes and
reeds; as the agility of the former very often asso-
ciates them with florid work in which the reeds have
no share. As to the brass, a good practical distinction
is between "light" and "heavy," irrespective of the
actual instruments employed; as the pianissimo of
the heavy brass may enter into effects rather outside
the traditional domain of those instruments. Two
lines will therefore be sufficient for the entire brass;
and, if the bass clef be used for the lower line (which
is the most practical way) it is of course on the understanding that the trumpet passages are really an
octave higher. The upper line will be nearly always
reserved for the horns; but the convenience of the
method lies in this;—that in the supposed first-sketch
the student does not wait to decide upon the special
instrument, but only upon the weight and character
of the effect desired; and that therefore the gentler
pulsations will be recorded on the horn-line, even
though on after consideration they might be transferred elsewhere. I am reminded in this of Tchaikov-

sky's remark to his friend, Kashkin; when he tells the latter how, though he was working hard at the instrumentation of " Eugene Onegin," he was really treating it as if it were the work of some one else. Such a description of the operation evidently presupposes a sketch—if not precisely like what I now propose, at all events of the same nature.

And now for the strings. So far, we have employed four lines only; to which we now add two, braced in the piano manner. These are to contain not necessarily the string parts proper; but, rather, all essentials of the composition not otherwise expressed. Used in this way, this department protects us from the loss of time consequent upon hesitation; as it provides a refuge at once for all thoughts the precise instrumentation of which does not instantly occur to the mind.

It follows from the preceding that the lower line will be reserved for the dominating rhythmic pulsation throughout. Not necessarily, or by any means, the drum part; in proof of which I need only remind the student that the rhythmic pulsation is constant; whereas the parts for all percussion instruments are (if I may so express myself) very much not so. The rhythmic pulsation is in one sense the foundation of the work; and therefore its position on the lower line is not only appropriate, but it also reflects the importance of this fact, by presenting it to the eye of the worker in a salient manner. In addition to this it is worthy of observation that, as only one indicated note is required for rhythmic purposes (rendering even a single line sufficient in cases where space is an object) this stave remains practically free, and affords ample opportunity overhead for figuring the bass as we go, and thus ensuring the progressions which spontaneously occur without waiting to translate the chords into individual parts.

I do not propose to touch the question of how far Tchaikovsky's blame of Schumann's instrumentation was deserved; but, treating the particular faults mentioned merely in a general sense, and, therefore, as likely to occur to anyone in course of study, they are easily traceable to the use of one or other of the extreme methods above mentioned. For, should the composition be first written for the piano, it is but a pen-and-ink sketch in origin; and, lacking the suggestiveness for choice of *timbre* which is the life and soul of an orchestral work, it will be driven to rely mostly upon degrees of strength for its contrasts. Or, on the other hand, should the full-score outline have been used throughout, there will be either no blendings of the groups at all, or the blendings will not really speak the composer's meaning; in consequence of his attention having been too much occupied with details during the act of composition.

The method which I have ventured to suggest is in no sense a pen-and-ink sketch; but rather a full-score of bare essentials. The limitation to essentials avoids cumbrousness on the one hand; whilst, on the other, it gives us the best chance of attaining to that brilliancy and transparency which Tchaikovsky complains of finding absent in Schumann. And it does this because, in consequence of subordinate work being postponed, no note is written without the want of it being first felt.

II

TCHAIKOVSKY AND FORM

THE student who already knows something of Tchaikovsky in the working will not be likely to impute too literal a meaning to his conversation with Serov's daughter; for the more lofty a man's inward conception of the true and beautiful the less apt will it be for any verbal description. Mere desiderata of the common-place order are altogether beside such questions: albeit, the ideas resulting from their fulfilment may usefully assist the imagination. To assist the imagination in this way is good; provided the nature of the assistance be that of an added facility. But an imagination for which such assistance is a necessity is not only one which nature has forbidden to soar: it is also one beset by innumerable dangers, and foredoomed to a halting decision; even within the limits of its humble scope.

The fates seem so cruelly to have ordered matters that, whilst some are ethereally wafted to the Empyrean, others need to console themselves with a faint approximation; and that, too, attained only by small and painful stages. Such are they who, by the constant study of desiderata, at last attain to notions (which the large class of similar minds is only too prone to endorse) of what the perfect work of art should be. Such are they who forget that, in following these methods—poor as is the distance which they are enabled to travel—they have not, even to its insignificant extent, the guarantee of being in perfect agreement with the more highly gifted.

I am led to these observations by the apparent divergence between qualities imputed to Tchaikovsky and principles which he himself constantly upheld. Either the sapients, on the one hand, have engaged upon doubtful courses, or Tchaikovsky himself must have been strangely in need of a more stringent self-examination. Time alone can settle the question; but the judgment of the student may, meanwhile, be substantially assisted by the encouragement of higher views of the more important art-questions involved. And, as these are too numerous to allow of an exhaustive enquiry in this place, I prefer the subject of *form* for illustration; on account of that being, at the same time, one intimately connected with either Tchaikovsky's idealism or his weakness (according to our way of thinking); and, also, one which, in mere course of treatment, is likely to prove of some lasting utility and benefit to the student-reader.

Firstly, let us gather a few of Tchaikovsky's own observations upon the subject. I do not pretend, of course, to deduce, from the mere profession of principles, that a man must necessarily have carried them out; but, I do insist that, in the case of a guileless nature like that of Tchaikovsky, it is proof positive of his intention to do so. The question which we have to try therefore is not whether or no he imperfectly realised one essential attribute of artistic perfection; but, whether his conceptions of it may not have been something different from those formed upon the ordinary school methods.

Now, on this particular question, we cannot fail to be attracted, in the first instance, by the admiration which was always excited in Tchaikovsky's mind by the contemplation of formal beauty in the works of others. Thus, in his praise of Beethoven's Eighth Symphony, it is the first feature which attracts attention. We need not be misled, however, into supposing that he therefore exaggerated its weight; as we fortunately know, from his *resumé* of Beethoven's merit, the exact order of importance in which he placed the various desiderata mentioned. Instead of quoting the words I give this, for the student's benefit, in tabular form; as most suited to his purpose.

1. Creative imagination.

   Tchaikovsky distinguishes between this and the merely inventive faculty. He classifies composers as:

   (a). Those who have principally relied upon invention: Schubert, Chopin, Dargomijsky.

   (b). Those endowed chiefly with imagination: Mendelssohn, Liszt, Balakirev, Berlioz.

   (c). Those—the truly great—who united both faculties in equal proportion: Beethoven, Mozart.

2. Perfection of form.

3.   Skill in the handling of musical means.

   (*a*). In development of themes.

   (*b*). In fullness and luxuriance of orchestration.

We have not to proceed far in the study of his opinions before becoming aware that his idea of form is not that of the school-men, but of the artist. Thus, Schumann (with whom, as we know, he could readily find fault upon occasion) is revered for his introduction of "a whole world of new forms"; which is interpreted as a striving towards the Ideal. And, in the case of Berlioz, notwithstanding that he qualifies his praise in many respects, he places depth of thought as allied to beauty of form in the very foreground. Later on, he alludes to the "formless" romantic school of Berlioz and Liszt; but this is a mere mode of expression, and arises from our having grown to a conventional restriction of the term "form" to include only certain established forms; instead of comprising, as it should do, the entire question. The ambiguity thus resulting leads us naturally to employ the term, now in one sense, and now in another, and the important point is rather for the student to observe that Tchaikovsky's admiration is not limited to that of the prescribed forms; being impartially excited by whatever form seems appropriate to the occasion. In other words, he does not confine himself to the worship of those traditional *cadres;* the faith in which constitutes a sort of musical orthodoxy. His stipulation is for *some* form; for form, that is, in its ordinary sense, and therefore as liable to variation in art as in material productions.

We all know that, to varieties of the latter, there is absolutely no limit. We do not hold up certain geometrical proportions to universal admiration; and then decree that all productions shall conform to them under pain of being denied the possession of all shape. But we do require that the outward semblance shall be in conformity with purpose and meaning. These features being granted we are equally ready to admit all forms; a mental attitude so simple and so ob- viously correct, that we can only marvel at the ap- parent difficulty of its application to musical creations.

But the natural desire of Tchaikovsky for apprecia- tion is alone sufficient to show how unlikely he was to disregard the question of formal beauty; for there is ample evidence of his having been aware of the prevalence of what may be called mechanical methods in its respect, and to be forewarned could not fail in such a case to produce its usual effect. In this con- nection he expressly tells us that great works of art are "less valued for creative force than for perfection of form"; and that Beethoven was regarded as the first of all composers, because of his successful fusion of the idea and its external expression; though all the world knows that there have been other musicians possessed of a greater volume of inspiration. Con- sequently, he absolutely knew that, in the fulfilment of his own ambition, it was pre-eminently a question not to be lightly disregarded.

All this leads me to a belief (which I hope in suc- ceeding chapters to induce the reader to share) that the divergence between what is often said of Tchaikovsky and his own expressed opinions does not in reality relate to form in the conventional sense, but rather to prime conceptions of what form should signify. It was fortunately so natural in him to discriminate, and, so to speak, subdivide this question that we can easily imagine him conceiving himself to be in perfect obedience to æsthetic requirements without close adherence to the recognised external features.

There are many passages in his writings which seem to bear out this idea. He alludes for instance to Schumann, in his First Symphony, introducing new methods of procedure "without departing from classical forms"; and thus proving that new ideas can be united to the "established traditions of form." In all these expressions there is the underlying stipulation of free choice in such matters.

But the point comes out specially clear in his judgment of Rimsky-Korsakov. In the course of this he accounts for his lack of enthusiasm by the view that this composer was wavering between what was modern, as compared with the old and archaic; and that the result of such hesitation was an "absence of form." His admiration was evidently not dependent upon the adoption of either classic or modern form; but was given in return for the fulfilment of an ideal conception apart from either, though partaking of both. If we can succeed in arriving at a correct view of this we shall better understand the apparently wavering nature of his work; which caused the Germans to deem him a representative of the ultra-revolutionary party, whilst in Russia he was often placed in the ranks of the retrogrades. He tells us, with charming frankness, that both opinions were equally without foundation; an avowal which the view I am adopting would lead us to expect.

It will now be necessary to enter upon more speculative reasoning; as Tchaikovsky's idealism, though somewhat indicated by his utterances, is not by them set forth in any sufficient detail. The enquiry will therefore leave ample room for an exercise of the student's own judgment; and, on that account, be of benefit to him independently of the value of the theories advanced.

III

TCHAIKOVSKY AND IDEALISM

CONSIDERING the ascendancy of programme music at the present day it is easy to imagine the unthinking lured into the belief that idealism is in the ascendant. Such folk perceive no humour in the aspect of a "man in the street," analytical programme in hand, *en route* to be tone-poemed. They might even be ready to dogmatise upon this as a sign of the wonderful advance accomplished in the true understanding of the tonal language : aye, and even perorate with pity of times gone by, before the supervention of this glorious flood of enlightenment.

If I were to be suddenly wafted *à la* Dean Swift to some curious country where the entire population were to be seen perambulating with the aid of crutches, and were similarly to be informed that all this constituted an improvement upon the old style of locomotion, my opinion would be very much the same as in the case of those whose enjoyment of music depends upon being told beforehand what was in the composer's mind. There are still some old-time musi-

cians who disfavour this sort of thing; but why do
so? Surely a wooden leg is a fine institution for
those who require it; and I for one at all events have
nothing to urge against the innocent use of programme plaster by those who feel its necessity; any
more than I should object to the application of reme-
dies for any bodily infirmity. Programme music has
come to stay, but only as an additional member of
the family; for it will leave the cultus of absolute
music exactly where it was in the beginning, is now
and ever shall be.

Are we to conclude that, because Tchaikovsky
allowed himself to go with this popular current, it
was therefore his ideal? Asked by Mme. von Meck
whether he had a programme in mind for the composition of his Fourth Symphony he plaintively
replies :—How can one describe those indefinite sentiments which fill one during the act of composition?
It would be vain for me to endeavour to express in
words that immeasurable sense of happiness.

But it is noteworthy that he overcomes this reluctance; and that gratitude to his benefactress impels
him to the endeavour. It is also keenly instructive
to note how he characterises the programme which
he has been at such pains to evolve, and with what
charming _naïveté_ he answers the momentous question
of what a programme really is; by confessing that it
is merely the "possibility" of a description in words
And, after all his pains, he is alarmed at the imper-
fection and vagueness of what he has written and

R

pleads that, at any rate, the Symphony is really an echo of his feelings at the time; but whether it can be " forced " into clear and definite sequences of words he does not know.

I pass by the contention that this was in the case of a work to which no title had been given; for, notwithstanding this, Tchaikovsky himself says that it is really the musical confession of the soul, from which the accumulated material flows forth in tones just as a lyrical poet expresses himself in verses. No one has ever doubted the effectiveness of the tonal language in illustration of a fixed idea, such music exhibiting merely a sub-division of a class standing mid-way between the absolute or " pure," on the one hand and the vocal or " mixed " on the other; by which latter term the union of tonal sounds with words of definite meaning is, in this connection, most appropriately described. The remaining subdivision of this class of music is composed of works in which the main idea is translated into detail and becomes a narrative or episode affording opportunity—some say excuse—for more express delineations—some say vulgarisms. But which ever may be our grove of thought, the following is the classification : —

1. The absolute :—or purely ethereal tonal language.
2. The interpretative :—
    (a). Of a parent idea suggesting mental pictures more or less fitted for tonal description.
    (b). Of a complete scheme, with phases arranged in panoramic succession.

3. The mixed:—or tonal language allied to words of definite meaning.

   (*a*). In which the rhythm of the text is alone considered; the tonal setting being a mere form of utterance.

   (*b*). In which the sense of the text is reflected by varying tone-colour.

These degrees are patent to the meanest understanding and the real question before us is this: In which of these does idealism take its highest flight? Which of these is the most æsthetic?

This is an enquiry which compels us to seek to form some conception of the latent feeling by which, not only Tchaikovsky, but every great composer has been actuated. In the case of Tchaikovsky we have evidence that he was perfectly alive to the fact that music could only ally itself with poetry at the expense of its own independence. It may be considered harsh, but it is scarcely too much to say that there are passages in his vocal music in which the words are rather set to the music than the music to the words; the fault evidently arising from a predilection in favour of the tonal language, and a disinclination to immolate it for the exigencies of verbal expression. It follows, therefore, that he idealised the absolute; as every inspired composer had done before him and will do to the end of time. If therefore the ardour of programmists leads them to conceive themselves in sole possession of the emotional they could not better prove the stultifying effects of material descriptions.

The ideal, therefore, of formal beauty is a subject to be treated from two very distinct points of view—

the one merely technical, the other purely æsthetic. With the former of these I have, for the present, nothing to do. The rules and principles which guide us to the attainment of symmetry relate to the mere act of shapening our production; of so ordering it that it shall outwardly and visibly conform to what is inwardly and spiritually needed. But conformity to the mere framework stands in the same relation to the æsthetic need as does obedience to the mere letter of a human law to a loyal fulfilment of the spirit of it. It is entirely with the latter form of obedience that we are now concerned.

How many of those who talk glibly of sonata-form have ever paused to enquire why this particular "shape," so to speak, of music should so charm and interest us that we can go on, as it were for ever, listening to compositions cast in the same mould without satiation or weariness? I am afraid that there are very few; and my reason for so thinking is that such an enquiry would effectively prevent much of our present-day criticism; in which the deviations from mechanical routine, which are inevitable in an inspired work, are regarded as imperfections of form. School books cannot deal with this. They cannot even do our thinking for us: still less can they teach us what to feel. But it is expressly the feeling which gives character to our work; and causes the production of one composer to differ so greatly from that of another, notwithstanding that the mere thinking part of the business is very much the same in both cases. Thus my conceptions on this subject may widely differ from those of another composer, yet both may be right. The reason why the majority of people remain ignorant of such matters is because it is not usual to disclose them : indeed, I do not remember having ever seen such confessions. Thus, I have something of the same embarrassment as Tchaikovsky when called upon to explain his fourth symphony; but I will overcome the reluctance in the hope of being of service; and lay some of these inward conceptions bare.

Once, a rebellious scholar asked me (he was one of those *enfant terribles* who cannot write in less than six flats or express their ideas in ordinary rhythms) why I so revered the Sonata-form.

"Because it is *true*," was my reply then; as it is my contention now. Once let us perceive this "truth" and we shall see how little the deviations from beaten track, either of Tchaikovsky or any other master, have to do with the spirit of the Sonata; in which alone its integrity consists.

The sonata enthralls us because of its truth to nature. To begin with, its repetition groups reflect the constant tendency in nature to return to a point of departure. Our very lives end as they began; in childishness and helplessness. With the termination of our school-days we are at the threshold of the "Durchführung" which is as the turmoil of our existence; its climax our zenith of success—or, mayhap, our moment of supremest suffering. But, whether borne along by happiness or misery, it is the flood-tide of our lives; the forerunner of calm; associated with either contentment or with resignation, as the case may be; as we return to pass the evening of our lives in meditation of the past.

But a single such analogy would constitute but a poor case in favour of the truth of this form. Its truth consists not in one, nor even in a multitude of such analogies; but in the fact that the Sonata is, in some shape or way, ever present to our eye and understanding. Every day of our lives has its dawn and its unfolding; its meridian and period of greater activity; after which its close in darkness as it began. And, just as is the mode of occupying our span of life is eternally subject to variation among untold millions of men, so is the receptivity of this form infinite and inexhaustible. The seasons of the year present us with a repetition of the same picture; either broadly, as in the varying landscape, or minutely, as in the separate life of every flower and insect. The difficulty is not to find analogies; but to escape them. Up and down the pages of the classics we find them, as in Shakespeare's sonata of the seven ages of man; in fact, I need but turn from the page at which I write to perceive a variety of material objects which, in their silent humble way, offer a like testimony. What wonder, then, that within this *cadre* should lie an endless sea of opportunities for tone-description? What wonder, then, that so inspired a writer as Tchaikovsky should, at one time, write a tone-poem, and at another a symphony? Depend upon it, the distinction about which it is now the fashion to make so much ado will, one day, pale into utter significance. All good music is absolute; as it is also descriptive.

Then again, as to deviations from correct form. Are our lives regulated to such a degree of mathematical perfection? And are we not perpetually overtaken by the unforeseen? To be true to itself the Sonata-form must recognise all this. The life to which I have alluded might, for example, instead of being allowed to ebb away in calm, be terminated by a sudden catastrophe. Would a tone-description to that effect be an infringement of form? Unfortunately, in such case, some precocious pedant would probably upstart with a lecture accusing the composer of lawlessness, as if he were a scholar at an exercise; and obviously unmindful of the effect which he is producing upon the minds of competents when they observe him thus madly rushing in where they would fear to tread.

IV

TCHAIKOVSKY AND NATIONALISM

THE unsophisticate student is quite an embarrassing personage to those who ardently favour the exclusive nationalism of the Russian composers opposed to the eclecticism of Tchaikovsky. Not only does eclecticism *per se* present itself to his mind in the light of an artistic virtue, but the necessity for any opposition between it and cultivation of the national element does not appear to him as obvious. This does not, however, prevent him from sympathising to the fullest extent, alike, with the love of art and with the patriotism of that devoted band and its adherents, who, headed by Balakirev, and impelled by the desire to elevate the musical importance of their country, have, since the formation of its plan, accomplished such great things. Neither does it prevent him from perceiving that their very exclusiveness has, after all, its utility.

But extremists, be they ever so well-intentioned, heroic or skilful, are never the most successful in scoring an actual advancement in this world; and, in the result, therefore, it may be fairly contended that the weak-kneed brother who could never be lured from his early loves, who adored Mozart to his latest breath, and whose eclecticism prevented him from seeing any inconsistency between the use of the "absolute" in classic form and that of the most daring programme innovations, has really accomplished much more on behalf of his country's musical fame than the whole of his compatriots put together.

The rare fund of national melody of which Russia is possessed constitutes the basis of this great movement; if indeed the musical upheaval which has been in progress since the time of Glinka may suitably be described by such a term. This composer, though appreciative of the beauty of folk-song generally, seems to have been fairly indifferent as to its origin; and in his "Romances" we accordingly find melodies emanating from Spain, side by side with those of his own land. Another composer of the same period, and of whom we now very seldom hear, was Verstovsky, then the director of the Moscow Opera. Just as the composers for the gipsy troops wrote music in the gipsy style, so Verstovsky gave a national colouring to his melodies, without laying the actually existing Russian melodies under contribution. In his "Tomb of Askold" there is a tune in polacca rhythm for the hero, quite in the style of those sung by the boatmen on the Volga; and a large proportion of the melodies in the whole work are in the minor, and reminiscent of old national airs. Besides that, there is a frequent recurrence of the song with choral response—another characteristic of Russian popular music; whether executed by the peasants, the gipsies or the Cossack companies. But, in all this, although a real impetus was being given to the national musical aspiration, it seems to have been fortuitous, as to the event. Moreover, it is not always easy to distinguish between time-honoured melody and that which has been written in imitation; so apt had the Russian composers of even fifty years ago become in echoing, through their own inspiration, the characteristics possessed by these tunes. And as, at that time, it was the habit of the Russian music publisher to call those airs "gipsy melodies" which had simply been written to order in the gipsy style, we have ample opportunity to observe that the gift for such imitations is a racial instinct. This, sooner or later, was bound to take form; for it never lacked more than the advantages to be derived from organization and development. The confederacy of Balakirev and his companions, therefore, is a culmination of this force; and furnishes the foreigner with a date with which to separate the two periods—that in which the latent instinct was unobservedly ripening, and that from which its cultivation has become a recognised national object and assiduously and designedly promulgated.

But we must not allow the rich imitative faculty of the Russian to divert our attention from the treasures of national melody which Russia undoubtedly possesses. It would, in fact, be difficult to discover any other portion of God's earth so richly endowed in this respect. The airs of other lands may

interest us by quaint melodic progressions, by peculiarity of cadence, or even by being constructed upon
scales no longer in vogue. But those of Russia,
whilst also possessing these features, have an added
rhythmic interest. It is no concern of our present
enquiry to trace this as an Asiatic emanation; but,
whatever may be its origin, it has familiarised the
Russian composer with an almost unexploited element
of musical beauty of which he has not been slow to
take advantage.

We see, therefore, that this, by its very nature, is,
although a national movement, one in which the whole
world is interested. For, if these traits be suitably
developed, not only will the Russian school be thereby
advanced, but the whole world will acquire a new
stage of musical enlightenment. And, though thoroughly appreciative of what has already been done,
we must ever remember that the mere quotation of
such melody, its incorporation with important work,
its adroit manipulation or even its successful development does not constitute this blessing. True it is
that Russian masters show the Kalmuck in all they
do, and that we feel that we are face to face with a
new school. But there are degrees of this feeling;
which sometimes become so faint that the characteristics for which we long are no longer perceptible. It
is in this respect that Tchaikovsky often fails; and,
were it not that what he gives us in exchange is so
apt to be extremely beautiful, our feeling towards
him would be different.

Now that we have awakened to these facts we begin

to take the view that it is the natural duty of a country so favourably situated as Russia to weld together
the European and the Asiatic. We see it embarked
upon the enterprise with an accumulated abundance
of folk-song; with a people the acuteness of whose
rhythmic perceptions impels them to unite the song
and dance; but above all with that indefinable racial
instinct in its composers which enables them effu-
sively to outpour thoughts of which the Westerns
would never dream.

In the meantime, however, I know not how to regard the eclecticism which is supposed to differentiate
Tchaikovsky from the nationalist composers otherwise than as a question of degree. In other words
they are all to some extent eclectics just as Tchaikovsky was to some extent a nationalist. The two
questions overlap; and, if Western influences are
abundantly evident in Tchaikovsky's work, does not
the Slav also make an effective appearance? We are
thankful that he drew so freely upon his own melodic
gift; but did he not also utilise the national store?
And, that the proceeding was heartfelt, is shown by
the fact that such resources are so frequently reserved
for important occasions. Thus, when he desired to
honour the memory of Nicolas Rubinstein he reverts
to the choral dance of the peasants at Vorobiev's
Hill; the andante of his first quartet is based upon
the singing of a workman; the finale of his fourth
Symphony contains a folk-song:—so does the
Serenade for Strings, the "1812" Overture, the
"Little-Russian" Symphony and so forth.

I have already alluded to Tchaikovsky's melodic gift; which, from our Western point of view, is the cause of his comparatively slight connection with the national movement. The divergence thus set up between himself and his compatriots might feasibly assume from their point of view the nature of a defection; whilst, from ours, it appears not only as a quality by which he is greatly endeared, but also the one of all others, perhaps, to cause his music to endure. But we cannot expect to find this opinion in his own writings. Avowedly, he seems to have regarded eclecticism as the dividing line; for, in his criticism of Rimsky-Korsakov, he expressly states what it is to be an eclectic in the best sense of the word, and in terms which sound like a musical confession of faith. He characterises the nationalists as free-thinkers; and prophesies (the wish being probably father to the thought) that Rimsky-Korsakov will ultimately leave them and become a faithful eclectic; which he thereupon expressly defines as "one who unites within himself strict classical forms and methods with that dazzling beauty of modern exposition wherein lies the imprescriptable quality of the new school." We have here no reference to the national store-house. The new school is on the contrary principally extolled for its technical equipment and reproved for not associating this with a more orthodox groove of thought.

But before concluding I have to refer to another source of distinction between Tchaikovsky and the others. A copious reference to folk-song may be much, and the Slav temperament may be more; but, even united, they are not everything. They are in fact of no avail unless consistent with the subject chosen; and might conceivably even amount to an intrusion and a disfigurement. A sincerely national composer of any country will be naturally impelled to choose *subjects* relating to his own land; and it must be confessed that in Tchaikovsky this feeling does not appear to have been very strong. The important tone-poems "Romeo and Juliet," "Francesca di Rimini," "Manfred," "Hamlet" and "The Tempest" eloquently testify to this fact, and leave in us the impression that his ambition tended in the direction of excellence alone. As he himself said when asked to state his ideals,—"My ideal is to become a good composer."

Such then are a few of the impressions caused by the consideration of Tchaikovsky in connection with the nationalist movement. The reader must not expect a verdict upon this question; because it is a case in which both parties are distinctly right. In art, just as in the material world, we are not all fitted for the same task. In every case wisdom consists in the pursuit of the natural vocation. If we Westerns in our capacity as onlookers are apt to regard Tchaikovsky with greater affection than the nationalists the preference is no reflection upon their splendid work. We even feel ourselves to be wrong occasionally: but our hearts are captivated though our reason may be unconvinced; and they bid us respond to the feeling and discard the thought. But does

this mean that we regard the onward Russian movement with less respect? On the contrary, the
achievements of Tchaikovsky provide us with a
happy halting-place in which to enjoy some of the
riches which have been already acquired. By-and-
bye when we have become sufficiently refreshed we
shall be ready to resume our journey and gratefully
to welcome the possession of any treasure accumulated in the meantime.

V

TCHAIKOVSKY AND INDIVIDUALITY

PRECIOUS indeed is the preservation of individuality to anyone aspiring to distinction as a composer. Better to be possessed of one good trait and that his own, than to be a participant in thousands of ideas which belong to other people. To imitate, for a pupil, is improving: for a composer, it is suicide.

I will not go so far as to say that those who sacrifice their individuality are insincere. Hero-worship sometimes assumes the form of mania; under influence of which we may innocently commit the greatest follies. But I do insist that the greatest protection against such errors is an absolute sincerity, a singleness of mind; and, not only the absence of all desire to appear to be what we are not, but a determination that we shall not appear otherwise than as we are, and, an equal determination to assert ourselves in that capacity.

This is precisely what I find admirable in Tchaikovsky. He adored Mozart; but did not imitate him. He could even find fault with him upon occasion;

and, indeed, it may be generally stated that his individuality enabled him to blame his friends or praise his enemies according to the immediate claim of the subject-matter upon his intellectual support.

The theory that a man's character is reflected in his music requires qualification; for it only applies to the composer who is entirely true to himself. In Tchaikovsky the emotional characteristics are those of a man who, though timid in many respects, was nevertheless resolved to live his *own* life; to state his own thoughts; and, for good or evil, so to commend himself to the judgment of his fellows.

Let the student who reads these lines reflect a little upon the change which would come over his own endeavours by dismissing the "*qu'en dira-t-on?*" What would have become of Wagner's doctrines had they been formulated in the mind of an Englishman? Physically courageous and shrewd in all matters of fact, our race yet lacks the moral courage to brook opposition in matters of art. Mere blatancy of assertion is not courage, but rather the contrary of it; and it is an unpromising feature of the new English school that it "whistles aloud to keep its courage up." The courage of the true hero is not deterred but increased in the face of opposition; and takes the form, not of assertion, but of achievement. Not the achievement which is usually called success (the word being used in the sense of popular appreciation) but that which lies in the *consciousness* of having done well; and in the belief that what is well done will be ultimately appreciated.

S

Tchaikovsky is *now* a popular composer; but what were his views of this popular appreciation when, scarcely beyond the threshold of his musical life, he reflects upon the struggles through which others have passed? I have no need to emphasise; in fact I should rather hesitate to employ terms so strong as those which Tchaikovsky selects in describing what he calls the "obtuseness, conventionality, ignorance and intrigue of that brutal collection of units which poets call the crowd." Then, again, he tells us that "the majority is always blind to fine gradations of artistic colouring. Bright tints, florid outlines and strong colouring—in short, whatever catches the eye—attracts their attention; but finished details and elegance of form escape the notice of these victims of blindness." Furthermore we have his opinion that whatever is worst in a work is that which catches the public ear in the first instance. And, finally, he holds up to admiration the heroism of those who "work out their own problem leaving the fruits of their labour for the pleasure and profit of future generations"; as contrasted with the egotism of those who strive only to astonish the world.

Herein is individuality; or, rather, a single phase of it, as exhibited by Tchaikovsky. Another consisted in his refusal to give either praise or blame merely because of the drift of general opinion; and in the courage with which he could give an account of the hope within him, notwithstanding all opposition. No amount of cajolement had any influence upon his opinion of Brahms; whom he considered "cold, dry, vague and nebulous." It must be admitted that Brahms was equally candid, however, for each master made a frank confession to the other that he did not like his music.

The sincerity of this is also shown in his opinion of himself as a conductor, and in his reply to the critic who described him as admirable in that capacity. He avows that, having taken up the bâton at forty-seven, he aspires merely to conduct his own works sufficiently well to pass muster. The subject lies outside the range of actual creation; but it emphasises his individuality that in faults and failings as in endowments he tolerated no illusions.

For these reasons therefore the music of Tchaikovsky may really be taken as an index of character; though that is not their most valuable application. What is far more important, especially for the young composer, to note is that it was by virtue of this individuality that his achievements were reached. Had he been dissuaded from its assertion his work might still have been technically excellent; but that is all. The human note would have been lacking. The human heart will not respond to the efforts of the music-maker; and, if we desire that our strains should be felt, we must first feel them ourselves. If we desire that they should, so to speak, "reach home," they must first come from home. Hearts, in fact, have a greater mutual sympathy than heads. We think variously; but we all feel very much alike. There is in Tchaikovsky the touch of nature which not only makes the whole world kin; but fills it with a gratitude, and a grateful remembrance.

How different is all this to the work of the imitator. And why is it that we, who are such pioneers in material affairs, should nevertheless feel the necessity of artistic leaning posts? There are, at this very present moment, ideas latent in the minds of Englishmen which, on account of being new, dare not be uttered. They will probably wait, and wait,—and still wait; until, say, some Teuton or Slav upsprings with their sudden discovery; when all the world will ring. But, for the remedy of this evil, Tchaikovsky gives us an excellent example. Let those who are capable of contemplating it aright take its lessons well to heart; and act accordingly.

I know that it may be urged that Tchaikovsky made occasional bids for the popularity he seemed to disdain; that the bright tints and florid colouring, which catch the eye, also made their impression upon his mind; as a means of success. But all this merely involves that he fell somewhat short of his own counsels of perfection—the common fate of all who strive. It does not touch the main lesson to be derived from his career, that he had, as he confesses, a very natural ambition to extend as far as possible his fame as a composer; especially as he combines with it the hope of successful service to the cause of Russian art. In one respect he knew too much. He had analysed the causes of popular assent too closely not to be tempted to their occasional use. But his opinion of the artistic value of the popular voice remained the same. When, for example, he is alluding to Serov's success with "Rogneda" he explains it on the ground that the public are not particular about æsthetics. All Serov's poverty of melody, want of organic sequence and weak declamation pass unnoticed; all his crude instrumentation and harmonies are forgiven; because he knew so well how to pile up sensational effects. Whatever may be the value of the criticism, its terms leave no doubt of Tchaikovsky's estimation of the approval of the crowd.

There are, however, many traits in Tchaikovsky's own music which prove that valuable as is his estimate of popular approval—the general truth of which can scarcely be disputed—it does not constitute the whole truth. To take only the conclusion of the "Pathetic" Symphony as an example; here is music for everyone. As he himself says, "there exist some rare compositions which possess the power of pleasing alike the educated and uneducated public." The existence of such compositions, however rare, proves their possibility; and the importance of the fact gives value to the enquiry why this should be. The reason is, that such works have always been produced by composers of strong individuality; and, even by them, at moments of intense earnestness. Herein lies the weakness of mere technical equipment, however perfect; that it cannot take the place of individuality, it cannot, so to speak, tell the composer what to say; but merely how to say it. There are some who look upon it as the mainspring of merely intellectual music; and so distinguish it from inspiration; through which the emotional is engendered. But, whether intellectual or emotional; whenever the trait of individuality is absent there will be no response.

Some of our younger musicians incline to regard an academic training as prejudicial to the individual character; but not only is Tchaikovsky himself an instance of the contrary, but his opinion was also contrary. Thus he considers that Glinka would have been a great symphonist had he not been deprived of a cultured environment. The point, however, is not one of any great importance to the student, for the unavoidable uniformity of academic training can never prevent individual effort; whilst on the other hand the emulation caused through being brought into contact with other aspirants is of the greatest advantage.

Of far greater importance is the necessity to keep our admiration of any one composer within reasonable bounds. This can easily be done by habiting ourselves to a wide range of literature. So surely as we allow the current of our predilection in favour of any one writer to become too strong, so surely shall we find ourselves unconsciously imitating him. The frequency with which this has already happened renders illustration unnecessary; but, without the warning, the treatment of individuality would not have been complete. Tchaikovsky's example does afford us much instruction in this instance; as his admiration was reserved for so few. With the exception of Mozart he was not fervent with regard to any composer. Of his praise of Beethoven there are many qualifications to be found in his criticisms; Bach, Handel, Chopin—all in turn come in for some degree of censure. Under such circumstances his individuality was never in any danger from this particular cause. As a critic he is in strong contrast to Schumann; whose opinions lost colour through the indulgence which prompted them. Tchaikovsky could easily consent to be silent, but not to mollify his terms; and in the result we can easily perceive that he was free of all desire to follow in the wake of others. This, however, is a luxury which few of us can be said to enjoy naturally; though it may be compassed by adopting reasonable precautions.

This brings the subject—if not to its end, at all events to the end of the space here allotted to it. It is one second to none in importance to the student; whilst the example of Tchaikovsky in its respect is one of the most fertile. Much might have been said of the traits of individuality exhibited in his works; so much so that the subject can only be satisfactorily completed by a reference to the various analyses. In these I shall, by means of direct illustration, draw the reader's attention to some mannerisms and weaknesses which, equally with points of merit, have to be included; but which leave our impression of Tchaikovsky in his relation to individuality, as above described, practically undisturbed.

VI

TCHAIKOVSKY AND CRITICISM

THERE are, as everyone knows, two kinds of critics; those who know nothing but how to write, and those who do know something but cannot write. As to the few—the extremely few—who combine literary with musical *creative* power there is, in the rare event of their electing to write criticisms, but one possible verdict: to wit, that they should know better. The gift of musical creation should be regarded as held in trust for the public benefit; and even the very best criticisms are dearly purchased at sacrifice of the opportunity for a new work. Therefore, much as I value Tchaikovsky's reviews, I would willingly exchange them for, say, another Trio, *à la* Op. 50. There are many of us whose vanity might easily extend to emulation of the former; but to whom that of the latter would not commend itself quite in the same way.

Yet, say what we will, the popular ear will ever be ready to attend to the man who has proved himself possessed of "Schaffungskraft." It does not follow that people invariably believe whatever he may happen to advance; but they certainly delight in hearing what he has to say—and that for various reasons. Such deliverances have not only a felicitous way of throwing side-lights upon work in which we are already interested, but also one of exhibiting underlying elements of value In reading them we feel conscious of there being something to read again; to ponder over, and finally to be the wiser for.

And so it is in the case of Tchaikovsky; whose sparse writings were so different in the eyes of their author to what they are in ours. Many of his sentences seem like sequences in rudimentary form. They seem to ask for development, seem to point to a necessary outcome; and, like the man who felt obliged to get out of bed in order to resolve a discord, we feel obliged to amplify them in order to reach a point of satisfaction. Thus, after all, it is not so much the criticism itself which interests us as what we may call the way-side observations. Like the mere narrative in the works of Thackeray the actual criticism, though ostensibly in the foreground, does not engage our thoughts equally with the philosophy which is interspersed; and thus it happens that, even in the event of holding contrary opinions, our pleasure is in no sense diminished.

In his judgment of contemporaries we need feel no surprise that Tchaikovsky should err. That one so different to them should, nevertheless, possess a fine discrimination as to their merit is not to be conceived. The consciousness of this prepares us for some surprises in the way of censure : censure, however, which always leaves us with the impression that it has been both kindly expressed and sincerely given. But, in his enunciation of principles the case is widely different. Whenever he starts to generalise we know that we are upon the point of receiving valuable advice.

Thus, while we may not feel inclined to go the whole way with him in his praise of Mozart, we can do no other than assent to the reasons which he gives for his admiration of "Don Giovanni." His observations, too, upon the influence of surroundings and the impress given, even to the greatest works, by peculiarities of the period at which they happen to be written are sufficient to inspire a whole volume of useful reflections. And, when he pictures Mozart's work as defying the hand of time, as awakening in us the same enthusiasm, and as touching our feelings as effectively, as in the days of our fathers and grandfathers before us, he does not present all this exuberance without the support of good reasoning. He is not even satisfied with appeal to the fact that Mozart's work, after a century's wear and tear, is now as fresh as ever; but he draws a methodical distinction between the mere technical details of a work and its essential substance. It is only the external features of a work which become old-fashioned. The depth of conception upon which it rests is born again with every succeeding generation. Time cannot change it, except in the sense of holding it up to greater veneration; for, when ages are between, we see it still more clearly. Nothing is so obsolete as that which has but recently gone out of date. A revival of the fashions of fifty years ago would be both offensive and ludicrous. The aspect of them would still be in the memory of some old inhabitants; who would unconsciously mix up the fashions themselves with the persons they remembered to have seen so bedecked. Those of two centuries ago have now a romantic interest; notwithstanding that, in their own day, they were held in no greater respect than ours. The moral of all this is that, if an artistic creation can live for one century, it can easily do so for twenty; this being pre-eminently a case in which it is " le premier pas qui coûte."

I can imagine certain readers interposing the observation at this juncture that the bulk of these principles might have been profitably applied to some of Tchaikovsky's own work. Perhaps so. And it would be ridiculous in me to pretend to any certain knowledge of the power of survival contained even in his finest creations. In such matters, however, experience is largely capable of strengthening our force of observation; and in this particular case it directs our attention to two qualities possessed by the leading works of Tchaikovsky in a very remarkable degree.

The first of these is an intense *human feeling*. His subjects are evidently selected with the deliberate intention that this shall be so; and cases where they are not declared are no exceptions. The only difference is in *us :* for we know the one, and not the other. The intensity of human feeling presented by the subjects is reflected in that of instrumentation and of harmony. Nothing but a faulty development could militate against the durability of such work.

The second of these is abundant *melodic charm*. Not only is this quality the one of all best fitted to stand the test of time; but it is so happily united to the glow of harmony and to the fire of instrumentation that, between the two, there is an ebb and flow which is perpetually renewed. I do not mean to the individual listener; of whom I should be very much inclined to say the same as Tchaikovsky did of Henselt: "he is nobody." I am thinking of succeeding periods; and of the power of these works to attract under all circumstances. For the time may quite conceivably come when even the most gorgeous instrumentation may pall. There may come a survival of the musical simple life: not the musical life of our fathers, but our own; divested of the superfluous. Ye gods! what a clearance of useless work will that day furnish, should it ever come. It is fearful to think of the consequences of such a "jüngste Gericht" upon the mountains of nonsense by which we are surrounded. In that dread hour even the finest work will be in danger; unless its clamour and its glamour are atoned for by melodic charm. In this respect Tchaikovsky has armed himself in a two-fold manner.

There are various gleams of such thought in Tchaikovsky's criticisms. Thus, in the case of Schumann, he has much to say which is derogatory; but which does not cancel his belief in the immortality of the work. History, he tells us, has not yet taken cognisance of Schumann : only in the distant future will this be possible. The *influence of time* upon musical creations seems to be ever present to his mind. Thus, Beethoven's seventh symphony "shines with the same radiance as when it astonished all Europe in 1812"; at which date Beethoven first took it from his portfolio. Haydn has "survived from the last century with difficulty." His ideal composer is one who quits the arena of life leaving the fruits of his labour for future adjudgment; just the contrary of Serov, for example, and in whose "Rogneda" Tchaikovsky says that the popularity of the numbers is in inverse ratio to their value. He had evidently no faith in the immortality of Berlioz's work; and retained always a keen eye to the classifications of history. Shall we then suppose that he was indifferent to the future of his own work; or that he did not take the utmost pains to infuse into it those qualities the durability of which he had so accurately observed in others?

Another feature of Tchaikovsky's criticism is the note of caution which pervades it. He is not demonstrative on the subject either of Wagner or of Brahms. Perhaps, on the contrary, the reader might deem it fairly demonstrative to apply to Wagner the term "prejudiced and obstinate, richly endowed but narrow-minded German." But context does not lend much strength to the expression, which is merely expletive. At the risk of being the first victim, I recommend to those of my readers who are prone to indulge in the perusal of criticism the following recipe.

Take a bundle of criticism; and first carefully

shake out all the expletives. The removal of these will enable you to perceive the facts, if any. Be sure that the facts are really such, as there are so many formations prepared in their resemblance; and that the opinions, if any, are not soiled by the intrusion of any foreign motive. You will then be prepared to form a judgment.

But what has this to do with the spirit of caution? A great deal. As expletives really mean nothing they are the most excellent means of holding a matter in suspense; and, depend upon it, not Tchaikovsky alone, but every one of us has more or less the habit of indulging in them whenever our minds are not quite made up. Their use is therefore a clear exhibition of caution; as is that, also, of generalities. We unconsciously seek refuge in these havens of rhetoric, when on dangerous ground. We feel something like Tchaikovsky at the Gewandhaus, a fear and trembling lest we "do something to blush for"; and, in our embarrassment, we have recourse either to neutral, or to exuberant, or to universal expression. This may not be so desirable as exhaustive criticism; but it is far better than making a mistake, and it still further exceeds in desirability the act of saying what we do not mean. Tchaikovsky could never be converted to either Brahms or Wagner. On the other hand he had no desire to run counter to the feelings of others. He expressed himself within the limits of this mindfulness; and there it ended.

The regretful moment has now arrived for me to part, for the present, with this delightful subject. My

endeavour has not been directed to any increase in
the estimation of Tchaikovsky by the merely technical musician. The latter has his standard; and,
armed with precedents, and compass, and rule, and
all his well-known formidable equipment he will proceed to judgment in spite of what I, or any one else,
may say. He wants the element of love infused into
his veins; of the love which is blind, and will take
no cognisance of those blemishes which he is at pains
to discover; and without the knowledge of which he,
also, would be far happier. My hope is to have succeeded in inducing the generous reader, without being
oblivious of his faults, to regard Tchaikovsky from the
the higher stand-point : from the stand-point of a man
who, in tonal-language, made himself the spokesman
of his fellows—and especially of their sufferings—
whose ambition it was to touch the heart rather than
to court the understanding. Those who address the
heart have a large and sympathetic audience; as well
as one that varies extremely little from age to age.
It is this feature in Tchaikovsky's music which
emboldens us to the belief that, for ages yet, it will
convey the same message; and ever meet with the
some response.

SUPPLEMENT (B).

ANALYSES OF SELECTED WORKS.

I

PIANO TRIO, OP. 50

I.—PEZZO ELEGIACO.   II.—TEMA CON VARIAZIONI.
III.—FINALE

THE first of these divisions is a lovely Sonata movement based upon a leading theme of elegiac character; befitting the composer's intention to honour the
memory of his departed friend, N. Rubinstein.

Its peculiar value to the student lies in the fact of
happily combining symmetry of form with rhapsody
of utterance.   People so usually suppose these two
characteristics to be at variance that the reader should
welcome any instance tending to show that exuberance
of feeling is unrestrained by the conditions of design.

For the purpose, therefore, of enabling this lesson

to be completely utilised I will here devote a few words to the *construction* of this movement; and show how its various bearings reveal themselves upon analysis—notwithstanding the highly emotional character of the ideas expressed—to be in complete accord with sonata-form requirements.

FIRST SECTION.	Bars.	RETURN GROUPS.	Bars.
Subject 1 - - - -	60	Subject 1 - - - -	41
„ 2 - - - -	26	„ 2 - - - -	26
„ 3 - - - -	24	„ 3 - - - -	24
Song group - - -	32	Song group - - -	32
(logically evolved from Subject 3.)		**CODA.**	
		Epitome of Durchführung in slackened pulsation, followed by revival of new subject on dominant pedal - - - -	
DURCHFUHRUNG.			
Thematic work to climax -	51		
Intermezzo, leading to new Subject (designed for recall in the Coda) -	71		63
		CADENCE.	
		(Tonic pedal) continued slackening of pulsation shown by reminiscence of Subject 1 in augmentation - - - -	29

If we examine this distribution carefully we shall arrive at a better understanding of some of Tchaikovsky's recorded observations. Take for example the happy idea of epitomising the Durchführung for coda purposes; of causing this operation to consist in removing the quicker rhythmic pulsations and of thus gradually preparing the mind for the mournful refrain of the leading subject in augmentation;

T

amounting really to a prolonged cadence. All this is purely an instance of the very quality which he attributes to Schumann; of "introducing new modes of procedure without departing from classical form."

If Tchaikovsky had written this movement in express illustration of the various proportions desirable in a sonata movement he could scarcely have adopted any better scheme. Thus, the Durchführung is slightly shorter than the total first exposition, the repetition groups being also somewhat abridged; but the abridgement of the latter is confined to that of the leading subject; evidently on account of this being destined to return in augmentation at the cadence. Then, again, the epitomization of Durchführung for coda might have somewhat distorted the form, but this is effectively guarded against by the new subject on pedal bass; tending, in the one case, to the return of the subjects, and, in the other, to the cadence. The logical evolution of song-group is also a feature; though it really belongs to that of the choice of the subjects. These are precisely what sonata subjects should be: simple and dignified, yet containing the mainsprings of passion and admitting of ready contrapuntal elaboration. In this connection it is easy to trace Tchaikovsky's resolve to produce a work of serious and systematic development; for such large employment of melodic progression *by grades* would be immediately taken by every contrapuntist as a sign that the composer "meant business"; and that he did not intend to be disturbed by any inversions or complications which might afterwards occur.

The subjects open as under : —

the fact being thus exhibited that the first subject
alone is in A minor; the remaining subjects being all
in one other tonality : that of the dominant, and
therefore major. The peculiar prominence thus con-
ferred upon the leading theme is no doubt intentional;
but the similarity of key of the remaining subjects
throws a light upon the composer's probable *modus
operandi*, which seems to have been some such formula
as here subjoined : —

by means of which several advantages are secured.
Firstly, there is sympathy without identity of rhythm,

secondly, there is the power of interchange of subjects for purposes of dialogue; and last, but not least, there is a reserve of material for almost endless contra-puntal devices.

The first subject is announced by 'cello in a four-bar strain, extended to eight by violin repetition in sub-dominant. The eight-bar complement is for *ensemble* with an interrupted cadence of three bars terminating with arpeggio figuration for 'cello; which is afterwards retained as accompaniment, while the piano repeats the whole quasi-16 bars in massive chords; the time-interstices afforded by the rhythm being filled in by a free violin melody. Tchaikovsky is always happy in his interrupted cadences; which, though the musician may regard them only as adroit workmanship, always charm the listener by appearing to be an integral portion of the phrase. The latter, in this instance, concludes as under : —

We now meet the first instance of a deliberately close adherence to sonata structure in the utilization of the first subject's capability of being completely harmonized by its own triad. The result of this is that, instead of modulating *within itself*, the fact of its complete and massive repetitions representing only one chord enables these to appear as units in a harmonic progression upon a grand scale; while the detail of all attendant figuration acquires thereby all the inherent charm of sequence. Such are some of the advantages resulting from the choice of a simple subject. By-and-bye the pulsation quickens in anticipation of second subject; but here it must be confessed that Tchaikovsky has not been so successful. Indeed his work seems somehow to recall his own censure of the "unsightly join formed by pasting thoughts together." I have already shown that the first subject stands aloof from all the others; which may account for the awkwardness of the transition in this case. However, taking the matter as it stands, we find ourselves ushered into the key of the dominant by a syncopated stringendo; the gain in speed being retained by the substitution of Allegro for the previous moderato.

The second subject possesses little interest in itself; and, considered as a melody, would certainly not testify much to Tchaikovsky's gift. But, if it originated in some such formula as I have suggested, the case would be different; as that would account for the bald manner of its announcement, and for the fact that all elaboration is held back. Every composer who has been through these experiences knows that those who have little resource are beset by an inclination to immediately display whatever they possess. But, where a wealth exists, there is often an indifference with regard to it; and its display, is, in any case, deferred.

The third subject is first announced by piano alone; and occasion may here be taken to remark that, throughout the work, the piano part, though masterly in conception, is frequently disfigured by instances of clumsy figuration. This, however, only affects the performer; as the result, with the exception of being occasionally a little ponderous, is satisfactory.

This third subject, consisting entirely of grades, is of course toyed with, contrapuntally. It canons in dialogue between violin and 'cello; and, finally, evolves a phrase which proves to be the material for song-group. This logical evolution is worthy of special notice, as it gives the finishing touch to the unity which characterises the whole movement. It is, moreover, rightly placed for purposes of the sonata-form; for the same process which evolves also develops, and enables the composer to reach a climax just sufficient to prepare for his diminuendo and thus to end first section.

In this way we arrive at the point where, in the old days, the repeat would have been inserted; and probably in this case it was also inserted in obedience to form, even although afterwards taken out in obedience to fashion. The only landmark in the work as published is the reversion to tonic key and preparatory meditation on the leading theme; quite the orthodox departure. The student, however, is recommended duly to repeat at this point, if he wishes to thoroughly master the work.

In every sonata the Durchführung is precisely the portion least open to criticism from the merely technical side. It has been the custom to allow far too great latitude in its respect; and the abuse of this liberty is a disfigurement in numberless cases. Here, however, the development is *real;* the climax being reached by methods which convince by their sincerity. The principal formal feature worthy of remark is the introduction of a new subject, destined to re-appear in the coda; for which purpose it is peculiarly appropriate, being constructed on dominant-pedal. It is a charming instance of Tchaikovsky's gift in the treatment of simple means, as the reader will perceive.

Sadly working its way it tapers off at last into the thinnest possible streak of sound; then a momentary silence and the parent key is resumed. The piano part is devoid of elaboration, the 'cello sighs a disconsolate answer to it at every bar; only the violin takes up the melody, and that upon its fourth string. In this sad home-coming we know not which to admire most, the sincerity of Tchaikovsky's intention, the inspiration of his work or the marvellous receptivity of the sonata-form which can so lend itself to every human purpose. The student is recommended particularly to note that Tchaikovsky has not thought it necessary to resume a note-for-note repetition of the first subject. He treats it in accordance with his intention—a method which generally results in the first part of the repetition being somewhat different to the commencement of the movement.

Little more remains to be said of this division. The ordinary transpositions follow; and thus, all being in order, we arrive at the Coda, which, as already described, consists principally of dominant pedal. The major is retained until just before the resumption of the first subject in augmentation. This takes place upon a tonic pedal diminuendo; and so the movement concludes.

II.—TEMA CON VARIAZIONI

This division is, to say the least, no less intimately associated with the intention of the work than the preceding. Not only is the theme itself reminiscent of a happy day spent with N. Rubinstein; consisting, it is said, of the very melody sung at the latter's invitation by the peasants at Vorobiev; but each variation is supposed to have been written by Tchaikovsky with special reference to some characteristic of his departed friend. It would be both difficult and undesirable to penetrate into such matters; besides

which the reader can well afford to confine himself to
the musical merit of such fine variations.

The rhythm is (2 X 3)+(2 X 3)+(2 X 4) ; or, otherwise, 6 + 6 + 8, considering the latter numbers as mul-
tiples of 2; as the whole theme consists of two-bar
phrases.   It runs thus : —

Ex. 5.

Russian composers are so adroit in the imitation of
their own national melodies that it is often difficult
to separate the crude air from its artistic presentment.
If the above is really an untreated folk-song its refinement is remarkable; for the symmetry afforded
by the continual two-bar phrases is just sufficiently

disturbed by the introduction of a new multiple to impart an exquisite grace to the whole.

Var. I. is a mere elaboration; clever and musicianly, but that is all. The violin sings the entire melody; the piano accompanies with a continual flow of semiquavers; rhythmical interstices being filled in meditatively by 'cello.

In Var. II. the time is changed to 3-4; the melody in its new rhythm being given to 'cello with highly interesting accompanying violin figures. But to me it seems that this variation contains some hidden meaning, for the reason that nothing is gained to the melody by the change of tempo; which seems to have been made simply to accommodate a new melody contained in the piano part. What the interest may be from this point of view I cannot say; but musically the effect is second-rate; for the piano part is of Tchaikovsky's heaviest description, and constitutes, with the 'cello, too great a weight against the violin figures for a perfect *ensemble.*

But with Var. III. a higher interest sets in. Pizzicato chords for both strings; light, when used alternately—emphatic when combined. The whole in amplification of a new version of the theme, brilliantly delivered by piano. The master is shown in the new material afforded us without any loosening of our grip upon the original theme.

Var. IV., in relative minor, changes the rhythm to 4 X 6; each alternate four-bar phrase being a replica of the preceding, but with a *tournure* adapting it to new requirements. The counterpoint is admirable;

but it shows Tchaikovsky again seeking safety in grades; as for instance : —

Ex. 6.

etc.

This procedure is, however, no fault; and it is only mentioned because constant recourse to it becomes a mannerism. But Tchaikovsky is practical; for these gradual progressions are both easy for the listener to follow and for the performer to execute, so that if the student feels inclined to imitate him in these respects he may fairly count upon reaping the same advantages.

We proceed, with very novel effect, to Var. V., *attaca*. The strings have a perfect fifth in monotone practically throughout the entire variation. It is accompanied by a bell-like florid version of the theme for piano, starting in diminution, but with a fastidious prolongation of the cadences giving, as in Var. III., a new rhythmical effect while still holding fast to the original theme. The tonality is C sharp major; and, at the conclusion, the 'cello, having sustained the tonic note throughout, continues to reiterate it (this time alone and in syncopation) the intention being to use it as the third in the chord of A and so pass on to the Tempo di Valse in that key. It seems to me

that such a tawdry effect should have been beneath
Tchaikovsky's dignity; but it is well atoned for in
the succeeding variation.

Var. VI. is delightfully graceful and possesses an
earnestness of purpose which is not immediately
apparent. We are at first attracted only by the flow
of the Valse movement; but shortly we have a sudden
transition to the key of C and a new distribution.
The piano now takes the valse-melody whilst the
strings deliver the original theme in unison.

Ex. 7.
Piano.

Theme (Strings in Unison).

Piano (bass elaborated.)

This variation is of considerable development, in
perfect form; and, by its final diminuendo effectively
paves the way for the entrance *ff*, of Var. VII., in 3-2.
The latter is a pompous declaration of the original
theme in which unison rushes of the strings come in to
complete the rhythmic outline. The effect, though
good, is scarcely novel, and therefore calls for little
remark; but the student will again observe the
counterpoint by grades as in the last example.

Var. VIII. is a tonal fugue of the good old sort.
There is no attempt at modernization: a thing to be
thankful for. All good honest work, clear as noon-

day and gloriously effective withal. For once, Tchaikovsky's inaptness in piano-writing is rather welcome;
for he has been content to let the hands play at an
octave apart throughout, with the result that the piano
part is the natural base of the structure. The fugue
is therefore in three real parts; a trio in the sense in
which good old Bach understood things. Then,
there are several strettos; a good organ point; (which
we should naturally expect knowing Tchaikovsky's
weakness in that direction) and perhaps the only
reproach to be made is that his *penchant* for the use
of grades in contrapuntal work causes him to use
figures with which we are already somewhat too familiar. Let the worst be said, however, it is a fine variation; and it is well placed, before the hushed lament,
con sordini, which now follows.

Var. IX. is principally characterised by the piano
part in which a very faint and rapid arpeggio ampli-
fies each sustained note of the dirge, and adds force
to the pathos and earnestness of its expression. The
sorrowful tale is first told by the strings alternately;
but they afterwards unite in a manner so suggestive
and so true to nature that it seems a pity that this
variation was not allowed to die away in the same
spirit; the feeling evoked being too real and sincere
to admit of any intrusion. Instead of that, however,
we have a modulation into the incongruous key of A
flat, for the purpose of introducing—a mazurka.

Var. X., the mazurka in question, must surely have
been written separately. Its faint connection with
the theme is scarcely sufficient to justify its presence

in the work at all: in addition to which, commencing as it does, with an uninteresting piano solo of 47 bars and leading afterwards practically to nothing, it seems difficult to regard it otherwise than as a disfigurement. Assuming the object to have been to disperse all clouds of melancholy, this may be admitted to have been accomplished; though not so well as might have been. Moreover, the silly reiteration of A flat, changing enharmonically to G sharp for the purpose of introducing the next variation in the key of E is not only a trick which has been worked to death, but it has been already used once before in this very work, in passing from Var. V. to the " Tempo di Valse."

Var. XI. calls for little remark, being merely the theme in a new dress appropriate for the suggestion of a dialogue in diminuendo with which to terminate the work. For, although the Finale is supposed to be a variation and coda, it really constitutes a separate movement. With No. 11, therefore, the variations terminate to all intents and purposes; and in spite of defects they must be pronounced to be one of the finest specimens of such work ever produced.

III.—FINALE

This movement must be considered apart from the Andante with which it concludes, and which is really the epilogue of the entire work. Its general character is contrapuntal; its style risoluto, with a semiquaver motion in Allegro, only slightly relieved; its form a close approximation to sonata—so much so that with a little indulgence it might be so construed. In

rhythm the eight-bar period predominates and is subject to very slight interruption of cadence, but there
are many instances of the two-bar phrase, due to the
introduction of reminiscences of the theme. The contrast afforded by the second subject

Ex. 8.

would have been insufficient but for the epilogue to
follow. This consists of the theme *fff* delivered by
the strings in unison against a very powerful and
elaborate piano arpeggio accompaniment. Commencing in upper octave the melody gradually
descends: pausing meditatively and for a length of
time upon the dominant; and finally subsiding into a
short funeral march. In this the violin and 'cello announce the original leading theme precisely as at the
beginning of the work. There is no cadence for
strings, the last note of which is that of the 'cello,
which sadly dies away upon the dominant, leaving
the piano to make its way to the conclusion alone.
This is done, perdendosi, on the mere triad; and there
is silence. Surely as we close the score we must feel
a reverence, as well as an admiration, for the composer.

II

PIANO CONCERTO IN B FLAT MINOR, OP. 23

I.—ALLEGRO.   II.—ANDANTINO SEMPLICE.
III.—ALLEGRO

I.—*(a). Allegro non troppo e molto maestoso.*
(b). Allegro con spirito.

THERE are two questions affecting this truly remarkable work in respect of which further enlightenment
would be extremely desirable. The first is:—" To
what extent was a disinclination to its revision created
in Tchaikovsky's mind by N. Rubinstein's original
hostility to it?" And the second:—" How far was
N. Rubinstein's subsequent enthusiasm in its favour
due to a desire to make amends for his exaggerated
criticisms?"

With regard to the first of these we know that
although, in his anger, Tchaikovsky vowed he would
not alter a single note of the work, he nevertheless did
revise and to a great extent re-write the solo part for
the edition of 1889. This proceeding is highly sug-

gestive when taken in connection with his previous refusal even to entertain any such idea; and it was not to be expected from human nature under such circumstances that the revision could prove as copious as it might have been in default of any feeling of *amour propre*. On the other hand the inherent beauty of its material, its novelty of treatment, and perhaps also the grand opportunity for technical triumph which it affords might well console Rubinstein for any reticence with regard to other features of the work; especially when aided by the reflection that, in the first instance, his strictures had undoubtedly gone too far. These two considerations must inevitably occur to those who study the Concerto impartially: that is to say, with neither the predisposition of the listener to be carried away by characteristic beauty, nor that of the virtuoso to regard a good field for personal display as the be all and end all of the matter.

The popularity of the work does not rest entirely upon the pleasure afforded to the listener. Not he alone but all the various parties to its production are propitiated. Even the most subordinate orchestral part is integral to the work; which for that very reason, stands almost alone among concertos and requires an explanation of its peculiar features before we can proceed to examine its detail.

The student will scarcely need to be reminded of the time when it was considered *de rigueur* to set forth in an orchestral introduction the thematic material of the entire first movement; and when the

U

entries of the solo (usually three in number and of which the third naturally aimed at the greatest intensity both of effect and display) were the signal for the orchestra to subside into mere accompaniment.

Nous avons changé tout cela; and, long before Tchaikovsky, it was already the custom to proceed with the business of the solo, if not immediately, at all events after a very short delay. Like most changes of the kind, however, this innovation produced effects which were not at first contemplated. No doubt, some of the old introductions were somewhat tedious; though that in itself was scarcely a reason for rushing at once to the opposite extreme. But, as reactions *will* be reactions in spite of all which we may urge, the critic is now called upon to reconcile himself to an altered state of things; for the modern concerto is something radically different from its predecessor.

It will be interesting to observe how what was apparently a simple innovation in the first instance led to structural changes. Formerly the solo entry took place after the subjects had been already set forth. It was therefore not called upon for a delivery of them; the composer being free either to dilate upon them or to adopt an entirely new departure. The endurance of the soloist was also then something to be economised; but now there is no need of the relief afforded by an orchestral tutti. On the contrary the muscular prowess of the present-day virtuosi not only knows no limit, but the greater the call upon it the greater the eagerness to prove that it is equal to the demand.

The natural result of all this is that the solo part of a Concerto does not now, as formerly, stand apart from the orchestra; but, on the contrary, strives with it in unfolding the work. It is as it were an orchestral part—an important one doubtless—but still as much an orchestral part as that of any line we might select from top to bottom of the score, the effect upon the composition itself being simply enormous; as the solo part is only occasionally—one might almost say accidentally, self-sufficient and requires continually to be taken in conjunction with the score before its meaning can be ascertained or appreciated.

It will be obvious that these remarks must necessarily apply to different works in varying degrees. Let the student therefore assume that to the Concerto of Tchaikovsky now under consideration they apply in their full force, and he will be somewhat prepared to approach that work from a correct point of view; which implies that he will not expect observance of the old regulations under such altered conditions.

The composer leads off with a pompous introduction in D flat, distinct from the first movement, although in deference to the tonality in which the work is cast it is prefaced by a few bars commencing in that key (B flat minor). This short section has sometimes been referred to as a subject of the first movement; but the reason for this is all the more difficult to conceive as its theme, given below, is never afterwards referred to.

Ex. 9.

The interruption of cadence (marked *) is an instance of Tchaikovsky's happy manner of imparting grace to the conclusion of his sentences. The Concerto so abounds with examples of this that it is impossible to do more than refer to them generally; but the student is urged to rhythmise the entire work for himself, when, if he aspires to musical creation and especially to the writing of a concerto he will soon discover the importance of the interrupted cadence in "provoking" as it were new departures for technical display. This feature of Tchaikovsky's Concerto is not only a revelation; but an answer to those who deem its rhythms to be erratic.

The announcement of the leading theme at once bears out my observation respecting the want of self-sufficiency in solo parts under the new conditions; the melody reaching the listener in this way:—

Ex. 10.
Piano.

Orch.

Such distributions naturally relegate the solo part to a mere position in the orchestra; though whether this be a defect or otherwise is a question entirely depending upon our standard of judgment, and therefore one in which I leave the student to make his own choice. His concern should lie principally with the dangers attending such a method—dangers which have unquestionably hampered Tchaikovsky in the present instance, for it cannot be seriously contended that there is a grain of inspiration in the whole first development of the leading theme, or in the approach to the second subject. Upon its arrival, however, the latter makes ample amends. It is in A flat; and is first announced by wood wind and horns in the following manner:—

Ex. II.

exhibiting Tchaikovsky's favourite melodic device of the under-changing note in the two opening bars. This, however, is a mannerism of which we never seem to tire; its application being made with invariable grace.

But we have now arrived at a very curious feature of the score in the shape of an unobtrusive passage for strings, con sordini; of identical note-succession with the third subject of the movement. I shall have occasion, in connection with the second movement, to say something of Tchaikovsky's habit of giving a foretaste of subjects to come; and therefore content myself with mere mention in the present instance.

The development of second subject is highly elaborate and leads us to a pompous episode in which the orchestra largely figures; and which, when recurring in the return portion of the movement serves as a sort of diving plank for the principal solo display—a purpose for which it is well fitted by its chromatic character.

Ex. 12.

In the first instance however the third subject is immediately introduced, which shows Tchaikovsky to have been not altogether unmindful of traditional arrangements. Another circumstance of the same description is that after due statement the third sub-

ject is allowed to terminate in A flat and is even
marked off by a pause, prior to the new departure.

Ex. 13.

This subject exhibits another of Tchaikovsky's pre-
dilections—the pedal bass; in the use of which he
must certainly be admitted to have been a past master.
At its conclusion we have arrived at a point corresponding with the free portion of a sonata; and the
working which now follows gives a good account of
itself in that capacity. Firstly, there are reminiscences
of the various subjects for orchestra alone; followed
by a display of the solo instrument introducing new
material, with which the various forces of the orchestra are, as it were, one by one induced to sympathise.
To begin with, the wood wind and horns are lured
into the circle; then the strings; and finally the brass;
in each case the adhesion being given bodily, as if
the members of each section had been previously
debating among themselves whether or no to subscribe
to the new announcements and at the last moment
had quite suddenly arrived at the decision to do so.
The drum is easily tempted to contribute its roll by
the pedal bass of the strings; which commences somewhat early in the struggle, and which consequently
affords time and opportunity for a splendid crescendo
with the grand tutti ushering in the return.

A question now arises as to the merit of Tchaikov-

sky's novel and fantastic treatment of the opening
theme. To avoid a note-for-note repetition of it may
be a proof of fertility of invention; but to invest it
with so much obscurity that we arrive at second subject almost without having had opportunity to realise
that a return is in progress is quite another matter.
This does not, of course, apply to the student with
the score before him; but an unprepared listener hearing the work for the first time would undoubtedly be
at a disadvantage.

In other respects the return groups afford us little
new material for observation. As already stated the
chromatic episode quoted above (transposed, of course,
and otherwise adapted to fit the occasion) provides
the point of departure for a magnificent solo display,
by leading up to reiterated chords of G flat; in which
the piano first alternates with the orchestra and is
finally left alone. The solo concludes with an
elaborate cadenza, of which the final undulations are
utilized as a diminution of third subject; in course of
which the latter enters with the wood wind. Meanwhile the solo instrument continues the same progression, increasing its motion and embroidering the
rising sequences of the strings until its strivings
gradually cause it to reach the tonic harmony when
with a few bravura chords of the entire forces the
movement is at an end.

The impression with which it leaves us is that, even
though there may be some things to regret, there are
infinitely more to admire and to enjoy; and, upon the
whole, there can be no question of the movement

otherwise than as one brimful of charm and
originality.

II.—ANDANTINO SEMPLICE

As this movement is of pastoral character we have,
naturally, important parts for the wood wind. For
the same reason the second oboe and flute fall practically into abeyance; the timbre of those instruments
being entirely required for melodic utterances. The
clarinets are, of course, freely used; but the bassoons
mostly contribute to the harmony alone, the one
melodic point given to this instrument being of no
great importance, and being apparently introduced
merely for the purpose of reserving effect for the
cantabile of two violoncelli soli later on. It joins the
first clarinet in octaves, however, in a dialogue with
viola and 'cello; playing also in octaves. This occurs
in connection with the melody of the prestissimo
which occupies the middle portion of the movement:
and which will be presently referred to. The instrumentation is so light that two horns might fairly have
done all the work required, whilst the parts for tym-
pani, two trumpets and three trombones each consist
of one note for the entire movement.

After four bars of strings pizz: (marking half-bar
pulsations) the flute announces the theme, the pizzicati
continuing and forming the only accompaniment.
Such simplicity scarcely prepares us for the richness
to follow; but a foretaste of which is close at hand,
as here subjoined.

The student will notice the interrupted cadence respecting which no more need now be said. It will be sufficient to observe that in four bars more we have arrived at what appears to be a second subject but which is rather to be considered as an elaborate counterpoint to the first. These four bars have a special interest; being a notable example of Tchaikovsky's habit of giving a foretaste of subjects to come. Thus, in a short time they furnish the sugges-

tion for the prestissimo already alluded to; and it has
always seemed to me that in some way this practice
was connected with his ideal conceptions of form—a
subject which I have treated in a separate chapter.
The effect is naturally inclined to appear fragmentary
to those who do not rightly understand it; which is
not surprising when we remember that the composer
evidently intended something of this kind, for there
is a sudden cessation of the solo instrument coupled
with the adoption of a totally new instrumentation.
Had he desired to merge this phrase into the surroundings such would scarcely have been the case.   The
important bearing of these points upon the construction of the movement compels me to adduce examples.

Ex. 15.

These are two of the four bars in question, the other
two being for the solo instrument and modulating into
D; introducing the counterpoint alluded to which is
exclusively for wood-wind.   In giving the student an
example of this I have taken the liberty of appending
the original subject which he must remember is not in
the score and is merely given in order to show how
one is in reality a counterpoint of the other, by presenting the two in combination.

The semi-quaver motion is at this point taken up by the solo, the drone fifth of the two bassoons being transferred to 'cello and bass whilst all the wood discourse in turn upon the two opening bars of the theme. So far so good; but who can deny that the entry of the two violoncelli soli is very awkwardly managed, or fail to regret that such a blur should have failed to pass under the composer's revision? Let the student judge for himself. The mind of the listener is comfortably settled in the key of D when the bar marked * occurs; which to make matters worse is a merely mechanical addition to the rhythmical phrase.

Ex. 17.

Two Violoncelli Soli.   etc.

The semi-quaver motion of the solo instrument continues as an accompaniment of the cantabile of the
'celli which is shortly well contrasted with the
delivery of the same subject by oboe solo. This
leads to the same interruption of cadence as in the
first instance; and thus introduces the prestissimo
intermezzo in the manner already described.

Some idea of the banality of the melody upon
which the latter is based as well as that of the style
of the elaboration adopted for the solo part may be
gathered from the following example:

Ex. 18.

but notwithstanding this triviality the result in
Tchaikovsky's hands is charming. Of course it may
be urged that this charm is entirely due to the instrumentation and that otherwise such poor material
would be devoid of interest. That may be so; but,
as matters stand, the interest is there. The solo part
does not now concern itself with the melody; being
engaged upon elaborative work mostly in moto perpetuo. A noticeable feature is that whenever it is
left free it immediately betakes itself to the four bars
of which so much has been said, until a sudden chord
by the entire orchestra starts it off upon a cadenza the
cross-hand arrangements of which remind one of the
fashions of sixty or eighty years ago. Tchaikovsky
had such a weakness for this antiquated style that he
sometimes seems to have worked on the principle of
never allowing a passage to be played by one hand
if it could possibly be taken by two. Still, the object
of the cadenza is attained—that of gracefully returning to the original theme, which with a new instrumentation and a beautifully graduated diminuendo,
brings the movement to a close.

III.—ALLEGRO CON FUOCO

This movement is constructed in rondo form upon two themes with an intermezzo, the several returns to the first subject and the approach to the coda being all provided with a Quasi Cadenza; which, in the latter case, is also appropriately preceded by an orchestral interlude. The divisions are all subject to the same form of internal arrangement; except that, in the coda, the order of the subjects is inverted; the second being taken first and the first being reserved for the close, with considerable effect.

The admirable order of this construction is well worthy of notice; and if we examine it even more closely we shall be amply repaid. Thus, the principal subject in the first instance modulates into G flat; in which key it is suddenly taken up by the entire orchestra. On the next occasion it modulates into A flat; this time being taken up similarly by the entire orchestra in that key. We might therefore suppose, naturally enough, that, on the next occasion, the same thing would occur with regard to some other key. But, not so. Such a view would leave out of consideration the approaching conclusion of the movement; and the consequent desirability of giving paramount importance to the tonic. Accordingly, in this case, the subject remains in B flat minor; the orchestra proceeding at once to second subject.

The subjects themselves do not present any features rendering examples necessary; and the solo part is cumbrous, though effective. There seems to have been a consciousness of this, if we may judge from the introduction of a new and lightsome counterpoint on the second entry of the theme. This undoubtedly does something for us in the way of remedy; but in truth we cannot reasonably expect a conventional solo to be evolved from such unpianistic material. It should suffice for the listener that as music, the finale is worthy of a work, which taken in its entirety is one of the most remarkable productions of the age.

III

SYMPHONY, NO. 6, IN B MINOR, OP. 74
(THE " PATHETIC ")

FIRST MOVEMENT

Adagio. Allegro. Andante. Moderato. Andante. Moderato. Adagio. Allegro. Andante

I PURPOSELY set forth at the head of this chapter the various changes of movement which occur during the first section of this work, in order to secure at once some visible indication of its erratic character. Noble as the creation may be (and of its title to be so considered there is no question) its claim to the name of Symphony is one based rather upon the respect due to its composer, who so entitled it, than upon any discoverable conformity either with symphonic form proper or with the conventions which have gradually accumulated round it.

The truth is that it was rare for Tchaikovsky to work at his best under formal restraint; and, with all our admiration for him, we have no reply to those who find an inconsistency between his professed deference to an academic training and the unscholastic trend of many of his own works. For, at first sight, it would naturally seem that he, who could so freely impute the defects of other composers to the lack of school advantages, should at least have exhibited to us in his own work a proof that these advantages were the mainspring of success. What he really has exhibited to us could scarcely have been less academic if his object had been to show that such training can easily be dispensed with, his success being, generally speaking, a fairly accurate measure of his disregard of it; and in no case is this more evident than in that of the remarkable work which I am now to treat. The circumstance is regrettable on account of the danger to young students of drawing the conclusion of being entitled to do the same; forgetful of the fact that with Tchaikovsky it was not a case of imperfect conception or of want of the spirit of obedience. His defection had a far deeper cause.

The question of a programme for this work is one to which I am induced to refer from deference to the many who attach importance to it; though, for my own part, I consider that it has none. The composer himself, though avowedly he *had* a programme, evidently deemed its revelation to be unworthy of much concern; and, after all, there may have been some method in this reticence. A work of such intense emotional character would, under any circumstances, have offered an alluring range to the imagination in devising a circumstantial frame-work to fit it. But, with the composer's act in constituting its programme an enigma, the enticement to solve the mystery became ten-fold. To those who are unaffected by such curiosity the interest lies rather in the light thus thrown upon the *force of the tonal language;* in which an emotional discourse goes home to the hearts of men all the more for not being pinned to any direct application. It is like an eloquent sermon in which each man traces the allusion to his own shortcomings, and in which he seems to hear the expression of his secret thoughts; wondering, the while, by what secret process the preacher can have thus succeeded in penetrating to the depths of his inner conscience. But the subject appertains rather to that which I am already treating in "The Tonal Language as an Instrument of Thought"; and cannot, therefore, here be encroached upon.

We start therefore with what I ask pardon for considering the *advantage* of being able to regard this work in the absolute sense; and which, from my point of view, is some compensation for the task of having to treat it as in form. We shall require some imagination in reconciling the panorama of its first movement to such conditions, but duty requires that we should make the most of whatever feasibility may appear.

We start, then, with a short Adagio. This, as compared either with the work in bulk or with the Allegro which immediately follows it, as, at all events, a perfect introduction. The thematic material which it broaches has just the requisite amount of reference to that of the Allegro in order to prepare the mind of the listener; whilst the lugubrious effect, due not only to its substance but to the mode of its instrumentation, is a key to the character of the entire work. The reference to the Allegro consists of an augmentation of the latter's principal motive, as here shown.

Ex. 19.
(a) as in Introduction.   (b) as in Allegro.

The hearer therefore starts with the expectation of a reasoned discourse; an expectation which he is free to retain for exactly sixteen bars, during which the first subject appears to be in orthodox course of development. But it now becomes quickly evident that fervid rhapsody is to be the mood; and the first impression caused by the *détour* reminds us of the feeling we are apt to experience when a speaker embarks with the evident intention of remaining calm; but for whom the temptations, offered alike by natural temperament and by the extent to which his feelings are engaged, prove to be too strong.

The first symptom of restlessness takes the form of a diminution of the theme—which the intelligent reader would naturally expect; as it is Tchaikovsky's well-known method of producing a palpitating rhythm. In this case, however, it is a "diminution" in more senses than one; being also of the nature of a dissolving view, for we are destined to hear no more of the first subject until the 11th bar of the Durch-führung. When we think of the extent of the work this means much; for we have still over 50 bars to travel before even reaching the second subject. But so it is; and the eclipse of the first subject is the more complete in consequence of several other features of importance now appearing. Were we treating a work of small dimensions the latter are sufficiently pro-nounced to be entitled to consideration as separate subjects, but their subordinate position in the present case excludes that possibility; and the momentary feeling is one of disappointment that the expectation raised by the coherence of the introduction and open-ing of the Allegro is not to be fulfilled.

Recovering from this, however, we are very soon converted to the composer's view; and, throwing aside the philosophic mood are ready to sympathise with his excitement. There is a lesson to be derived from this, for there is rhapsody *and* rhapsody; and the listener unconsciously discriminates between what is manufactured and what is sincerely felt. The former is akin to the ebullition of the paid agitator; but the latter is an ecstatic voice; and the lesson to which I refer is, that these distinctions are precisely the same in the tonal language as in any other.

From the moment that we accept the rhapsodical style of utterance the point of view is changed; for, now, instead of looking for homogeny, we regard it as more human in Tchaikovsky that he did not employ the same figurations for the new features; as he might easily have done without sacrificing the trend of his intention. In order to make this clear I subjoin some features of this portion of the work; giving, in each case, the passage in the figuration which Tchaikovsky has selected for repetition.

Ex. 20.
Thematic material.

Of these the last is the most prolonged; continuing, at last in diminuendo, until it tapers off with the 'cellos alone; who murmur it as an accompaniment to soft chords of the trombones and tuba.

It may, of course, be claimed that the third portion of the above example is a reference to the leading theme; and its assignment to the brass might appear to give colour to this view. But, had this been so intended, Tchaikovsky would certainly have given the motive integrally; for no composer would ever dream of including redundancies in such circumstance. On the other hand, the opposite view requires little support in argument; for everything points to the rambling character of the work, in proof of which I need only instance the extravagant amount of modulation. In doing so I will take the second portion of

the above example; which occupies exactly sixteen
bars. During that short time there are changes, in-
volving much care in the instrumentation, and being
in every sense complete modulations, into no less than
seven different keys; as under : —

MINOR KEYS.	MAJOR KEYS.
C♯. G♯. D♯. F♯.	E. A. B.

The object of thus fringing so many tonalities is
not very apparent, as the composer is evidently steer-
ing for a suitable introduction of his second subject.
It is only when we reach the latter that we perceive,
by the beauty of the contrast which it affords, that all
this restlessness was not in vain. We perceive also
the meaning of the gradual descent of the figure; not
to the double-basses, but to the 'cellos only ; with their
murmur which, though equally expressive of discon-
tent, is more associated with calm and resignation.
The *pp* of the brass; the final slackening; and the
plaint of the uprising cantabile passage for violas all
show that the rhapsody is not that of a composer
attempting to produce an effect; but of one who gives
you his actual emotions. Nine out of ten writers
would have allowed the harmony of A dominant to
prevail during the last few bars, in order that the
second subject might be heralded according to Capellmeister traditions; but there is an exquisite sadness in
the viola slowly toiling up to the very note upon
which the next subject is to begin; even indicating its
very chord, and then having, as it were, to take refuge
in the sympathy of its companions. Points like this
easily account for the popularity of the work and

render it independent of a programme; for we have all passed through experiences which these heartfelt strains are capable to express, and silently—perhaps unconsciously—we make the application as the notes go by.

But what can be said of the message of consolation which the violins and 'cellos united have now to offer. If, anywhere in this world, the pure tonal expression of sincere condolence is to be found, it is here. In its presence I confess to a reluctance to appear upon the scene, as it were, with a dissecting knife; for it seems almost of the nature of an inhumanity to tear these delightful bars asunder and to seek to account for the feelings which they evoke. There are only twelve of them; though fortunately they are destined to recur, with more ample instrumentation, later on. Only twelve; and I am afraid that even *they* will assume much smaller proportions, as a result of the examination to which it is my duty to submit them. But they deserve a greater respect on that account; as I shall presently show by the aid of the following extract, taken from my published piano arrangement of this Symphony.

Ex. 21.

Firstly, let us give our attention to the conflict set
up between the accentuation of passion and that which
consists of mere rhythmic emphasis. Tchaikovsky's
method in this case is of the utmost value to other

composers; for he shows them exactly how to obtain a greater intensity of expression than lies in the power of any amount of sforzando to offer. This method consists in changing the position of the bar lines; and of thus converting the *de jure* first-beat into the *de facto* third. Were the sforzando applied to the first beat it would monopolise the situation of that emphasis; and thus prevent its separate existence. But, being applied to the third, the natural accent of the bar still remains alive as a rival emphasis; and absolutely compels a greater degree of intensity. Every player in the orchestra, if only from habit, will accentuate his first beat; and, as the result of doing so, he creates a competition between the two. The listener therefore does not hear the bar as written; but as I have indicated overhead in the above example. Yet, had it been written in that way, the effect would not have been the same; for the reasons I have given.

Next, we have the instruction to be derived from the smallness of material. During the twelve bars in question the melody of the first two bars occurs no less than four times; as the student will perceive, by comparing the brackets marked (a) and (b). These are *integral* repetitions, notwithstanding differences of cadence; and the remaining four bars are, in reality, only two; as will be clear to the reader if he will compare the two situations marked (c) and (d). Therefore the whole thing consists of *four bars;* and it either is, or ought to be, of the closest interest to every musician to find out how it is that Tchaikovsky has succeeded with a mere fragment of simple music in obtaining such truly marvellous results.

When, a short while ago, I explained this melody as one of "condolence" I had these very repetitions in mind; and its beauty is due to the fact of being, in virtue of them, absolutely true to nature. The appeal is to *one great reason* for the appeasement of sorrow; and the differences of cadence clearly indicate the desire to give to this, each time, a more soothing expression. It is not so much a question of mere difference of cadence as of increased persuasiveness; which I shall show when I come to the technical side of the matter. In the meantime let me also point out that Tchaikovsky has exhibited to us in this melody the grand distinction between a repeat which is a mere repetition and one which is not. The last four bars absolutely *require* to be repeated; for, without repetition, the message which they contain would have been flagrantly incomplete. It is therefore a test of the intensity of a phrase, that it should demand a two-fold utterance.

As to the technical aspect of all this it is even more wonderful to note that these bars, which so excite our admiration, are nevertheless full of the well-worn mannerisms at which we should so love to grumble— if we dared. They are practically all upon a pedal-bass; and it seems half absurd to "enthuse" over that of which we have already had so much. But, how could the passionate appeals marked (*) have been given without the effect of that augmented octave between clarionet and double-bass for which a

stationary bass could alone provide the occasion?
Under any other circumstances, what is now so thrill-
ing would have been mere cacophony. So, as his dia-
tribe will not apply, the critic becomes half angry
with the master; whose novel fault consists in using
his chosen implements with such consummate skill as
to turn the laugh against his accusers.

The same experience awaits us if we turn now to
those ultra-persuasive cadences; and ask "whence
come they?" From that simple device which I have
elsewhere described as the "under-changing note"; a
mere trick, which Tchaikovsky has already worked *ad
nauseam;* and of which we should be quite justified in
feeling tired. But how can we give expression to this
feeling with the conviction (as at †) that this expedi-
ent is precisely what was necessary? Is it not beautifully expressive of the gentle hand pressure of a
consoling friend? And why therefore should we
trouble ourselves about scholastic proprieties? Rather
let us admit that the artful craftsman has gained the
day; and, since we are already inwardly conscious of
being disarmed and taken captive, frankly allow
Tchaikovsky the use of his mannerisms while he is
capable of investing them with such charm and
interest.

We have now arrived at the first moderato indicated
at the head of this chapter; with which, therefore, in
the next, the subject will be resumed.

III

SYMPHONY, NO. 6, IN B MINOR, OP. 74
(THE "PATHETIC")

FIRST MOVEMENT (*continued*)

In the last chapter we had arrived at the first
moderato of the opening movement; which is practically an intermezzo, separating the two announcements
of the second subject. In describing the latter I had
full occasion to call the reader's attention to Tchaikovsky's masterly use of the mannerisms to which he
was most addicted. But we must not conclude that,
in the Symphony before us, these methods are invariably attended with an equal success. As a preparation for the fuller instrumentation of the second
subject, there occurs, for example, a "moderato
mosso"; embodying some neat little tricks which I
should not like to say are altogether free from char-
latanism. A very short extract of this will suffice

Ex. 22.

to exhibit Tchaikovsky's insidious method in the use of grades; and, though dissimilar in purpose, it reminds one of Rossini's use of the chromatic scale for modulative purposes. This frequently consisted of a wandering passage in neutral semitones until the sense of tonality was destroyed; after which it was open to him to arrest its progress in any desired key. So, in the above example, the stealthy creeps of the flute are answered by bassoon; while the strings, with what is really sostenuto harmony, obtain a fantastic motion by means of saltando bowing. This also is neutral, and may easily be tacked on to anything; besides which the neutrality of grade-work may be used to simulate contrapuntal features which do not really exist. Thus at the 5th and 6th bars of the moderato, and frequently after that, we have grade passages in this form : —

Ex. 23.

given by the wood-wind. Now, from the phrasing, the unwary might be inclined to imagine that this has something to do with the second subject. Such, however, is not the case. Over and above all this, we have to face the rigidly mechanical arrangement of the moderato; which I shall now describe.

First, we have eight bars; of which four are similar to Ex. 22, and four to Ex. 23. The last four are further characterised by an ascending grade passage for the brass, and rounded off by a rapid scale passage for first violins; the saltando bowing continuing of course in the middle strings. If we have accomplished nothing else, we have at least travelled from D to A; so, back we go again to our saltando and scales; and, in another eight bars, it is scarcely surprising to find that we are in E. Back again; but no more sequence now, evidently for fear of getting too far away from the key; so, instead of it, we have a descent of the wood-wind and horns by grades, and in notes of half-bar length. Each of these is duly measured out to the requisite amount of saltando; and this goes on for no less than an octave and a half of the compass of those instruments. Happily, however, we are in the mood to forgive anything; for we know that we are only waiting for the return of the lovely second subject, which this time appears upon the scene in more gorgeous attire, and provided with an extended diminuendo marked "moderato assai" to which I shall have to refer in connection with the Durchführung to which it leads.

In considering the development there is a difficulty in taking up the symphonic stand-point. If we hold that the free portion terminates with the return of the first subject in the original key we shall exclude the climax; which comes later on. But the latter is of supreme importance and, for that reason, it will probably be better to deem Tchaikovsky to have dispensed with first subject in his return groups, on the ground of its having been so largely utilized in the development. Whether or no this was the case, the interpretation is feasible; and it certainly lies in the interest of the reader desiring an intelligent survey of the movement to include the climax with the middle portion of it. This means that under this heading we have to deal with 144 bars; the orchestral display contained in which is so magnificent that I must risk being charged with punctiliousness rather than fail to give good account of it. I must also ask the reader to use the score for reference.

A. (bars 1 to 10). The more ample instrumentation of the second subject has already betokened a fortification of spirit; and its prayerful conclusion, so full of the language of supplication and entreaty, as clearly indicates the imminence of the fray. The expression of earnestness derivable from repetitions which are integral to the meaning of the phrase is here again in evidence; as the following will exemplify:

Ex. 24.
Moderato assai (in continued *diminuendo* until the *Allegro*).

But, independently of the *exact* repetitions thus indicated, the reader will observe that there are several others, offering mere differences of detail; so that, in the result, 10 bars of subject-matter really extend to 19; during which the streak of sound grows less and less, in preparation for the contrast with the orchestral outburst of the new departure. The latter, as indicated above, continues its four-bar phrase in rising sequence. But, suddenly, when its third working is but half-way through, it is, as it were, forcibly and violently interrupted; and this furiously eloquent intrusion will account for the portion we are discussing amounting to *ten* bars; which may be dissected as 4+4+2. At the moment of interruption every instrument is not only busy, but engaged *ff* in that part of its compass capable of offering the maximum of resonance. The crowd are commanded to make way for the first subject; with which the violins enter, playing "feroce" upon their G string, and accompanied by an equally determined figuration of the violas; who come to the assistance of their comrades in the most pointed manner by supplying the rasping semiquaver motion wherever the first subject fails to do so. It is fine; for it seems to speak. There is absolutely nothing vague about it; and it wants no programme.

B. (bars 11 to 29). This is a fugato on first subject; the mere counterpoint of which is insignificant. Moreover, for all its nineteen bars, there are really only four, as under : —

Ex. 25.

considering that all you have to do, in order to reproduce the entire fugato, is to give an inversion of the
above in A minor; a repetition in E minor; another
inversion in B minor; and then form a sequence of
the figuration at the last bar; carrying it on for three
bars more. The effect, however, is immense; but it
all harks back to the dignity of the original entry;
and once more Tchaikovsky shames us by the simplicity of his means.

C. (bars 30 to 45). The alternating sequence
between strings and wood-wind, which has just been
formed from the figuration derived from that portion
of the subject marked * in the above example, has
now arrived at an altitude at which flutes and clarinets playing in octaves and supported by the upper
strings are sufficiently assertive to counterbalance
trumpets and double-reeds. These accordingly make

a pompous entry with the grade-work to which Tchaikovsky was so partial; and upon which he now concentrates the interest by appointing that every instrument not engaged in its assertion shall have a stationary part. The figuration, for example, is stationary; so also is the part for the lower horns and trombones. The lower strings, too, even including the violas, have nothing but continuous tremolo; and yet, with this almost childish simplicity, we have an amount of orchestral excitement and agitation difficult to surpass. But it is all rhapsodical; and, as I have already alluded to the power of grade-work to simulate contrapuntal features which it does not really possess, I shall take no notice of any fancied resemblances to second subject. The rhythm, too, is plainness itself; not only 4+4 but divided in such way that the first half contains the working above described whilst the second embraces the descending figuration and diminuendo. It is rather laughable that the cadence of this period is the supposed quotation from the Russian requiem. One would not have supposed it possible for the me est t not to know that, for the allusion to have been anyt. ng more than a coincidence, it would at least have begu a sentence. Still, the coincidence may not have been displeasing to the composer, when the character of the whole work is considered; in the event, that is, of his having even noticed it at all.

D. (bars 46 to 70). These twenty-five bars are three 8-bar periods, of which the second receives a one-bar extension. Intensity of expression is secured in the

usual way, as the following germ of the adopted progression will sufficiently indicate:

Ex. 26.

This is, of course, followed by diminution; which,
in its turn is (equally of course) the signal for a
gradual crescendo. When this crescendo has ripened
to *ff*, and (equally of course) when the passage has
simultaneously reached its highest point it is evidently (in Tchaikovsky's mind) time for an organ-
point. He does not therefore charm us in the least by
the means which he employs; but by his splendid
manipulation of them. Here, for instance, we have a
C sharp pedal; not only full of effect, as such, but
completely fulfilling its object in restoring to us the
reposefulness necessary to prepare the mind for the
return. It is charming to note how this reposefulness

is increased by the simple device of a one-bar extension at bar 62; a clear case of "masterly inactivity." Then comes a gentle warning in triplets by the horns. This appears at first at the rate of only once in each bar; but soon it becomes more frequent and in all the range of compositions with which I am familiar I know of no more artistic expression of the fact that the first subject is about to re-appear.

E. (bars 71 to 84). The returning first-subject first shows itself in a removed key; and by the infrequency of its recurrences gives the effect of an augmentation.

Ex. 27.

The reader's acquaintance with Tchaikovsky's methods will now enable him to foresee that this augmentation is a mere "backing"; for the purpose of giving greater effect for the onslaught to come. He will also readily guess that several grades of diminution await him; and that there will be a gradual ascent and crescendo before the final burst. Accordingly, of the 14 bars involved, four are employed as above; in what is practically an augmentation. Then, four are devoted to the subject at its natural tempo and with the rise of a 4th. Then, two bars are occupied by a diminution in first degree; with continued rise and commencement of the inevitable crescendo. Then comes the second degree of diminution; with its palpitating effect of being contained in a single bar. But the advent of the third degree is naturally the signal for every form of excitement; and, during the three bars of its continuance, the score presents the orchestra to the mind's eye as a veritable hive of industry. Only to glance at it makes us breathe more quickly; but we have scarcely time to realise the feeling when the first subject is upon us—for all that it is worth. That it will now be torn to tatters goes without saying. In other words, we all know the "recipe"; and may even indulge our vanity to the extent of laughing at it. But it sadly appears to me that the laugh is in favour of the man who could *produce* these wonderful results; entirely without any mysterious aid. There could not after all be a better proof that it is the poetic instinct, and not the musicianship, which makes the composer.

F. (bars 85 to 106). I shall leave it to the reader's imagination to picture how, in these wonderful bars, the rival orchestral elements seem to contend for supremacy. What is most marvellous is that the grand climax is still to come : a climax which may be readily accepted as the maximum of orchestral fervour. According to all accepted ideas of the general fitness of things this pinnacle of excitement could only be justified by being the herald of something extraordinary. And what, think you, is the novel feature for which all these grand preparations are made? *Still another organ-point!* An organ-point this time of 38 bars, moreover. But, note well the master. In the final approach to the climax just referred to the uprise and crescendo was far more rapid than had previously been the case. We travelled through a swift whirling sequence from *pp* to *ff*, and we traversed two octaves of space, recruiting all idle instruments on the way; all within the time occupied by three short bars. It was as if, with one final mad rush, at last the heights were to be stormed. But, with the attainment of the climax, we are *there;* and the length of the succeeding pedal is commensurate with the importance of the achievement.

G. (bars 107 to 144). These are the 38 bars of organ-point. Flutes, clarinets and upper strings, though previously content with a rhythmic subdivision of the time, now run hither and thither; for the march rhythm is no more. This fact is rendered most patent by the brass having changed their attitude to one of wild exclamation. But soon, as might easily be foreseen, the tendency is towards diminution in all respects; and, alike in altitude, in force and in speed, there are indications of nearing the point of well-earned repose. The result is that, although the basses have been grumbling along continuously with their tremolo F sharp, it is only at the eighth bar that we really become conscious of them; and of their fagot companion in the wood-wind. We know of course that it is about time for the grade-work to set in, but we are too much engaged with the matter of Tchai-

kovsky's discourse to trouble about his mode of expression; and, for my own part, I make note of the
fact that in my treatise on the latent power of fixed
progressions I shall be able to appeal to him in support of the principle—"the simpler the means, the
greater the resource." In the meantime the reader
may, without danger to himself, take this principle
for granted; and the following new exposition of
grade-work as an illustration of it.

Ex. 28.

Wood wind and Str.

That we are now approaching the end of the Durchführung the selection of F sharp for the organ-point
sufficiently indicates; and the rate of approach may

naturally be measured by that of the intensity of the over-head working. With the arrival at pp, we feel in every sense prepared for the re-introduction of the second subject; not, this time, so much for the expression of condolence, as for that of mutual congratulations upon a successful issue. Accordingly the fastidious under-changing notes which so aptly express this feeling now literally swarm. No mere extract can adequately convey the loveliness of treatment; and the following bars are therefore offered only as a sample of its features from the purely technical side : —

Ex. 29.

The coda-like continuation of this subject is such a perfect piece of orchestration that closer examination seems continually to reveal more beauty in it; and the very satisfaction engendered by it is probably the reason of the final andante being sometimes considered *de trop*. Some ground for this view is presented by the fact that the string-parts consist of the complete scale of B repeated by the strings pizz.: no less than eight times; while the attending motives are distinctly commonplace. But, if we accept the whole as merely a prolonged cadence, not merely in association with what immediately precedes it but rather in connection with the entire movement, our judgment will be different.

It has been said of Tchaikovsky that his music often sounds better than it is; as distinct from that of Brahms which is described as often better than it sounds. But the weak point of such reasoning is that it begs the question of a standard of excellence. In the meantime, therefore; and, while the sapients are making up their minds, it is well to remember that, as the proper study of mankind is man, the merit of the creative musician must ever be in proportion to the amount of human feeling with which he is capable of investing his tonal utterances.

SECOND MOVEMENT

Allegro con grazia

In embarking upon the analysis of this movement I am conscious of some advantage as the author of a treatise upon the very scope of composition of which it affords such a perfect example. When my manual "How to Compose within Lyric Form" was written, although I knew that the principles which it enunciates for the student's guidance would find easy confirmation, I scarcely hoped ever to find in any *one* movement of a great master such a complete and accurate corroboration of every detail of my statements that extracts from his work would as fitly have served to illustrate my text as those which I wrote specially for the occasion. The consequent satisfaction I enjoy reminds me of a kindred sentiment expressed by Dr. Prout when he tells us that, upon completion of one of his theoretical works, he found his principles to be in complete accord with those of a professor of Greek at Moscow University; and that he felt, on that account, strengthened in the belief that his views were sound.

The bar-rhythm of this movement is $\frac{2}{4}+\frac{3}{4}$ ($=\frac{5}{4}$) and its chief characteristic during the first section is the division into triplet-quavers of the third crotchet. In $\frac{5}{4}$ there is a danger lest the listener remain unaware of the exact location of the bar division. Duple and triple measures present no difficulty; as bars of such ordinary kind naturally distribute into equal portions. But, in the quintriple, the impossibility of equal bar-subdivision creates an option between 2+3 and 3+2; coupled with necessity to avoid mixing the two. Inexperienced writers largely rely upon emphasis; precisely the means which good composers most seek to avoid. They know that mere accentuation is but a crude method of raising the rhythmical importance of a beat; and that to fall back upon it is to make everyone else as wise as themselves. That there is no necessity for such crudity of style Tchaikovsky herein amply proves; for, whenever the second division of his bar is marked off into single beats, he continues, by the simple device of triplet-division of his third crotchet, to compass the requisite rhythmic salience by automatic means; the result being that both player and listener are surprised to hear a five-beat rhythm flow quite naturally, which can obviously never be the case if a strenuous accent is allowed to become necessary. The true ground for surprise, however, is that this delightful rhythm should be so little culti-vated; as it contains a veritable world of music within itself.

The following example exhibits the two essential parts of the opening theme :—

Ex. 30.

and enables me also to call attention to the aptness of the choice of a triplet-division in this instance; the character of the second portion of the bar, which it commences, being also triple. We may therefore conclude that, had Tchaikovsky exercised the option alluded to in the other direction (that of $3+2$) he would have made a *duple* division of his fourth crotchet; in order that, here also, the beat-division should correspond with the character of the second portion of the bar which it is designed to open. This leads me to a statement of musical fact likely to be of service to many of my readers.

There is a natural tendency to the expression of gaiety in the musical as in the poetical tri-syllabic foot. When mingled with the dis-syllabic this gaiety develops into humour; and, of this humour, there are two degrees. When the dis-syllabic foot comes first we have the lesser of these two degrees; and this is the rhythm which Tchaikovsky has chosen in this instance. His triumph consists in the fact that the movements, in spite of the natural tendency of its rhythm, is not humorous; but exquisitely graceful and expressive. He has, therefore, revealed to us that our conventional notions regarding this rhythm, though correct as to natural tendency, are incorrect as to constancy of the humorous feature. As he has not set himself to overcome the humorous tendency at its greatest $(3+2)$ I will now exemplify this rhythm for the student's benefit; by taking Tchaikovsky's

own favourite grade method and applying it to a
descending scale,

Ex. 31.

in which the fourth crotchet is halved, so as to correspond with the duple character of the second portion of
each bar. I fancy that Tchaikovsky himself must have
learned something from the discovery of a means of
rhythmic prominence independent of mere emphasis;
as it seems so natural that a composer should, after
such a successful application, proceed, not only to
apply the same means in other instances, but also to
enlarge the idea so as to meet the requirements of
other cases. My ground for so thinking is that an
extension of the same principle constitutes the most
salient feature of the next movement; which I shall
explain when I arrive at that point.

In exhibiting the beauties of the movement now
under review it is with reluctance that I again allude
to the inevitable grade-method; but there is really no

escape from the reference, Tchaikovsky having again by its employment, converted what ought theoretically to be a reproach into what we know practically to be a feature of great merit. By the time that earthly rhythms are no longer our concern and when (partly as the result of our absence perhaps) the world has grown very much wiser, our successors may laugh at such paltry expedients. But, in the meantime, and for the entire career of the very youngest of us, there will never be better means of securing ready acceptance for a $\frac{5}{4}$ movement than those which Tchaikovsky has adopted—well-worn as they are:—to wit, grade "Stimmführung" and pedal bass.

The mere construction of this movement will not detain us; as it entirely consists of the ordinary square-built periods and sections of lyric form. I say "lyric form" advisedly; not professing to know what the common expression "song-form" may stand for. Lyrical poetry is a class of which the song is merely one exemplification; and, as what is true of poetry may be fairly taken to apply also to metrical music, it follows that the song has no more monopoly of this class than of the corresponding poetical category. In this movement, the form being so simple, our business completely lies with the contrast of periods and sections; with the logical transitions and coda-diminuendo. To assist the consideration of these, therefore, I will first indicate the opening of the Trio Section.

Ex. 32.

Str. and Fl.

Tymp. Fag.

When, in " How to Compose " I explained variety
of means, I passed in review the contrast of periods
in the several respects of construction tonality and
figuration; explaining at the same time that, although,
for purposes of instruction, I brought these contrasts
all closely together, either one or other of them would
generally suffice for a particular movement. And so
it happens; Tchaikovsky's chosen means of contrast
in his first section being figuration only. This figuration, moreover, so completely accords with my definition that I am tempted to a quotation.

" Figuration, in the accepted musical sense, is a sort of embroidery consisting of pattern-work subordinate to the main
design. In unskilful hands it is generally deficient in sense
though assertive in sound. In those of a good composer it is
both delightfully subordinate in point of sound and interesting
intellectually."

Every pupil in composition is so familiar with what
I am wont to describe in short as the " dominant-
weld " that its employment in an important work for
purposes of figuration would scarcely commend itself

z

to him. Yet here we have a great master delightfully adorning his theme and contrasting his periods by this simple means; to which he imparts beauty not only by the grace of its introduction but by the mode of instrumentation; as, for example, in the crossing of the horn parts.

Ex. 33.

The Trio-section contains no figuration; and again my manual description figures it exactly, stating that

"The Trio-figuration, *if any*, will be exceedingly plain, except may be, during the intermezzo, when, as the object is to grow naturally into the returning first section, the re-appearance either of the theme itself or of its figuration will be foreshadowed."

These provisions are all literally fulfilled; for, after the single repeat of the first eight bars at D, C, of Trio, an intermezzo occurs; and, surely enough, while continuing the Trio character, it is intermingled with a foreshadowing of the return. Thus:—

Ex. 34.

This intermezzo provides the only instance in the movement of a yielding on Tchaikovsky's part to his usual inclination in favour of prolongations of the phrase. Previous to its commencement the phrases have been of invariable four-bar length; but they now proceed as here shown :

$$(2 \times 4) + (1 \times 7) = 15.$$

or, in other words, the eight-bar period requisite to fill the cadre is first made to throb at two-bar distance; when the further diminution to a one-bar rhythmic pulsation becomes, as it were, logically due. But, as the number one is neutral, the rhythm is now unregulated; being somewhat of the nature of a cadenza. This is shown by Tchaikovsky's use of the irregular number, seven; and these bars, though forming a delightful adornment, are not integral to the movement; but are merely designed to increase the hearer's interest in the return of the opening theme.

It only remains to speak of the Coda; which I cannot better describe than in words, written without reference to this movement, yet applying to it in every detail.

"The Coda, is in spirit, a repetition of the first period or periods according to the dimensions of the work. It therefore partakes of the same mode of figuration; though in respect of *quantity* there is a great difference, as, the general character of the Coda in this instance, being to decline towards the end, the figuration, like the quantity of tone, will be less and less. It is generally necessary to break away from sequence as tending to an exciting third phrase which is not required, but in which, on the contrary, there should be but a slight reminder of the figure; and none whatever of the fourth, in order that the theme may be allowed undisturbed to fade into pianissimo."

Ex. 35.

So reverent a conclusion, by almost provoking an "ainsi-soit il," completely proves its independence of $\frac{5}{4}$ conventions. May I also be pardoned for adding "so-mote-it-be" to the support of my book; which Tchaikovsky has so unconsciously, and yet so completely, given in this movement.

THIRD MOVEMENT

Allegro molto vivace

In dealing with the previous movement, and in reference to Tchaikovsky's adroit production of rhythmic salience independently of emphasis, I alluded to an extension of the same principle later on. It is obvious that, if systematic subdivision of a particular beat whilst the surrounding beats remain intact gives it a rhythmic prominence without the aid of accent, a reserve of power exists for the increase of that prominence by the addition of emphasis whenever desired : that is *one degree*. But, in the next place, if the emphasis when given be not applied to the actual percussion of the beat but reserved for the subdivision of it, its abnormal situation will impart to it a still more striking individuality : that is *another* degree. And, finally, if the prominence thus secured be *isolated* by removing the percussions of the succeeding beats, it follows that a maximum salience will be attained : that, of course, is the *last* degree. Now all these *nuances* would as naturally occur to anyone quietly reasoning the matter as they do to me in course of this examination. Therefore the surmise is reasonable that Tchaikovsky either intuitively; or, if by reasoning, then by some such process as I have indicated, evolved the first subject of this movement;

Ex. 36.

which the reader will at once perceive embodies all
the features I have severally mentioned. The union
of so many logical consequences in the one theme
can scarcely have been accidental, notwithstanding
that the composer's fervour would prevent him from
applying the *sang-froid* with which we, as mere onlookers, arrive at our conclusions.

Tchaikovsky's consciousness of strength must have
been great for him to conceive the possibility of so
vast a movement, based, practically in its entirety,
upon this one bare theme; destined in his mind to
emerge, with the daring prominence thus so well contrived, from a filigree texture of orchestration in
"moto perpetuo." This texture, I presume, is a sample
of that which Sir Hubert Parry had in mind when
recently lecturing upon the subject; a kind which he
then described as "subtly made of diversely coloured
strands." Though only one kind among many, it
possesses the two important qualities of being both
representative of modern developments and in itself
of a highly refined character. The latter trait in particular enables it to form the very finest possible background from which to cause a march-like theme to
emerge with full force; so that we seem herein to
follow the composer's procedure to the further step
of completing his design by the selection of a texture

most calculated to give vivid expression to the same principles which had guided him in choice of theme.

This question of texture is one which lies at the very root of modern musical progress. It is one to which I have devoted many years of my life; and in illustration of which it is my ambition to complete the task of many vigils. The gratification was therefore keen on finding that Sir Hubert Parry had addressed himself to this subject; and only the fear of digression withholds me from more copious reference to his golden observations. Suffice it to say that, in this instance, Tchaikovsky, having secured the requisite lightness for his texture by a rapid staccato triplet motion and apparently conscious of the necessity of a somewhat greater solidity than could arise from strands proceeding all in the same direction (especially when temporarily the theme being merely in expectation the texture is alone under observation), had recourse to two methods, one of which he applies to the strings and the other mostly to the wood-wind. That of the strings is the reservation of a portion of them for an apparently capricious crossing of the main lines; and that of the wind a setting of normal quavers of the common time bar against its triplet subdivision. If the latter occurs but rarely it is because thematic working in other parts provides the required normal quaver motion and consequently sufficiently solidifies the texture without such aid; just as the capricious extra string parts also disappear upon entry of the theme: unquestionably for the same reason. Nothing would be easier than to illustrate all this; the only difficulty being to know where to stop. Therefore, considering that the score is so easily accessible, I will content myself with one example.

Ex. 37.

These, being the opening bars, occur while the texture stands alone. They therefore exhibit fairly well the features referred to. But, needless to say, there are many refinements of orchestration equally deserving of quotation; but for which the reader must necessarily be referred to the work itself. Enough, however, has been said to make him understand why in the latter part of the movement the texture wholly disappears; in the sense, that is, in which it has so

far been described.   In homely language the thematic
material, by its gradual crescendo, has outgrown the
texture which first fondled it.   The lightness of the
latter would now be of no effect; even if the instruments necessary for its production had not already
been commandeered for the general onrush.   Yet
Tchaikovsky's unerring æsthetic instinct causes him
to find room for reference to it just before the final
cadence; precisely upon the same principle as the
figuration was treated in the last movement.

I will now resume the subject of texture as concerning this movement, the reference on this occasion
being to its influence upon the actual composition.   A
very slight knowledge of the tendency of texture in
other cases leads us to separate in our minds those in
which the subject-matter is subject to the texture
from those in which texture is subject to the subject-
matter.   But I am conscious that many of my readers
may never have turned their thoughts in this direction.   For their sakes, therefore, I will give just one
homely instance of each description.

If I examine a tapestry I shall find that merit in
execution will not altogether have cancelled a certain
subservience of design to texture.   The curves of
outline and the *nuances* of colour will alike retain some
evidence of their freedom having been restrained by
the necessities of the ground surface.   Defects of
execution will render this even more apparent; for
the very measure of excellence in this case is the
degree of the artist's triumph over such difficulties.

If, on the other hand, I take a cheque-form in which

the name of the bank is presented in endless repetitions of letters so extremely small that they only court attention when examined very closely I shall find that, at a small distance from the eye, the effect is that of a ground-work or tint. In drawing such cheque I shall write the amount of it as if no texture existed; and, therefore, ruthlessly overstep its details. This is an instance from everyday life of texture subservient to subject matter.

Now in musical creation the option lies open to us of choosing either of these methods. Probably the reader will agree with me that perfection of beauty can alone consist in ascendancy of the subject-matter; but that need be no hindrance to our appreciation of good work in the opposite direction. The Tchaikovsky movement under consideration is a case in point; for the composer has allowed his texture to be the real master of the situation, and has chosen his subjects not so much independently as in order to accommodate it. He has, therefore, to my mind, chosen the less artistic of the two methods; and the measure of his triumph, as in the homely instance which I gave, is the degree in which he has succeeded in cancelling the angularity with which he set himself out to contend.

It was necessary to give instances of human work, fitly to compare with that of the composer. But no perfect human work exists; and, therefore, neither of the cases mentioned presents an ideal to our minds. For this we must go to Nature; which provides us with ample instances of texture subservient to design,

and yet not marred by, or in any sense in collision
with it.

This preamble is necessary to the examination of
the movement, and will at once explain why, in spite
of Tchaikovsky's great gift of melody, its subjects
are so deficient in that respect. Not one of them
could give the slightest pleasure apart from its surroundings; to the influence of which it entirely owes
whatever attraction it may possess. I have already
explained the method by which Tchaikovsky attained
a maximum of rhythmic prominence for his first subject; (see Ex. 36) a feature of which his work must
for ever remain a convincing example. Now, my
opening remarks will make apparent the analogy between this prominence and the overtrampling of
texture; of which, in this movement, the *sforzando*
of its first subject provides the solitary instance. With
this one exception the texture is entirely predominant,
and the remaining subjects derive their nature as such
merely from systematic recurrences; but for which they
might fairly be regarded as mere accompaniment to
the endless motion. Often the texture subsists entirely
alone; presenting to the mind's eye a *tabula rasa* upon
which we wait in expectation for something to be
written. The result is that when it ceases, and when,
after the inevitable pedal, all these subjects are re-
assembled and paraded in march-form, the effect is of
the wildest description. No other than a defiantly
assertive conclusion would have been possible to this
movement; and no other than a lordly masculine instrumentation would have sufficed to ally subjects

which sometimes actually require wrenching into position.

An instance of this occurs when Tchaikovsky breaks away from the pedal just mentioned; and when, by the adoption of a series of furious scale passages between the strings and wood-wind alternately, coherence is absolutely thrown to the winds. But what we are accustomed to regard as incoherence may sometimes be the most suitable treatment; and that is preeminently the case in a movement like this, where, between the various subjects, neither any mutual sympathy, nor any graceful contrast exists. Therefore, whether we approve of these or no, we can do no other than applaud the treatment.

Examples of such features are scarcely necessary; but there are some clever cases of *volte-face* in motion which I must exemplify; as the work is so valuable for reference in this respect. One of these occurs just after the entry of the principal subject in E; as under:—

Ex. 38.

pp e stacc.

and is to be commended for its very audacity. It is
the walk of the sentinel who allows himself a fixed
number of paces; upon completion of which he suddenly swings round upon his heel to make the return.
But it is also the writing of a man sure that what he
had written would be played first, and criticised
afterwards; for I venture to think that, if some passages in this work had been first submitted to censor-
ship, they would scarcely have survived the ordeal.
Here, for instance, is one: this time a case of *volte-
face* more remindful of the rapid turns in a mad
dance; and in which the composer has had the sublime assurance to make his strings and wood-wind
discuss matters in this way.

Ex. 39.

Four times.

The process of thought seems to have been that,
as the octave of twelve semitones divides mechanic-

ally at the augmented fourth, and, as a one-bar "whirl" was desired, brevity commended what I can only call a surgical division. Scruple, we know, is not always common sense; and, while one man is searching for an anatomical division, another, with a hatchet, will extemporise his own—and all is well. But had the composer not been so adroit with his instrumentation, he would have heard something more of this. As it is, the contrast of *timbre* comes happily to the rescue; the ordinary listener is cajoled; and only professional sifters like myself know what has really happened.

The boldness of treatment therefore by which the whole movement is characterised is thus in keeping with the frank manner in which the subjects emerge; for, in the one, there is no pretence of any regard to proprieties; and, in the other, no attempt of alliance with the dominating texture. An exception however occurs at the appearance of the first subject in E; and where the reposeful feeling thus induced derives great effect from contrast.

Ex. 40.

Thus the sense of unity in Tchaikovsky seems to have resulted more from intuition than study; for only intuition can have suggested this repose as a necessary support for the incongruous progressions to follow. Under cover of it, however, he fearlessly commits himself to some of the strangest chord parades that the student can have ever beheld. One example must suffice; as they so abound that the reader, with score in hand, will have no trouble in their identification.

Ex. 41.

These observations are by no means intended to imply a reproach. They point rather to examples of how the masterly hand can so transform the aspect of such features that, by their remaining in agreement with context and intention, it is impossible for them to be adversely regarded. In this case even the

commonplace conclusion of the movement is good;
for it immediately follows an abstruse progression to
which it administers an effective antidote, by allowing the tonic harmony absolutely to predominate for
the last eighteen bars. These bars merely look
lengthy; for, in the hearing, they do no more than
emphasise the fact that the turmoil is over, and, in
so doing, help us to the feeling of satisfaction with
which it was meet that so noble a movement should
conclude.

FINAL MOVEMENT

Adagio lamentoso

This movement is framed upon two subjects; the
first of which, in each of its three recurrences, remains
constant to the parent key of B minor, and the second
of which occurs, first in D, and is afterwards utilised
to complete the work. The first subject thus retains
its original sadness of character throughout; the recurrences differing only in intensity of expression.
But the second, at its first appearance, partakes somewhat of the consolatory nature of the second subject
in the first movement, and, by so doing, confers a
depth of meaning upon its return; the inference being
irresistible that at last all hope is gone.

The actual material of these subjects is extremely
spare; and the frequently repeated phrases and extensions by sequence continually remind us of the
first movement, where it was shown to be not only
one of Tchaikovsky's mannerisms but also one of his

greatest merits to confer such inherence upon his repetitions as to render them compulsory for completion
of the musical sentence.   It is doubtful if any other
composer has been so sensible of this important means
of expression; and it is also doubtful whether he has
left us any better illustration of it than this movement affords.   The first subject is as under; the
rising sequence indicated being subjected to his usual
method of diminution, and culminating in a *ff*, which
sadly subsides; leaving the listener in expectation
of a repetition of the plaint.

Ex. 42.

The intensity of expression attained at the second
entry is remarkable; the effect produced by the whole
body of strings approximating to that of *portamento*.
A similar treatment characterises each appearance of

A A

the wail of this opening chord; though the instrumentation is ever changed in the direction of being
rendered more agonising and pathetic. The plainest
instance is therefore the first, which I subjoin; and in
which I recommend the student to observe the crossing string parts by means of which the individuality
of each is disguised and the whole chord-mass made
mysteriously to rise and fall like the utterance of a
single voice.

Ex. 43.

To unite rhapsody with method is something akin
to a contradiction in terms; and yet I know not how
otherwise to embrace the fact that on its second appearance this fervid theme is subjected to a falling
sequence in evidently designed apposition to its
former treatment. This time, however, the melancholy character of the movement renders the direction
of the sequence one from which return is unnecessary;
and it accordingly falls and falls—in apparent hope-
lessness. It is worthy of note as a symmetrical
feature that this treatment is precisely of the same
length as the preceding; in addition to which Tchai-

kovsky's purpose was wonderfully served by a fall
which enabled him, without undue exuberance, to impart a ray of hope to the second subject which now
follows. Such features are of great value; for his
methods lie so frankly on the surface that those who
run may read them. This is again exhibited in the
the second subject itself; for it consists, as before, of
a short phrase of which the repetition is integral; and
is again followed by a rising quasi-sequence.

Ex. 44.

In less masterly hands monotony would follow;
but here refinement is shown in the fact that this time
the sequence is merely imitative; besides which a
variety of treatment results from its working round
for an eight-bar repetition. This repetition is an application of the same principle on broader scale; the
broadening of the scale naturally resulting in the

justification of a greater number of repetitions. In the second of these instances we have a genuine rising sequence, which both invites and receives an increase in sound-volume. In the third, the crescendo continues; being now associated with an increase of movement. At the conclusion of the fourth the maximum of intensity towards which we have all along been striving has been attained, restraint is abandoned, and the strings, at last, literally scamper away from the rest; their descent being capped by a staccato chord *fff* for the entire orchestra, as if the tension had become unbearable. The human meaning is so clear that the musician does not stop to consider how far the means of its attainment coincides with orthodoxy. It is a just principle of rhetoric that the reason should be convinced before the feelings are appealed to. But, here, our feelings are taken captive too suddenly to allow of the application of rule; and to feel we ought to scoff only makes our praise the more sincere.

The pause which follows, the fragmentary allusions to the second subject, and the renewed wail by the entire strings of the opening subject I regard as too great a triumph of musical expression for any literary description. The only justifiable feeling in their presence is one of reverence. Some might suppose that so fervid a writer would now take advantage of the situation in favour of rhapsody; but not so. The first subject proceeds very strictly in order, its original simplicity being far more eloquent. Only on the second repetition is a departure permitted; and,

even then, the same mode of extension is adopted as
that already applied to the second subject. Again we
have the rising sequence, the attendant crescendo and
stringendo, the diminution, the change of tempo: all
of it so stale and yet so ever new. We begin to
wonder why no organ point, when lo! with the change
of tempo here it is. First on E, but only *en route*
to F♯; upon which, as the dominant of the parent
key, it rests in order to indicate that the end is near.
And, in company with the pedal we recognise another
old friend in the grade work; beginning with the low
E of the bass trombone and creeping in crotchets
slowly upwards with occasional semitonic division to
accommodate the harmony. When the trombone compass is exhausted Tchaikovsky's faithful fagot friend
is standing by to see that no cavil shall arise about
the join. In the meantime the strings, in a sequence
of passages with feminine endings and played in
tremolo have been working in contrary motion to the
uprising grade-work. The pedal is a sure foundation
for the otherwise too changeful harmonies; and the
lack of punctuation, which would otherwise occur at
each alternate bar, is well supplied by wood and brass.
The whole presents the phenomenal combination of
regularity with "rhapsody of rhapsody." The goal to
which we are tending is equally clear; for the whole
orchestra is in progress of convergence upon the
dominant pedal. And with it comes the agonising
wail of the first subject which has already been so
intensely expressed that we do not even suspect the

existence of any greater pathos. But let the reader judge.

The same one-bar sighs with which the hope elicited by the second subject was abandoned; and now all concern with life is ended. A funereal semitonic sequence in four-part harmony for trombones and tapering off to *ppppp* prepares us for the dirge of the second subject in minor on tonic pedal; and this continues to end of the work. The simulation by means of grade work of contrapuntal features which exist not was with him to the end; as the following pathetic dialogue will show.

Horns and clarinets accompany the descent for a time, but at last the strings are left alone; the last to desert them being the bassoon; who was also first to join them in the opening movement. Even the violas have fallen away before he departs; leaving the 'cellos and basses all alone. They divide up as if to keep one another company; at odd moments there is a faint pizzicato from some of the double basses. Finally, these also disappear; when the tonic harmony, at the lowest pitch at which it could possibly be orchestrated, continues faintly for a moment—so faintly that we are scarcely conscious of its disappearance. But it is gone; and the spark of life is out.

I have endeavoured in my notice of this work, by a disregard of conventionality, to enable the reader to benefit by such truth as my opinions may happen to contain; and have therefore pointed to some features not conscientiously to be described as admirable in themselves. But my sense of the greatness of the composer is in no way dimmed by these strictures; and the greatest reward to await me would be to know that I had added to the number of his admirers.

IV

SYMPHONY NO. 5, IN E MINOR, OP. 64

FIRST MOVEMENT

" A FINE symphony—wrought of little." Such, I
remember, was my first impression of this work; and,
although spontaneous utterances of the kind made
without weight of responsibility are peculiarly liable
to after-modification, a closer scrutiny in this case has
entirely failed to produce its customary effect. Many
have been my previous occasions to refer to Tchaikovsky's sparse thematic material; but, in the Symphony before us, that characteristic is accentuated to
a degree requiring some preliminary observations on
the general subject.

To what extent is it permissible that a symphony
should be of monophonic character?

Is a prevalence of single-voice material consistent
with the ideal conception of the form?

Granted, a composer with great melodic gift and
vast orchestral command, and the means of affording
interest and pleasure is at once secured. Alike to

the gaping crowd and to the musician of refinement
these powers appeal; but there is a difference. The
latter soon recovers from his beguilement, but the
former cannot do so. After the first flush of emotional excitement is over and the critic returns to
investigate matters he is apt to find that he has fallen
in love with the beauty which is but skin deep. The
complexion tints have been so charming that, in their
contemplation, he is liable to have forgotten the
question of character; and, though his reason may
warn him, he can never quite eradicate the memory of
the pretty face. Hence the work of Tchaikovsky
often secures from us a kindlier handling than our
cool philosophy would justify.

Had he possessed a contrapuntal power equal to his
gifts in other directions what might this symphony
have been? His mood during its composition was
evidently of the kind most suitable to an immense
achievement. He began for example with set pre-
caution against the tendency to rhapsodise, anchoring
himself straightway to a theme-pivot round which the
entire work was to revolve: as who should say—
" This must and shall be homogeneous."

Ex. 47.

The *naïveté* of those who regard this feature as of
hidden meaning exemplifies how little is generally
known of the routine of the composer's work-shop.
To the real student the procedure is not only clear,

but rather too much so; and, like the seam of a garment, though necessary it was not desirable to be brought too much in evidence. The kind of unity to which it gives rise is not the ideal conception of that high quality; because it does not correspond with the exemplifications of it to be found in the beautiful productions of Nature. True it may be that Tchaikovsky has been specially happy in the recurrences of his parent-theme. For that he excites our admiration in another way: for his workmanship, but not his inspiration.

But before we commend too greatly the resource displayed in workmanship it may be well to pause for a moment to consider, as first in order, the prudence exhibited in selection. A theme, for instance, such as the above, of which every accentuated note is an integral of the tonic harmony, presents that feature of neutrality of which this composer was ever so fond. Whether this fondness was that of real affection or rested upon mere convenience is indeed highly debatable. For my own part I have long since concluded that it was due to a conscious limitation of power; and it is better for those who admire him as sincerely as I do to make this confession, in order thereby to be the more free to dwell upon the many beautiful features of his work. Of such limitations there were several; the principal being that he seemed to feel the necessity of clinging fast to the simplest material. Whether he could have extricated himself successfully from the contrapuntal maze we do not know; but, within the range which was self-prescribed, the touch of his hand was magical; and I turn now to the more lovable task of exemplifying this.

Changing the stand-point therefore and regarding this symphony as an example of the masterful employment of simple means I quote the opening subject of the Allegro which may or may not be construed as a form of that of the Introduction, already given.

Ex. 48.

Subject I.

In either case the conclusion is the same, as the spirit of the parent theme is undoubtedly present. This the student may easily realise for himself by taking the bass of the latter and applying it to the above extract. I notice that Berezovsky describes this movement as based upon two subjects only; though, in reality, there are four. For purposes of analysis, however, there is liberty to construe according to the amount of detail in instruction, and I am naturally led to the greater subdivision. Besides that, it is often equally permissible to regard certain material as either subject-matter or episode; in which case the decision should rest partly upon the amount of development accorded to each theme by the composer himself, and partly upon the vocation which he has assigned to all such work in the home-coming. The latter is an even better test than the former; just as, in our wanderings, though we may make innumerable friendships, we re-assemble only our own kindred for the homeward journey; and each individual presence in that company is a token that it is of one who belongs to us. Accordingly (though with all respect to those who think differently) I discriminate as under.

It will be observed that, of these subjects, the first and third are of agitato, and the second and fourth of cantabile character; whilst between the last two there is a deficiency of tonality-contrast, needless to say of adverse influence in course of the work—a conspicuous example of which occurs at each entry of fourth subject. In accordance with Tchaikovsky's predilection we have foretastes of the third subject as early as bars 15 and 19 of the Allegro; such references being generally a sign that the subject so alluded to is destined for a subsequent position of

importance. This we find also here to be the case, for
the theme in question is not only used as such but its
opening bar is freely taken (if I may be forgiven for
so stating) whenever a stray instrument appears to
have nothing very particular to do; and copious
advantage is also taken of its neutral character to
wed it to the first subject in such a way that this fact
may account for these two subjects having been construed as one. The reader will scarcely require to be
told that its rhythm is a rather too forcible reminder
of Weber's Concert-Stück, but that may readily pass.
The important feature is that Tchaikovsky, though
he does not trust himself far afield, makes such
wonderfully adroit use of the advantages of keeping
close under the family roof-tree that we are lost in
wonder to discover such fine effects to be close at
hand whilst so many of us have been going long
journeys in search of them.

I must refer the reader to the chapters in which I
have described his diminutions in view of quicker
rhythmic pulsation; his repetitions which fail to
weary, through belonging to the musical sentence;
his simulations of counterpoint by the aid of grade-
work; and mannerisms generally. All these are, of
course, freely utilised in the symphony before us;
and, as usual, with excellent effect. The peculiarity
is that diversity of subject has deprived the Durchführung of its special interest. It is the only portion
showing a free modulation and presents the defect
that just when the more critical listener is promising
himself a real symphonic climax he finds him-

self back again; and has to face the whole parade
of subjects, merely transposed for the return. The
manner in which the Durchführung is introduced is
sufficiently amusing to justify an example, in which I
give, parallel to one another, the repeat which in old-
time form would have occurred, and the actual new
departure.

Ex. 52.

Such transparency of method positively endears this
composer to us; not, of course, by proof of genius,
but by the candour with which it seems to take us into
his confidence. An equal frankness is exhibited in
the abridgment of the first subject on the return;
where diminution is called in aid to form an upward
sequence in order that the tonality may be so raised
as to permit the transition to second subject to take

place in the desired key of G sharp minor. He must have known that every garden critic who came that way would be sure to observe how all this was done; and the delightfulness of not caring appeals to us as an amiability. [The passage is too long for quotation but the student will find it comprised within bars 320-328 of the Allegro].

The abridgement of first-subject thus alluded to constitutes the only difference between the return groups and the original statement; but the Coda, especially when considered in relation to the scantiness of the Durchführung, is somewhat extended. The actual proportion is 95-56 as against 188-166 for the two statements and 37 for introduction—this for the student who desires to gauge accurately the distribution of the movement. The Coda is a diminuendo, thrown into contrast by preparatory rise, and worked in Tchaikovsky's mournful manner—down and down to lower strings and bassoon. But the sadness of the ending is entirely consistent with the character of the movement; of which even the sprightly motion, though graceful, is never joyous. The contrasts afforded are not so great as those to which Tchaikovsky in other works has accustomed us. Not that those of timbre or volume are wanting; but that of varying intensity of feeling. This is no doubt partly caused by similarity of style in the subjects themselves; but to a greater extent by the composer's evident resolution to remain steadfast to the symphonic form, by which he was debarred from those higher flights more propitious to the full display of his genius.

SECOND MOVEMENT

The delightful melody of which this movement is the glorification attenuates all regret which shortcomings of the composition might otherwise occasion, for the sincerity of its discourse is too entrancing to admit of simultaneous contentions about principle. Our contention is rather with the kind of feeling we experience at the contemplation of beauty in tears; for we are compelled to sympathise even if we do not agree. It requires a stern resolve to enquire into the real merits of this creation; for, however we may view it as a symphony-movement, there can never be any doubt of its lyric beauty. But, if the ideal of the symphony is to be maintained, there is no alternative; and I will give my reasons for this.

All art is to some extent religious. Whether specially directed to the praise of the Creator or not it is a striving of the human soul heavenward. In music the symphony is the supreme expression of this feeling and its vocation is therefore to voice the aspirations of humanity—not those of an individual. There are those who imagine this view to exist merely in advocacy of contrapuntal display—a strange error. Counterpoint is merely an incident arising from the necessities of poor humanity for the use of rule and gauge in all its feeble accomplishments. The plaudits of the crowd in favour of an individual do not form the aggregation of voices of the symphonic ideal; which is a form of expression for the absence of which it is beyond the power of embroidery, however ingenious, graceful or varied, to atone. Such features as these more rightly appertain to the Suite than to the Symphony. To write in the latter form is the gravest responsibility which lies open to the creative musician to undertake. Dvořák said of Tchaikovsky that he could not write a symphony—but only suites; and, although I cannot go so far as to say that, I am evidently actuated by a similar thought.

It will be remembered that the Haupt-Motiv of this symphony pulsates at minim-distance; the crude-form of Ex. 47 being as follows:—

Ex. 53.

and it is obvious that all recurrences must be subject to this condition. That the intermezzo of this movement has been so constructed I shall have no difficulty in showing; and nothing could better demonstrate the accuracy of Tchaikovsky's æsthetic perception than the fact that he actually *commences* the movement with an introduction by the lower strings precisely in minim pulsations; precisely, that is, in the measured throb of which he so well knew the after-importance. The arch suspicion is here forced upon me that probably not one per thousand of his hearers have been technically aware of the reason for this.

Inwardly to feel it to be appropriate is not at all the same thing; for, when one knows the true inward meaning of these lugubrious chords, they actually *sound* differently. After eight bars of this character the first horn announces the principal subject; thus : —

Ex. 54.

its complete statement occupying 36 bars, in four-bar phrases, similar in rhythm to the above. The fourth of these is subject to a diminution of one bar, to allow of the plaintive oboe-introduction of a fore-taste of the next subject. This habit of Tchaikovsky, so often alluded to, should not be classed as a mannerism however; for the reason that it was probably due to his original ideas on the subject of form. It is worth the student's while to note that the bar thus lost is compensated for by an extension of

one bar in the sixth phrase; so that in rhythmising
the work he must be careful of this. The re-introduction of the subject at the seventh phrase is
naturally with a different instrumentation; as the
following extract from my piano-arrangement will
show.

The score being so accessible, I have thought it well
to present this passage in a manner suitable for
clavier; in order to enable the reader more readily to
gather the effect. The ninth phrase, introducing
second subject is less happy; for, truth to tell, it is
one of the "unseemly joins" with which Tchaikovsky

reproached other composers. But a speedy forgiveness awaits him for the sake of what follows.

Ex. 56.

This lovely theme is continued for 16 bars only; though in reality occupying 21 of the score. The difference arises from the fact that the second phrase is subject to an extension of three bars of grade work in contrary-motion for the entire orchestra (minus trumpets and drums) and leading to a burst of the above subject; the opening bar of which is made to form a falling sequence, resulting naturally in diminuendo. A cadence is arrived at with a single phrase; but out of this cadence a further integral two-bar phrase is formed. This is first given in the original key and afterwards used for the purpose of modulating into F sharp minor to begin the intermezzo. It is subjected on each occasion to an extension of one bar; and the whole distribution may be exemplified as under : —

Ex. 57.
Bars 60 to 66.

Cadence of previous bar used
for new two-bar phrase.

Repeat, producing one-bar
extension,

Repeat, producing one-bar
extension.

Commencement of Intermezzo.

minim-pulsation, necessary for the later
introduction of Haupt-Motiv.

The method here pursued is something akin to that adopted in the "Pathetic" Symphony, and which the reader (if he refer to Ex. 27) will find described as a rhythmic "backing"; but the object is not the same, being in this instance to return to a slower pulsation. This use of the same method for various purposes is what justifies Tchaikovsky's mannerisms—indeed, were an adequate space at my command, I should be tempted to show that they are thereby considerably more than merely excused.

The subject of the intermezzo, now constructed upon the minim pulsations to which we have attained, is distinctly common-place; and, saving one interval, entirely of grades. Yet it befits the situation completely: whilst the facilities afforded by the grade-work enable the composer to modulate with such entire freedom that he passes through the most various tonalities with an unaccustomed rapidity, free of all fear of incongruous transition. As it would be impossible to do justice to this intermezzo in the form of examples I shall content myself with quoting the bare subject of it, and for the rest refer the student to the score.

Ex. 58.
Clar.

After two such four-bar phrases the restlessness begins. The opening bar of the above, luxuriantly harmonised, is provided with a descending grade-bass calculated to work in sequence. By this means four phrases are formed, modulating to an extent which renders it difficult to say what key they fail to fringe, when suddenly the instrumentation is thinned down to oboes and bassoons with a simple running passage of the first violins only. At this point we who know Tchaikovsky regard the sequel as a mere matter of course. The stray instruments of each department rally round their comrades, the more ponderous being the last to appear. Everything uprises—strengthens—quickens, and finally bursts upon that which has all along been our calculated destination—the Haupt-Motiv. And the determination so expressed is the more resolute in consequence of the tiresome obstinacy of that organ-point over which the said parent-theme persists in forming a chord of the second which absolutely refuses to resolve. Even after the full orchestra has spent its passion and the strings resume the original movement preparatory to the re-introduction of first-subject it still tantalises us for two bars, before condescending to pass into the chord of the sixth; which, according to all musical decorum, it should have done long before. Now, let the critic, *if he can*, find fault with the supposed mannerism of the organ-point. It would be easy enough to do this were the case an ordinary one; but it is not so. Whether it be really good to tie up a whole symphony to a single theme is quite another matter. Granting the necessity, could there be a better means? That is the question— and the only possible answer is that there could not.

Little remains to be said of this movement, as the return differs from the original statement principally by variation of embroidery and figuration; features which, however interesting from other points of view, offer no fresh material for analysis. At the point corresponding to that of resumption of the minim pulsations a symmetrical feature occurs in the shape of a re-introduction of the Haupt-Motiv. The working of it, however, is not of Tchaikovsky's best; but the Coda diminuendo which follows is all the more perfect for presenting no new feature. Perfect instrumentation goes without saying; and the second subject, to which the Coda is devoted, is touchingly eloquent in such simple form. In this, as in all else, it is the human feeling which we most value; and which causes Tchaikovsky to be so esteemed, not only by those who know his failings, but by them, perhaps, most of all.

THIRD MOVEMENT (*Valse*)

When Shakespeare in praising the rural life claimed for it the beautiful advantage of finding "tongues in trees and books in the running brooks" he did not, as far as we know, contemplate its enjoyment alternately with that of the luxury of court surroundings. The truth of his reference to the good to be found in unexpected places and to the opportunities associated with humble life is shown by its power of ready application to other subjects; and, in the sphere of art, a disdain for the merely gorgeous and an appreciation of the beauty of more unpretentious work is the natural reproduction of his idea. There are tiny gems the detail of which is perfect; the material rich in suggestion; and the outline capable of indefinite expansion. There are also flowers by the way-side, from contemplation of which wonderful lessons may be drawn. On the other hand there are inflated and overgrown orchestral movements, which, like the *parvenu*, are only made to appear respectable by the aid of fine clothes; for not every character at court is of courtly character. But there are also grand works, conceived by master minds, for direct expression by the grand aggregation of musical means. The delights of each sphere are equally real—equally honourable: but they are opposed. To find "tongues in trees and books in the running brooks" the first condition is that we should actually be in some place where trees and brooks are to be found. We cannot, at one and the same time, enjoy the range of vision offered by two different standpoints in art, any more than in every-day life; and, if the attempt to unite the pleasures of court and country are found to result in both indifferent pageantry and realism, so will the attempted union of two different styles in art as surely prove to be of adverse influence upon both.

Such are the thoughts with which I approach the contemplation of a "Valse" within a Symphony. Either this movement must be held, by the caprice of its composer, to have hoisted a flag to which it was not strictly entitled; or the whole work has been incorrectly described. No one can "valse" while engaged in realisation of the symphonic ideal; and the manifestation of any such desire would be a sure proof of his not being in a fit condition of mind for the purpose. It is therefore refreshing to note that, in spite of his curious choice of a label for this movement, Tchaikovsky has equally found this to be impossible. It is perhaps right that (whether by courtesy or the adoption of an accomodating scale of judgment) we should not absolutely refuse to admit the title; but the fact remains that this is simply an ordinary graceful movement in $\frac{3}{4}$; from which the more characteristic accentuation allied with other dance forms is absent, and which falls under the "valse" category merely by virtue of that fact.

Tchaikovsky

Ex. 59.

This point cannot too greatly be insisted on, as it relates to features of the question which are continually taken for granted; and thus continue to remain but imperfectly understood. The most usual dance forms in ¾ are the Valse, Mazurka, Minuet and Polonaise. The Mazurka gives a rhythmic importance to its second beat; whilst the Polonaise adds emphasis to the first, partly by subdivision of the other two. The Minuet gives more individuality to each beat; and the "Valse lente" is consequently in danger of approximating to it too closely: should the composer be unmindful of this fact. With these, and a few other slight exceptions the whole residue of ¾ movement goes to the "Valse" category; for the simple reason that the absence of characteristic rhythm causes the wafting effect inherent to the triple measure to be allowed to take its course. [The student will find a treatment of this subject in my manual "How to Compose Within Lyric Form," Chapter XII.] It is therefore permissible to regard this movement as one of the mere "Tempo di Valse" character, in which the middle portion was deliberately reserved for a rapid bar-subdivision in moto perpetuo; and for the purpose of securing the scherzo-like effect with which that contrast was bound to be associated.

The view thus indicated of the composition of this movement is strengthened by the fact that the capricious portion of it both begins and ends quite suddenly, and is not treated by that process of gradual evolution in which Tchaikovsky so greatly excelled; and from which he therefore did not refrain from any lack of aptitude to apply it, had it fallen within his intention to do so. Not only so, but the in-coming of the caprice is preceded by phrases in syncopation which compel a slight rallentando; with the evident intention of adding to the sprightliness of the new departure as here shown.

Ex. 60.

The effect of this intermezzo is truly excellent; not, as some might think, in spite of, but rather because of its being built upon absolutely nothing. My readers will probably smile at such a peculiar combination of ideas; but I must really insist that after all this "humour" question is a very serious affair. "Serious"—I mean—for those behind the scenes; and who are responsible caterers for the great public in front. The latter requires only to be amused; but the former must closely discriminate after the manner of a *chef-de-cuisine* in order to avoid the introduction of ingredients unsuitable to the dish which is being actually served; however suitable these might be for some other occasion. The humour of the eccentric or grotesque must not be confused with that of the merely playful; and a great master is always well displayed in the writing of a fine scherzo, for the reason that whether the fun proceed from the ponderous character who is unconsciously humorous or from the gay dog who regards everything in life from the most cheerful aspect available a vast reserve of inventive power is necessary. But there is a mild form of humour the main trait of which is an utter *nonchalance;* and the musical expression of which would be completely ruined by the slightest intrusion of thought and calculation. When therefore we find ourselves, as now, in the presence of music of this description, to reproach it with lack of idea would be to find fault with the very fact constituting the composer's opportunity to give over his entire orchestra to the merest

frolic. An idea most welcome at some other time
would here but play the part of *trouble-fête*, by dis-
turbing the innocent course of our enjoyment.
Tchaikovsky proves his æsthetic perception in giving
us this movement strictly unadulterated. Herein he
has also well illustrated his own dictum that to
orchestrate is to "distribute"; for, though we are held
in rapt attention by the continual semiquaver motion,
it comes upon us from all quarters with such adroit
fusion and charming contrast that, short of absolute
knowledge to the contrary, we should imagine the
orchestra to be disporting itself without calculation,
after the manner of an extemporaneous performance.
The result is perfect of its kind; for Tchaikovsky
knew so well how to obtain rhythmic prominence
without emphasis that, notwithstanding the continual
semiquaver motion, the "Tempo di Valse" movement
abides, sometimes, however, crossing the bar-line. I
here give an example of each kind, accompanied by
the crude-form, and showing that the simple expedi-
ent for retention of the effect of emphasis is a
momentary crescendo and diminuendo with its climax
at the moment of percussion of the beat; by which
means not only the rhythmic object is attained but an
element of humour is introduced which no listener
can have failed to notice and to appreciate.

Ex. 61.

(a)

Of the return and Coda there is little to be said; for the usual reason that so little new feature is presented. But total exception must be taken to the introduction of the Haupt-Motiv; which is not only mechanically effected but which is not even a correct quotation, as the rhythmic proportions of the original are not observed. Time is the basis of all music; and, therefore, if the time-relation of the notes of a subject be not preserved the quotation cannot stand. In the original motive the time-relation between the sustained notes and the remaining portion of the bar was as 3 to 1. In the present version the relation is, however, 2 to 1:—utterly disfiguring the whole passage as the following example will show.

Ex. 62.

(a) Time-relations.

Original version of Haupt-motiv.

(b) Time-relations.

Valse version of the same.

That a subject does not consist of mere note succession is proved by the fact that, in the valse-version, all dignity of the original theme has completely vanished; without being even compensated for in any other way. I am at a loss to know whether; or, on what ground, the introduction of this parody of the original theme can be defended, other than that of deferential submission to the composer's will. The feebleness of the Coda is also a consequence of the intrusion; but, however regrettable this isolated circumstance may be, it is powerless to eradicate the charming impression of the movement, and especially of the intermezzo; the enjoyment of which is perfect whether indulged in as listener, performer, student or critic.

FOURTH MOVEMENT (*Finale*)

This movement, though last in order was probably the first to be written; as the parent-theme of the symphony, to which it is principally devoted, and which in every other phase has appeared more or less in the light of a "canto-fermo," the introduction of which was due to exigency, now for the first time assumes what appeals to us instantly as its form of origin. This circumstance at once bids fair for the success of the whole movement; and it may be freely stated that the promise thus held out is well redeemed. The section consists of an Allegro vivace (alla breve) of 414 bars, preceded and followed by a maestoso of 57 and 32 bars respectively; exclusive of a short subsequent Presto and concluding reminiscence of the first movement. The material of each maestoso is the same; being the Haupt-Motiv in the

major, told in a march-form extending to several
eight-bar sentences, which, though subjected to occasional overlappings and extensions, are sufficiently
exhibited, as to subject-matter, in the following
quotation.

Ex. 63.

The instrumentation of the second maestoso is far
more full and elaborate than that of the first, as
might easily be divined. But besides that there are
differences of character due, in the first instance, to
greater subdivision of the beat value on the second

occasion. Another difference of character arises
through the figuration being first kept systematically
below the subject and afterwards being allowed to
soar aloft; while the trumpets ("a 2, *fff*, marziale,
energico, e con tutta forza") deliver the final message.
All this work is of that orderly and disciplinary
species which, though it may offer no ground for
special remark, is of great value as indicating the
composer's method. For this reason I exhibit, as
well as the small space at command will allow me,
the four degrees of intensity to which Tchaikovsky
thus attained.

Bx. 64.

These observations leave me free to deal absolutely
with the Allegro; which, though lying between two
important recurrences of the Haupt-Motiv, really
constitutes the movement from the scientific point of
view. The march-theme, however effective, presents

merely a new example of the employment of resources within the reach of every composer; but there is that about the Allegro which is Tchaikovsky's very own, and with which therefore it is a pleasure to have to deal.

Attention is immediately arrested by the sparseness of material, in which respect Tchaikovsky has on this occasion positively eclipsed himself. Let the reader possess himself of the following rhythm; repeat it with any melodic, harmonic or contrapuntal devices which may occur; never suspending it (except during introduction of the Haupt-Motiv) until about two hundred such repetitions have been completed; and he already knows the rhythmic outline of the movement.

Ex. 65.

My duty, therefore, entirely lies with the question of how this rhythm is applied; a task as easy for me to fulfil as the explanations involved will be easy to comprehend. But let me first guard the reader against the error of supposing these remarks to be indicative of blame; as such an exposition of the composer's methods might rather naturally lead him to conclude. The diametric contrary is the fact; for, if this movement is a triumph (as, in any event, its effect would entitle it to be considered) it is all the more so for its simplicity of basis. The great majority of those who listen to it know only of its power; which they applaud. They would applaud still more, could they realise the wonderful use made by the composer of the most simple means.

The opening subject, as subjoined, is the first application of the subject-rhythm; each bracketed passage being twice played.

Ex. 66.

The four following applications of the same rhythm are similarly repeated; so that, independently of the extreme simplicity of the material employed this simplicity is practically doubled by the fact that the first 24 bars are in reality only 12. This feature of playing everything twice is part of the character of the movement, and manifests itself again in the episode leading to second subject; for, although variety is imparted by its length extending to four repetitions of the subject rhythm, these four repetitions are just as religiously subjected to repetition in their turn as was the former single utterance. A mere modification of the ending in order to favour the introduction of second subject is the only permitted difference; as here shown.

Ex. 67.

The superficial observer may perhaps be tempted to
feel contemptuous at such apparent servility of
method. Let him be cautioned; for, in reviewing
Tchaikovsky, it is highly dangerous to proceed to the
open disclosure of any such impressions. Far better
is it to wait and probe; for a too great simplicity on
the surface is generally found to indicate an underlying æsthetic motive of importance. In this case,
for example, a reference to Ex. 65 will show that the
subject-rhythm contains the germ of repetition within
itself; so that, in causing the majority of phrases to
be twice performed, the composer has been acting in
simple obedience to the requirements of the scheme
upon which the whole composition is founded. These
keen perceptions are precisely what most entitle him
to the rank of a great composer; and a further
delightful instance of this special power is shown by
the short sample of infinite canon, of which the
second subject consists. The canon itself is one
which the merest student might have written. Its
matter therefore courts no admiration; but the selection from the composer's armoury of an instrument
so suitable for the purpose on hand is the act of a

master in the craft. The "round" (by which title
the infinite canon is more popularly known) at once
implies that it contains the germ of repetition within
itself—precisely the feature of the subject-rhythm
which the composer had in view; and therefore, of all
means at his command, the most beautifully appropriate, as shown in the following example.

Ex. 68.

I have extended the canon for one bar in order to
show that the composer, in obedience to the same
principle, proceeds to a further repetition in the key
of D; so that the canon in question, though of only
four-bar length, occupies 16 bars of the score. Far
from tiring of such repetition our interest is not only

maintained but increased; as a consequence of the innate coherence of the whole procedure. I have heard it questioned whether Tchaikovsky will ultimately take rank with the giants of our art, and will not deny the existence of some reasons for doubt. But it is remarkable that those who know his failings think little less of him on their account; whilst those who do not know them may be trusted to remain enthusiastic, for the abundant reasons brought to light by the analysis of this movement.

The subject-rhythm next assumes the character of an ostinato bass; the introduction of which is as masterly in instrumentation as its subsequent employment is ingenious in design. The effective appearance of a feature of this description depends upon its *immediately* arresting the attention of every listener. Unless this be thoroughly well done the ostinato, by occasionally running counter to the harmony elsewhere prevailing, will be of intolerable effect. But, if its real character be *at once* recognised, a delight will ensue from its very preversity. This is precisely what happens; as is here shown.

Ex. 69.

This extract commences at the climax of an uprising passage in which the whole orchestra is engaged; the ostinato being at once given over to all the double-basses, 'cellos and both bassoons in unison and supported by the drums; for which purpose time has

previously been given to tune the C drum down to A.
It is obvious that these collective means, even if un-
assisted, would be somewhat boldly assertive; but,
aided by the silence of the remaining orchestra at the
strong beats of the bar, and by its gradual reduction,
the hearer becomes thoroughly initiated. Yet the
danger of obscuring the ostinato was evidently still
in the composer's mind; as is shown firstly by his introducing the new subject at a pitch far removed
from it. Next, the intermediate harmony is, with
evident intention, but lightly represented. Thirdly,
and most important of all, the accompanying strings
not only divide the bar with triplets (thus preventing
any simultaneous percussion from taking place with
the second and fourth beats of the ostinato) but they
are altogether suppressed at the first and third beats,
when a simultaneous percussion would otherwise have
occurred. The result is that, although the harmoniza-
tion is perfectly apparent, the ostinato makes itself
felt precisely as if performed alone. A grand lesson.

Space will not allow me to deal exhaustively with
this portion of the work; but the above example exhibits the first widening of the wedge, and therefore
faintly indicated the nature of treatment; until
finally a gradual crescendo and uprising sequence
heralds the entry of the parent-theme. This as
already stated is signalised by cessation of the subject-rhythm; the cessation becoming as it were a
negative means of conferring prominence upon the
entry; a four-bar extract of which is here given.

Ex. 70.

The Haupt-Motiv now monopolises the situation for 32 bars; minus two, for an anticipated return of the first subject. The features which then follow are of similar interest to those already described; whilst the Presto following the second maestoso is a glorification of the episode leading to second subject and is followed by a reminiscence of the first movement to conclude the work. There is therefore nothing to add; scarcely even a final tribute to the merits of this great work, my appreciation of which must already be abundantly evident.

Should, therefore, the lessons which I have attempted to draw from it result in benefit to the student, the consciousness of having been of practical service will be added to the pleasure of that which was already a labour of love.

INDICES FOR STUDENT USE

———: o : ———

I

LIST OF TCHAIKOVSKY'S WORKS IN THE ARRANGEMENT OF OPUS NUMBER

Op. 1. No. 1. Scherzo à la russe. 2. Impromptu. Two piano-
forte pieces dedicated to Nicholas Rubinstein.
Op. 2. Three pieces for pianoforte. Souvenir de Hapsaal. 1.
Ruines d'un Château. 2. Scherzo. 3. Chant sans paroles.
Op. 3. The Voievoda : an opera of which only two numbers
exist. 1. Overture. 2. Entr'acte and Air de Ballet.
Op. 4. Valse Caprice. For pianoforte (D major).
Op. 5. Romance. For pianoforte (F minor). Dedicated to
Mlle. Désirée Artôt.
Op. 6. Six songs. For voice and pianoforte.
Op. 7. Valse-Scherzo (A major). For pianoforte. Dedicated
to Madame A. Davidov.

Op. 8. Capriccio (G flat). For pianoforte. Dedicated to C. Klindworth.

Op. 9. Three pieces for pianoforte. 1. Rêverie. 2. Polka de Salon. 3. Mazurka de Salon.

Op. 10. Two pieces for pianoforte. 1. Nocturne. 2. Humoresque.

Op. 11. First String Quartet (D major). For two violins, viola, and violoncello. Dedicated to M. Serge Ratschinsky.

Op. 12. The Snow Maiden (Snegourotchka). Music to a fairytale by Ostrovsky. 1. Introduction. 2. Dance and Chorus of Birds. 3. Monologue of the Frosts. 4. Carnival Chorus. 5. Melodrama. 5a. Entr'acte. 6. Lel's Song. 7. Lel's Song. 8. Entr'acte. 9. Chorus of Blind Gussleeplayers. 10. Melodrama. 11. Folk Chorus and Chorus of the Courtiers. 12. Choral Dance of Maidens. 13. Jester's Dance. 14. Lel's Song. 14a. Lel's Song. 15. Brussilio's Song. 16. Appearance of the Wood Demons and the Shadow of the Snow Maiden. 17. Entr'acte. 18. March of the King of Berendei and Chorus. 19. Finale.

Op. 13. First Symphony (G minor), "Winter Day Dreams." 1. Allegro tranquillo : "Dreams on the High-road in Winter." 2. Adagio cantabile : Dreary Land, Land of Mists. 3. Allegro scherzando giocoso. 4. Finale : Andante lugubre.

Op. 14. Vakoula the Smith. Opera written for a prize competition organised by the Grand Duchess Helena, afterwards rewritten and published as The Caprices of Oxane.

Op. 15. Triumphal Overture on the Danish National Hymn. For full orchestra.

Op. 16. Six songs.

Op. 17. Second Symphony (C minor), on Malo-Russian Themes. 1. Andante sostenuto. 2. Andantino marziale. 3. Scherzo. 4. Finale.

Op. 18. The Tempest (F minor). Orchestra-fantasia on Shakespeare's play. Dedicated to M. Vladimir Stassov.

Op. 19. Six pieces for pianoforte. 1. Rêverie du Soir. 2. Scherzo humoristique. 3. Feuillet d'Album. 4. Nocturne. 5. Capriccioso. 6. Thème original et variations.

Op. 20. The Swan Lake. Ballet in four acts.

Op. 21. Six pieces for pianoforte, on one theme. Dedicated to Anton Rubinstein.

Op. 22. Second String Quartet (F major). For two violins, viola, and violoncello.

Op. 23. Concerto for pianoforte and orchestra (B flat minor). Dedicated to Hans von Bülow.

Op. 24. Eugene Oniegin. An opera in three acts. Libretto adapted from the poem of A. Poushkin.

Op. 25. Six songs. Published by V. Bessel and Co., St. Petersburg.

Op. 26. Sérénade mélancholique (B minor). For violin and orchestra. Dedicated to Herr L. Auer.

Op. 27. Six songs.

Op. 28. Six songs.

Op. 29. The Third Symphony (D major). 1. Introduction and Allegro. 2. Alla tedesca. 3. Andante elegiaco. 4. Finale: Allegro con fuoco (tempo di polacca).

Op. 30. Third String Quartet (E flat). For two violins, viola, and violoncello. Dedicated to the memory of F. Laub.

Op. 31. Slavonic March. On national themes. For full orchestra.

Op. 32. Francesca di Rimini. Orchestral fantasia from Dante's *Inferno*. Dedicated to M. Serge Taneiev.

Op. 33. Variations sur un thème rococo (7 variations and coda). For violoncello, with orchestral accompaniment. Dedicated to M. G. Fitzenhagen.

Op. 34. Valse-Scherzo (C major). For violin and orchestra.

Op. 35. Concerto (D major). For violin and orchestra. Dedicated to Mr. A. Brodsky.

Op. 36. The Fourth Symphony (F minor). For full orchestra. Dedicated "to my best friend." 1. Andante sostenuto. 2. Andantino in modo di canzone. 3. Scherzo. 4. Finale: Allegro con fuoco.

Op. 37. Grand Sonata (G major). For pianoforte. Dedicated to Herr C. Klindworth.

Op. 37a. The Seasons. Twelve characteristic pieces for pianoforte.

Op. 38. Six songs, with pianoforte accompaniment.

Op. 39. Children's Album. Twenty-four easy pieces in the style of Schumann, for pianoforte.

Op. 40. Twelve pieces for pianoforte (medium difficulty. 1. Etude. 2. Chanson triste. 3. Marche funèbre. 4. Mazurka. 5. Mazurka. 6. Chant sans paroles. 7. Au Village. 8. Valse. 9. Valse. 10. Danse russe. 11. Scherzo. 12. Rêverie interrompue.

Op. 41. The Liturgy of St. John of Chrysostom. For four voices (soprano, alto, tenor, and bass), with pianoforte accompaniment.

Op. 42. Three pieces for violin, with pianoforte accompaniment: Souvenir d'un lieu cher. 1. Méditation. 2. Scherzo. 3. Mélodie.

Op. 43. First Orchestral Suite. 1. Introduction and Fugue. 2. Divertimento. 3. Intermezzo. 4. Scherzo. 5. Gavotte.

Op. 44. Second Concerto for pianoforte and orchestra. Dedicated to Nicholas Rubinstein.

Op. 45. Capriccio italien. For orchestra.

Op. 46. Six duets. For two voices and pianoforte accompaniment.

Op. 47. Seven songs, with pianoforte accompaniment.

Op. 48. Serenade for string orchestra.

Op. 49. The Year 1812. A solemn overture, written for the opening of the Cathedral of Christ the Redeemer, Moscow.

Op. 50. Trio for piano, violin, and violoncello. Dedicated "to the memory of a great artist" (Nicholas Rubinstein).

Op. 51. Six pieces for pianoforte. 1. Valse de Salon. 2. Polka peu dansante. 3. Menuetto scherzoso. 4. Natha-Valse. 5. Romance. 6. Valse sentimentale.

Op. 52. Russian Service (first vespers). An attempt to harmonise the church canticles (for mixed choir).

Op. 53. Second Orchestral Suite. 1. Jeu de sons. 2. Valse. 3. Scherzo burlesque. 4. Rêves d'enfant. 5. Danse baroque (style Dargomijsky).

Op. 54. Sixteen songs for young people, with pianoforte accompaniment.

Op. 55. Third Orchestral Suite. 1. Elégie. 2. Valse Mélancolique. 3. Scherzo. 4. Tema con variazioni (12 variations).

Op. 56. Concert-Fantasia. For piano, with orchestral accompaniment. Dedicated to Madame Sophie Menter.

Op. 57. Six songs, with pianoforte accompaniment.

Op. 58. Manfred. Symphony, in four tableaux, from the dramatic poem by Byron. Dedicated to M. Mily Balakirev. 1. Lento lugubre: Manfred in the Alps. 2. Vivace con spirito: The Spirit of the Alps appears to Manfred. 3. Andante con moto: Pastorale. 4. Allegro con fuoco: The palace of Arimane. Manfred amid the bacchanalian revels. Evocation of the shade of Astarte. She predicts the end of his mortal woes. Death of Manfred.

Op. 59. Dumka. Russian rustic scene. For pianoforte.

Op. 60. Twelve songs, with pianoforte accompaniment. Dedicated to Her Majesty the Tsaritsa.

Op. 61. Fourth Orchestral Suite (Mozartiana). 1. Gigue. 2. Menuet. 3. Preghicra. 4. Theme and Variations (10 variations).

Op. 62. Pezzo Capriccioso. Morceau de Concert. For violoncello, with orchestral or pianoforte accompaniment.

Op. 63. Six songs, with pianoforte accompaniment. Dedicated to His Imperial Highness the Grand Duke Constantine.

Op. 64. The Fifth Symphony (E minor). Dedicated to M. Ave-Lallement of Hamburg. 1. Andante: Allegro con anima. 2. Andante cantabile. 3. Valse: Allegro moderato. 4. Finale: Andante maestoso: Allegro vivace (alla breve).

Op. 65. Six melodies to French words.

Op. 66. Sleeping Beauty. A ballet preceded by a prologue (30 numbers).

Op. 67. Hamlet. Ouverture-Fantaisie for full orchestra. Dedicated to Edward Grieg.

Op. 67a. Hamlet. Overture, melodramas, marches, and entr'-actes. For small orchestra.

Op. 68. Dame de Pique (Queen of Spades). An opera in three acts and seven scenes.

Op. 69. Iolanthe. A lyric opera in one act.

Op. 70. Souvenir de Florence. Sextet for stringed instruments. 1. Allegro con spirito. 2. Adagio cantabile. 3. Allegro moderato. 4. Allegro vivace.

Op. 71. Casse-Noisette (The Nut-cracker). Fairy ballet for orchestra, in two acts (15 numbers).

Op. 71a. Suite for full orchestra, adapted from the score of the Casse-Noisette ballet. 1. Ouverture Miniature. 2. Danses caractéristiques: (a) Marche; (b) Danse de la Fée Dragée; (c) Danse russe, Trépak; (d) Danse arabe; (e) Danse chinoise; (f) Danse des mirlitons. 3. Valse des fleurs.

Op. 72. Eighteen pieces for pianoforte.

Op. 73. Six songs, with pianoforte accompaniment.

Op. 74. Sixth Symphony, "Pathetic" (B minor). Dedicated to M. Vladimir Davidov. 1. Adagio: Allegro non troppo. 2. Allegro con grazia. 3. Allegro molto vivace. 4. Finale: Adagio lamentoso.

Op. 75. Concerto No. 3 (posthumous). For piano and orchestra. Dedicated to M. Louis Diemer.

Works without Opus Number

Romeo and Juliet. Overture-fantasia after Shakespeare, for full orchestra. Dedicated to M. Mily Balakirev.

Romeo and Juliet. Duet (soprano and tenor). Posthumous work, completed from sketches left by the composer, and orchestrated by S. Taneiev.

Elegy in memory of J. Samarin. For string orchestra.

Solemn Coronation March. For orchestra. Composed for the coronation of the Emperor Alexander III. at Moscow.

Solemn March. For full orchestra (posthumous).

Military March. For military band. Dedicated to the 98th Regiment of Infantry.

Impromptu—Caprice. For pianoforte.

Valse-Scherzo. For pianoforte.

Impromptu. Published in the album of old students of the Conservatoire dedicated to A. Rubinstein, St. Petersburg, 1889.

Impromptu (Momento lirico). For pianoforte (posthumous).

Perpetuum mobile. Finale of Weber's Sonata in C major, arranged for left hand only.

Five songs, with pianoforte accompaniment (published separately).

Hommage à A. Rubinstein. Chorus a capella, composed for his Jubilee, 1889. Words by Polonsky.

Chorus for male voices. Dedicated to the students of Moscow
University.
Chorus (The Nightingale). For mixed choir.
Night. Vocal quartet. Music arranged from Mozart's Fantasia
for Piano (No. 4).
Love and Nature. Vocal trio (posthumous).
Nine church choruses for mixed voices.
Hymn in honour of SS. Cyril and Methodius. Chorus a capella
on an old Slavonic melody.
Mazeppa. Opera in three acts.
Moscow. Cantata for solo, chorus, and orchestra. Written for
the Coronation of the Emperor Alexander III.
The Oprichnik. Opera in four acts. Published by W. Bessel
and Co., St. Petersburg.
Joan of Arc. Opera in four acts.
The Enchantress (Charodeïka). Opera in four acts.
Le caprice d' Oxane (Cherevichek) : Two little Shoes. Origin-
ally published as Vakoula the Smith.

Recent Posthumous Works

Overture to the Drama *The Storm*, by Ostrovsky. Composed
in 1865. Published by M. Belaiev, Leipzig, 1896.
Fatum (Destiny). Symphonic poem. Composed in 1869.
Belaiev, Leipzig, 1896.
Op. 78. The Voievoda. Symphonic ballad. For orchestra.
Belaiev, Leipzig, 1897.
Op. 79. Andante and Finale. For piano and orchestra. In-
strumentation by S. Taneiev.
Sonata in C sharp minor (containing the Scherzo which was after-
wards used in Symphony No. 1.)

Except where it is otherwise stated, the works are published by
P. Jurgenson, Moscow.

D D

II

CLASSIFIC ACCOUNT
OF
TCHAIKOVSKY'S WORKS

I

FOR PIANO SOLO.

Op. 1. Two pieces, dedicated to N. Rubinstein. 1. Scherzo à la Russe. 2. Impromptu (originally "Capriccio").
Op. 2. Souvenir de Hapsaal. 1. Ruines d'un Chateau. 2. Scherzo. 3. Chant sans paroles. (Ref. p. 18).
Op. 4. Valse Caprice in D.
Op. 5. Romance in F minor, dedicated to Mlle. Desirée Artôt.
Op. 7. Valse Scherzo in A, dedicated to Mme. A. Davidoff.
Op. 8. Capriccio, dedicated to C. Klindworth.
Op. 9. Three pieces. 1. Rêverie. 2. Polka de Salon. 3. Mazurka de Salon.
Op. 10. Two pieces. 1. Nocturne. 2. Humoreske.
Op. 19. Six pieces. 1. Rêverie du Soir. 2. Scherzo humoristique. 3. Feuillet d'Album. 4. Nocturne. 5. Capriccioso. 6. Thème original et Variations.
Op. 21. Six pieces on one theme, dedicated to Anton Rubinstein. 1. Prelude. 2. Fugue. 3. Impromptu. 4. Funeral March. 5. Mazurka. 6. Scherzo. (Ref. p. 34).

Op. 23. First Concerto (with orchestra) in B flat minor, dedicated to Hans v. Bülow. Analysis, 288. (Ref. p. 41, 214, 215).

Op. 37. Sonata in G, dedicated to C. Klindworth. (Ref. p. 78).

Op. 37a. "The Seasons." 12 characteristic pieces. 1. January. At the Hearth. 2. February. Carnival. 3. March. Song of the Lark. 4. April. Lily of the Valley. 5. May. Starlit Night. 6. June. Barcarolle. 7. July. Song of the Reapers. 8. August. Harvest Song. 9. September. Hunter's Song. 10. October. Autumn Song. 11. November. Troika. 12. December. Christmas. (Ref. p. 54).

Op. 39. Children's Album. 24 easy pieces. 1. Morning Prayer. 2. Winter Morning. 3. Hobby Horse. 4. Mamma. 5. Toy-Soldier's March. 6. The Sick Dolly. 7. Dolly's Funeral. 8. Waltz. 9. My New Dolly. 10. Mazurka. 11. Russian Song. 12. The Rustic Accordeon Player. 13. Russian Dance. 14. Polka. 15. Italian Song. 16. Old French Song. 17. German Song. 18. Neapolitan Song. 19. Nursery Tale. 20. Witch in the Wood. 21. Sweet Dreams. 22. The Lark's Song. 23. The Organ-grinder's Song. 24. At Church.

Op. 40. Twelve pieces of moderate difficulty. 1. Etude. 2. Chanson triste. 3. Marche funèbre. 4. Mazurka. 5. Mazurka. 6. Chant sans paroles. 7. Au Village. 8. Valse. 9. Valse. 10. Danse Russe. 11. Scherzo. 12. Rêverie interrompue.

Op. 44. Second Concerto (with orchestra), dedicated to N. Rubinstein. (Ref. p. 74).

Op. 51. Six pieces. 1. Valse de Salon. 2. Polka peu dansante. 3. Menuetto Scherzoso. 4. Natha-Valse. 5. Romance. 6. Valse sentimentale.

Op. 56. Concert Fantasia (with orchestra), dedicated to Mme. Sophie Menter. "Quasi-Rondo," "Contrasts."

Op. 59. Dumka: Rustic Russian Scene, dedicated to A. F. Marmontel. (Ref. p. 98).

Op. 72. Eighteen pieces for pianoforte. 1. Impromptu. 2. Berceuse. 3. Tendres reproches. 4. Danse caractéristique. 5. Méditation. 6. Mazurka pour danser. 7. Polacca de Concert. 8. Dialogue. 9. Un poco di Schumann. 10. Scherzo-Fantaisie. 11. Valse-Bluette. 12. L'espiègle. 13. Echo rustique. 14. Chant elegiaque. 15. Un poco di Chopin. 16. Valse à cinq temps. 17. Passé lointain. 18. Scène dansante (Invitation au trepak).

Op. 75. Third Concerto (with orchestra), dedicated to Louis Diemer. Posthumous work; of which the 2nd and 3rd movements (Andante and Finale) orchestrated by Taneiev, and sometimes mentioned separately as Op. 79.

Impromptu-Caprice (written for the Gaulois album).

Valse Scherzo in A (posthumous).

Impromptu (published in the Album of old students of the Conservatoire, dedicated to A. Rubinstein, 1889).

Impromptu (momento lirico), posthumous work, finished by Taneiev.

Perpetuum-mobile, for left-hand alone, being the Finale of Weber's First Sonata (posthumous).

Sonata in C sharp minor (posthumous).

II

FOR STRINGS.

Op. 11. Quartet No. 1, in D; dedicated to M. Serge Ratchinsky. Moderato. Andante. Scherzo. Allegro-finale. (Ref. p. 27).

Op. 22. Quartet No. 2, in F; dedicated to the Grand Duke Constantine. Adagio and Moderato. Scherzo. Andante. Allegro-finale. (Ref. p. 33).

Op. 30. Quartet No. 3, in E flat; dedicated to the memory of F. Laub. Andante and Allegro moderato. Allegretto scherzando. Andante funèbre. Allegro finale. (Ref. p. 53).

Op. 48. Serenade for String Orchestra. (Ref. p. 74, 85, 215).

Op. 70. Sextett (dedicated to the St. Petersburg Chamber Music Society), entitled "Souvenir de Florence." Allegro con spirito. Adagio. Allegro moderato. Allegro vivace. For 2 violins, 2 violas and 2 violoncellos. (Ref. p. 101, 102).

Elegy for String Orchestra, in memory of J. Samarin.

III

FOR ORCHESTRA.

(a) SYMPHONIES.

Op. 13. Symphony No. 1, in G minor. "Winter Day Dreams." 1. Allegro tranquillo (On the high road in winter). 2. Adagio cantabile (Dreary land; land of mists). 3. Allegro scherzando

List of Works 405

giocoso. 4. Finale—Andante lugubre. (Ref. p. 14, 15, 16, 17, 19).

Op. 17. Symphony No. 2, in C minor, on Malo-Russian themes, dedicated to the Imperial Russian Musical Society, Moscow. 1. Andante sostenuto. 2. Andantino marziale. 3. Scherzo. 4. Finale. (Ref. p. 38, 167).

Op. 29. Symphony No. 3, in D. "The Polish." 1. Introduction and Allegro. 2. Alla tedesca. 3. Andante elegiaco. 4. Finale—Allegro con fuoco (Tempo di Polacca). (Ref. p. 31, 51, 52, 167).

Op. 36. Symphony No. 4, in F minor, dedicated "to my best friend" (Madame von Meck). 1. Andante sostenuto. 2. Andantino in modo di Canzone. 3. Scherzo. 4. Finale—Allegro con fuoco. (Ref. p. 58, 73, 167).

Op. 64. Symphony No. 5, in E minor, dedicated to M. Ave-Lallement, of Hamburg. 1. Andante: Allegro con anima. 2. Andante cantabile. 3. Valse: Allegro moderato. 4. Finale—Andante maestoso and Allegro vivace (Alla breve). Analysis, 360. (Ref. p. 98, 103, 167).

Op. 74. Symphony No. 6, in B minor. "The Pathetic," dedicated to M. Vladimir Davidoff. 1. Adagio—Allegro non troppo. 2. Allegro con grazia. 3. Allegro molto vivace. 4. Finale—Adagio lamentoso. Analysis, 305. (Ref. p. 60, 98, 105, 106, 107, 108, 109, 112, 113, 139).

(b) SUITES.

Op. 43. Suite, No. 1. 1. Introduction and Fugue. 2. Divertimento. 3. Intermezzo. 4. Scherzo. 5. Gavotte. (Ref. p. 78, 199, 224).

Op. 53. Suite, No. 2. 1. Jeu de sons. 2. Valse. 3. Scherzo burlesque. 4. Rêves d'enfant. 5. Danse baroque (style Dargomijsky). (Ref. p. 86).

Op. 55. Suite, No. 3. 1. Elégie. 2. Valse mélancolique. 3. Scherzo. 4. Tema con variazioni (12). (Ref. p. 91, 213, 215).

Op. 61. Suite, No. 4, entitled "Mozartiana." 1. Gigue in D. 2. Menuet in D. 3. Preghiera (Ave verum). 4. Theme and 10 Variations. (Ref. p. 98, 118).

(c) TONE-POEMS.

Op. 18. "The Tempest." Fantasia in F minor, dedicated to M. Vladimir Stassov. (Ref. p. 38, 39, 40, 41, 113, 167).

Op. 32. "Francesco di Rimini," Fantasia from Dante's Inferno; dedicated to M. Serge Taneiev. (Ref. p. 56, 57, 108, 113, 167, 356).

Op. 58. "Manfred":—Four Tableaux from the dramatic poem by Byron; dedicated to M. Mili Balakirev. 1. Lento lugubre (Manfred in the Alps). 2. Vivace con spirito (The spirit of the Alps appears to Manfred). 3. Andante con moto : Pastorale. 4. Allegro con fuoco : The Palace of Arimane (Manfred amid the Bacchanalian Revels. Evocation of the Shade of Astarte. She predicts the end of his mortal woes. Death of Manfred). (Ref. p. 91, 167).

Op. 67. "Hamlet":—Ouverture fantaisie, dedicated to Ed. Grieg. (Ref. p. 93).

Op. 67a. The same for small orchestra, together with 16 incidental pieces, consisting of melodramas, marches and entr'actes. (Ref. p. 93).

Op. 78. "The Voievoda," Symphonic Ballad. (Although the score of this work was destroyed by the composer, it has been restored through the medium of the band parts which remained at Moscow).

"The Storm," Overture in C minor, written for the Drama of Ostrovsky. Early work. Posthumous. (Ref. p. 13).

"Fatum" (Destiny), Symphonic Poem. Early work. Posthumous. (Score also destroyed by composer and restored by means of the parts). (Ref. p. 21, 45, 50, 103).

"Romeo and Juliet," Ouverture-fantaisie, dedicated to M. Mili Balakirev. Early work. (Ref. p. 22, 23, 24, 91, 108, 222).

(d) MARCHES.

Op. 31. Slavonic March on National themes. (Ref. p. 55).

Solemn March, composed for the Coronation of the Emperor Alex. III. at Moscow.

Military March : dedicated to the 98th Regiment. For Military Band.

Solemn March. Posthumous.

(e) OVERTURES.*

Op. 15. Triumphal Overture on the Danish National Hymn. (Ref. p. 52, 55).

---

* For "Hamlet" (Ouverture-Fantaisie), "The Storm" (Overture in C minor) and "Romeo and Juliet" (Ouverture-Fantaisie) see under heading of Tone-poems.

Op. 49. Solemn Overture, written for the opening of the Cathedral of Christ the Redeemer, Moscow. "The year 1812." (Ref. p. 52, 74, 78, 222, 224).

(f) CAPRICCIO.

Op. 45. Caprice Italien. (Ref. p. 74, 78).

IV

OPERAS.

Op. 3. "The Voievoda." Completed and produced; but, score having been destroyed by composer, only the following portions survive: Overture, Entr'acte, Air de Ballet. (Ref. p. 11, 18, 19, 20, 21, 44, 104).

Op. 14. "Vakoula, the Smith." Written for the Grand Duchess Helena's prize competition. Afterwards re-written and named "Cherevichek" (Two Little Shoes); but also known by the title of "Les Caprices d'Oxane." (Ref. p. 19, 36, 37, 78, 168, 169).

Op. 24. "Eugene Oniegin." In 3 acts. Libretto adapted from the poem of A. Poushkin by Shilovsky in collaboration with the composer. (Ref. p. 58 to 67, 71 to 73, 76 to 78, 88, 100).

Op. 68. "Dame de Pique" (Queen of Spades). In 3 acts and 7 scenes. Libretto based on the story of Poushkin; by Modeste Tchaikovsky. (Ref. p. 99, 100, 119).

Op. 69. "Iolanthe." A lyric opera in 1 act on Hendrik Herz's drama "King Réné's Daughter." Libretto by Modeste Tchaikovsky. (Ref. p. 101).

"Undine." Libretto (on a poem by Shukovsky) originally written by Count Sollogoub for the composer, Lvov. Destroyed by the composer. (Ref. p. 25, 29, 38, 103).

"Mandragora." Tchaikovsky was dissuaded from continuing this work—principally by Kashkin. The only surviving portion is: "Chorus of Insects" for boys' voices S.A.T.B. and orchestra. (Ref. p. 24).

"The Oprichnik." In 4 acts. Libretto by the composer; based on tragedy of similar name by Lashetchnikov. For sketch of the text see p. 45: music p. 46. (Ref. p. 21, 25, 31, 44, 60, 107, 139).

"Joan of Arc." In 4 acts. Libretto by the composer, based on Schiller's play. (Ref. p. 76, 78, 79, 80).

"Mazeppa." In 3 acts. Libretto compiled from the material offered in Poushkin's poem "Poltava." (Ref. p. 86, 87, 88, 90).

"The Enchantress" (Charodeïka). In 4 acts. Libretto by Shpashinsky, author of the drama. (Ref. p. 98).

V

BALLETS.

Op. 20. "The Swan Lake." In 4 acts. Written for the Imperial Theatre, Moscow. Plot by Begichev, stage manager. (Ref. p. 54).

Op. 66. "Sleeping Beauty." Consisting of 30 numbers, in illustration of the fairy tale. Arranged by Marius Petipa, the ballet-master. (Ref. p. 101)

Op. 71. "Casse-Noisette." In 2 acts, consisting of 15 numbers, in illustration of the Dumas rendering of Hoffman's fairy tale. Arranged by Marius Petipa, the ballet-master.

Op. 71a. "Casse-Noisette" Suite, adapted from the above and consisting of: (a) 1. Ouverture-miniature. (b) 2. Marche : being children's entrance in Act I. 3. Danse de la fée-dragée (sugar-plum fairy dance from Act I). 4. Danse Russe (Trepak) from the divertissement of toys and sweets in Act II. 5. Danse Arabe :—For *coffee* in the divertissement. 6. Danse Chinoise :—For *tea* in the divertissement. 7. Danse des Mirlitons :—Whistle-pipe dance. (c) 8. Valse des Fleurs. (Ref. p. 60, 73, 101, 113).

VI

VOCAL WORKS.

(a) Songs with Piano Accompaniment.

Op. 6. Six Songs.

Op. 16. Six Songs.

Op. 25. Six Songs. (Ref. p. 53).

Op. 27. Six Songs. (Ref. p. 53).

Op. 28. Six Songs.
Op. 38. Six Songs. (Ref. p. 53).
Op. 47. Seven Songs.
Op. 54. Sixteen Songs for young people.
Op. 57. Six Songs.
Op. 60. Twelve Songs, dedicated to H.M. the Tsaritsa.
Op. 63. Six Songs, dedicated to the Grand Duke Constantine.
Op. 65. Six Melodies to French words.
Op. 73. Six Songs.
Five Songs, published separately without Opus number.

(b) DUETS.

Op. 46. Six Duets, with piano accompaniment.
"Romeo and Juliet." For soprano and tenor. Posthumous.
Completed from sketches left by the composer and orches-
trated by S. Taneiev.

(c) TRIO (S.S.A.)

"Love and Nature." Posthumous. Written for Madame Walzeck.

(d) QUARTET (S.A.T.B.)

"Night." Arranged from Mozart's 4th Fantasia for piano. (Ref.
p. 119).

(e) CHORUSES.

Chorus a Capella. Hommage à A. Rubinstein. Composed for his
Jubilee, 1889. Words by Polonsky.
Chorus for male voices, dedicated to the students of the Moscow
University.
The Nightingale, chorus for mixed choir.
Chorus a capella; on an old Slavonic melody. Hymn in honour
of St. Cyril and Methodius.

(f) CHURCH CHORAL WORKS.

Op. 41. Liturgy of St. John Chrysostom. For S.A.T.B. with
piano accompaniment. (Ref. p. 74, 75).
Op. 52. Russian Service (1st Vespers). The Church Canticles
harmonised for mixed choir.
Nine Church Choruses for mixed voices.

(g) CANTATAS.

"Moscow." For solo chorus and orchestra. Written for the Coronation of the Emperor Alex. III.

"Ode to Joy" (Schiller). Examination cantata in MS. (Ref. p. 8).

Op. 12. "The Snowmaiden" (or Snow Queen)—*snegourotchka* —choral music to a fairy tale by Ostrovsky. 1. Introduction. 2. Dance and Chorus of Birds. 3. Monologue of the Frosts. 4. Carnival Chorus. 5. Melodrama. 5*a*. Entr'acte. 6. Lel's Song. 7. Lel's Song. 8. Entr'acte. 9. Chorus of Blind Gusslee Players. 10. Melodrama. 11. Folk Chorus and Chorus of Courtiers. 12. Choral Dance of Maidens. 13. Jester's Dance. 14. Lel's Song. 14*a*. Lel's Song. 15. Brusilio's Song. 16. Appearance of Wood Demons and Shadow of Snow-Maiden. 17. Entr'acte. 18. March of the King of Berendei and Chorus. 19. Finale. (Ref. p. 25, 32, 33).

VII

FOR VIOLIN.

Op. 26. Serenade melancolique in B flat (with orchestra), dedicated to L. Auer. (Ref. p. 50).

Op. 34. Valse Scherzo in C (with orchestra).

Op. 35. Concerto in D (dedicated to A. Brodsky) with orchestra.

Op. 42. Three Pieces with piano accompaniment; entitled "Souvenir d'un lieu cher." 1. Meditation. 2. Scherzo. 3. Mélodie.

VIII

FOR VIOLONCELLO.

Op. 33. Variations (with orchestra) sur un thème rococo; dedicated to M. G. Fitzenhagen. 7 Variations and Coda.

Op. 62. Pezzo capriccioso; Morceau de Concert (with orchestra or piano), dedicated to Brandukov. (Ref. p. 98).

List of Works 411

IX

FOR PIANO, VIOLIN AND 'CELLO.

Op. 50. Trio in A minor, dedicated "to the memory of a great artist" (N. Rubinstein). 1. Pezzo elegiaco. 2. Tema con variazioni. Analysis, 272. (Ref. p. 33, 85, 204).

X

ARRANGEMENTS AND LITERARY WORK.

The principal of these are : Treatise on Harmony. (Ref. p. 31, 75). Translation of Gevaert into Russian. The Critical Essays referred to in Part II. of this work. Arrangement for piano duet of 50 Russian melodies. Orchestration of an overture by Laroche. Arrangement for piano duet of Rubinstein's overture "Ivan the Terrible." Diary of the tour in 1888 (Part III. of this work).

ANALYTICAL INDEX

E E